Breakthrough customer service
658.812 BRE

D0569693

Breakthrough Customer Service

Breakthrough Customer Service

Best Practices of Leaders in Customer Support

Editor and Contributor

STANLEY A. BROWN

Partner in Charge
International Centre of Excellence in Customer Satisfaction
Coopers & Lybrand

John Wiley & Sons Canada, Ltd
Toronto • New York • Chichester • Weinheim • Brisbane • Singapore

John Wiley & Sons Canada Limited
22 Worcester Road
Etobicoke, Ontario
M9W 1L1

Canadian Cataloguing in Publication Data

Main entry under title:

Breakthrough customer service : best practices of
    leaders in customer support

Includes bibliographical references and index.
ISBN 0-471-64232-0

1. Customer services.   I. Brown, Stanley A., 1946–
HF5415.5.B73   1997   658.8'12   C97-931692-8

Production Credits:
Cover & text design: JAQ
Cover Illustration: Freedman & Associates
Printer: Tri-Graphic Printing Ltd.

Printed in Canada
10 9 8 7 6 5 4 3 2 1

CONTENTS

BREAKTHROUGH CUSTOMER SERVICE....Do we really need it? What does it look like? And how do we achieve it?

Businesses around the world are driven by competition. The facts are simple: companies that can compete stay in the marketplace; companies that can't, are short-lived. That's nothing new. What *is* new, however, is the attitude of the companies that are now leading the race. Their philosophy is "If it ain't broke...break it."

The business world is changing rapidly, and organizations must be willing to do more than just keep up. They need to initiate change and recognize that what puts them ahead today will be regarded as normal tomorrow. Moreover, companies must focus not only on changing their own organizations, but on changing their industry as a whole.

Let's face facts. Customers are becoming scarce commodities. Everybody wants more, but we are not gaining them at the rate we did even 10 years ago. We cannot simply pitch products and services to the masses; nor can we afford to start selling to one customer at a time. Conventional strategies and practices no longer work. And selling more of the same products and services will only incite competitive retaliation and perhaps lead to lower prices and margins.

We need a new strategy, one that builds on a strong foundation of fundamentals yet creates that degree of differentiation that leads to long-term success. The organization must be transformed. But in what area? Product? No, it will be copied in short order. Price? No, you don't want to be just the lowest-price provider. The answer is customer service. That gives an organization perhaps the last strategic edge! And the strategy needed to defeat the competition in the race must be *break-through customer service*, which must endure as a source of competitive advantage.

Breakthrough customer service is not a single thing. It is not . . .

- A title
- A group
- Smile training
- A one-time change
- An advertising slogan
- A complaint-handling group
- Just being nice to customers
- The latest corporate direction
- A customer service department
- Customer-contact employee training
- Spending as much as possible on service
- A few simple changes that are easy to accomplish

Many organizations tinker with customer service. They may implement one or two of the catch phases mentioned above, create a lot of fanfare, and then, unfortunately, watch the program flop. And maybe that is the problem to start with. Breakthrough customer service is not a program but a complete change, a metamorphosis of the organization.

Not all organizations are the same, nor are all customers; and therein lies the first challenge. What must change within the organization may be different for each company and possibly for each customer grouping.

Breakthrough customer service is not about giving *more* service; it is about giving *differentiated* service. It is not about sending your staff on a training program or any other quick-fix program; it is about changing the culture of the organization from the top down. It is not about creating huge databases filled with customer information; it is about managing the customer relationship. It is not about using the latest technology; it is about using the right customer-friendly technology. It is about being an organization that is easy to do business with, in a way that cannot and, in the short term, will not be duplicated by the competition because you have changed the rules and own the issues that are key to the customer.

As the authors of this book explain, breakthrough customer service is a long-term initiative—a journey, not a week-end trip. And it requires doing a combination of things more effectively, from properly defining strategy to focusing on people, processes, and technology.

Companies that do this should expect superior returns to shareholders. Study after study has shown that companies with superior service enjoy higher returns on sales, greater returns on investment, and increased market share over companies with inferior service.

So breakthrough customer service is something to strive for, but where do we start? The very nature of the topic requires a depth of knowledge and expertise in each of the areas that contribute to breakthrough customer service. That in itself is a challenge since some of these topics have over the years become so well-documented and complicated that several books have already been written on them. (For those of you who will be stimulated to read more on the topic, I have provided a list of some of the latest or relevant books, magazines, and newsletters in Appendix One.)

Breakthrough customer service is all about best practices. Therefore, why not ask those most knowledgeable about best practices in their fields of expertise to share their experiences? The best of the best have been asked to contribute to this book, to provide real-life, anecdotal proof that it is possible. If you want to grow and improve, learn from the best practices of others—steal shamelessly from them. With some minor adaptation, they will work within your organization's culture.

This is a book of contributions from organizations, leaders, and individuals who provide and teach best practices in customer support, including

- Organizations in North America and the United Kingdom, such as Eastman Kodak, British Airways, and AlliedSignal.

- Organizations that have won awards (Ritz-Carlton, AMP) and people who have judged these awards.

- Organizations that seek to use the latest technology (mbanx, Travelers Insurance, and others that are just beginning to climb the technology ladder).

- Academics at the University of Texas and at the University of Wisconsin-Madison.

- Leading consultants and thinkers from Coopers & Lybrand in Canada, the United Kingdom, and the United States.

- Best-practices suppliers, associations (the ICSA [International Customer Service Association], ASQC [American Society for Quality Control], and APQC [American Productivity and Quality Center]), and industry magazines and newsletters that have their pulse on selected industries and relevant practices.

The book starts with a focus on strategy. **Part One, Best Practices in Creating a Strategic Approach to Customer Service** provides a framework for starting the process to achieve breakthrough. But even more, it provides perspectives from leaders of both service and manufacturing organizations on why they became personally involved in creating value for their customers. This part also contains the latest research on leader-driven organizations.

Part Two, Best Practices in Creating and Using Measurements and Standards to Achieve Excellence in Customer Service deals with the ways organizations tap the voice of the customer to establish meaningful standards and measurements. They use methods that range from traditional customer research to best practices in benchmarking. The authors in this part explain why creating and using measurements can help to define how the company should act and how it can become closer to the customer and achieve breakthrough customer service.

Part Three, Best Practices in Achieving Process Improvement deals with the processes that make it all happen. While strategic planning is an important first step, companies will not be successful unless they examine the processes that touch the customer. The contributions and stories in this part provide insight for both companies just getting started and those that are more advanced.

Part Four, Best Practices in Using Technology to Achieve Breakthrough Customer Service focuses on the different components of technology that affect an organization's ability to achieve enhanced customer satisfaction. The authors of this part provide perspectives on organizations that have wrestled with challenges such as which technology to choose.

Part Five, Best Practices in Workforce Management: The Importance of the People Factor is concerned with the intellectual support required for creating excellence in customer service. In this part, the authors describe the effect of empowerment and the roles of cross-functional teams, training, and leadership, using best-practices case examples.

Part Six, Bringing It All Together: Best Practices of Industry Leaders provides case studies of a number of industry segments: financial services, the public sector, hospitality, airlines, and transportation. Many of these companies exemplify not one but several of the concepts described in earlier chapters.

Following the six main parts of the book are three appendices that provide useful tools and resources. Appendix One, as mentioned, provides a list of books and other publications that I recommend for those interested in exploring in more detail the topics discussed in this book. Appendix Two provides a chapter index and cross-references. For each main tool, major concept, and key enabling technology discussed in this book, cross-references are provided to those chapters that give more depth or best-practices examples. Appendix Three provides a list of the book's contributing individuals and organizations, and how to get in touch with them for further information.

HOW TO READ THIS BOOK

This book is not intended to be read from cover to cover in sequence. It does not provide a single methodology to follow religiously. It is a collection of thoughts, and first-hand experiences on a number of subjects. Use the Table of Contents, and the cross-references provided in Appendix Two, to pick the articles that have most relevance to your organization. If you need more information, I offer you three options:

1. Contact the authors of the articles (names, addresses, and phone numbers are provided in many cases); they will be pleased to talk to you.

2. Use the resource list in Appendix One; it's not exhaustive, but it is a good start.

3. Contact me directly at <stan.brown@ca.coopers.com>. I'd be delighted to hear your thoughts and concerns, or perhaps give you some additional direction or put you on the mailing list for Coopers & Lybrand's quarterly newsletter, *Customer Focus*.

At the beginning of this preface, I spoke about what breakthrough customer service *is not*. In closing, let me summarize what I believe breakthrough customer service is.

It is

- Invisible

- Synergistic

- Customer-focused, not product-focused

- Process- and people-oriented

- Organization-wide

- Not magic

- The result of investment, patience, hard work, and commitment

- Innovative (thus based on best practices)

Best-practices organizations are really hard to copy. They don't excel in only one best practice; it's the combination of practices that together create their uniqueness. Consider for a moment Wal-Mart, Home Depot, Southwest Airlines. What's unique about these organizations? Their closest competition appears to be very similar to them. No single thing distinguishes them, no single thing you can see. It's a mix of practices, enabled by technology, with a pinch of organizational culture thrown in—invisible to the untrained eye.

How an organization can achieve breakthrough customer service is contained in the chapters that follow. Take up the gauntlet and rise to the challenge.

S.A.B.

ACKNOWLEDGEMENTS

CLOSE TO EIGHT years and a few gray hairs ago I wrote my first book. It was an exhilarating, but onerous experience, and one that I had no desire to repeat. Yet two years after that, and twice more over the next four years came successive books and similar declarations that each would be my last and my family would not have to endure my inattentiveness any longer. Probably the only reason that this book ever came to be is due to the fact that I have a short-term memory and I conveniently forgot the magnitude of the task and my previous declarations. I also have a considerate family, and some good friends and associates that I can count on.

There is an old Beatles song which appropriately describes how this book came to be: "...with a little help from my friends." Without these friends and their dedication and commitment, this book would not be what it is today.

I would like to acknowledge and express my deep appreciation to the many people who made this project possible.

To my associates at Coopers & Lybrand, and in particular Mike Stoneham, and David W. Smith, for their encouragement and support.

To the best practices organizations mentioned throughout this book for their willingness to share their experiences and lessons learned.

To my colleagues, clients and to my team at the Centre of Excellence in Customer Satisfaction for their insight, assistance, and contributions.

To my editor, Karen Milner, and her associates at John Wiley & Sons Canada, Ltd for including me in their family.

To the individuals that read this book and for their desire to provide Breakthrough Customer Service.

Most of all to my family, in particular my wife Rhonda and children Lowell, Brian, Cynthia, and Neil, for their support during those lost weekends and vacations.

Thanks to all of you.

Part One

Best Practices in Creating a Strategic Approach to Customer Service

OVERVIEW

The beginning is the most important part of the work.
—Plato

Just what exactly is strategy? And how will it affect the service that our organization is capable of delivering to our customers?

These are just two of the questions most frequently asked by management today. To find some answers, let's start where the best-practice leaders start. In Chapter 1, Michael Hanley, in discussing how to build customer service into a strategic plan, defines strategy as whatever a company does to sustain and grow its business value. According to Hanley, "Strategy is made up of decisions and actions, not plans and reports. Strategy is rapidly creating and sustaining value, not just thinking about it." The article continues with a step-by-step approach to help your organization create a breakthrough strategy that embraces customer service at its core.

Rather than leave you with a single perspective on such an important element of breakthrough customer service, we follow this article with one by Steve Yearout, who reveals the secrets of improvement-driven organizations, in Chapter 2. This article presents a second perspective on the elements needed to create and implement an effective breakthrough strategy, based on a North American study on best practices of improvement-driven organizations. Once again, this is not a theoretical approach, but rather one that is based on the best practices of others, tried and true. Consider the following: To be successful, an organization must be innovative. But innovation, if you're bold enough to attempt it, is nothing more than "stealing," since the best ideas are already being used by other organizations, perhaps in other industries. Learn from them, then adapt them to the culture of your organization—that's the creative component necessary. Your challenge is to keep an open mind and learn from the plethora of best practices that we present here. Read about what others are doing, massage their methods, and mould them to fit your organization—or even fit your organization around them.

But is a well-planned strategy enough? The answer should be obvious. No. A strategy created without benefit to, or input from, the customer is of little value to any organization and its customers.

So what is "value"? And more important, what is "added value"? Moreover, how should that drive an organization's strategy and direction? Hugh Bolton, chairman of one of Canada's leading accounting/tax/consulting organizations, gives his views on this subject in Chapter 3. His perspective on "exceeding customers' expectations" is contrasted somewhat with that of Jerry Fritz of the University of Wisconsin-Madison. According to Fritz (Chapter 4), you must strive to exceed expectations, yet Bolton and his clients suggest that adding value is not that simple. Within both these chapters, senior executives from some of North America's most respected and profitable organizations provide you with their views on what they expect from the organizations that supply products and services to them. But both authors agree, an organization's strategic breakthrough in customer service cannot be one that is created in a vacuum; it must be flexible, focused, and driven by the needs of its customers.

Once you know where you want to go, you will need a path to get there. As Confucius said, "Success depends on preparation. Without such preparation there is sure to be failure."

So rather than forge ahead into uncharted paths, why not use a road-map that will lead you around the potholes and avoid the roadblocks? Part One closes with Jim Sierk's perspective in Chapter 5 on becoming customer driven. From his work as Baldrige Award judge in reviewing some of the world's leading organizations, and as a senior executive with AlliedSignal and Xerox, Jim Sierk's message is simple—an organization must be customer driven. Rather than just stop at that, however, he goes on to offer insight on how he has made this a cornerstone of his breakthrough approach to customer service.

Without exception, our authors present you with a common perspective. Listen to their message. It is clear and resounding. An organization must have a direction and a goal, otherwise it will never succeed. Remember what the Cheshire Cat in *Alice in Wonderland* said, "Any road will get you there if you don't know where you're going."

Read on.

S.A.B.

Customer Service as a Basis for a Breakthrough Business Strategy

Michael Hanley, Coopers & Lybrand, Chicago, IL

COMPANIES IN ALL industries around the world are in a race, but there is never a winner. In fact, most companies, over time, will lose. Nonetheless, it is possible to be in the lead for long periods of time and to create significant value for shareholders and employees. Even for the leading companies, the race gets more difficult every year, with bigger, stronger, and smarter competitors. In addition, strong competitors who have been in other races suddenly join your race with strength, technology, and a new approach to the market. They often become instant leaders.

The conditions during the running of the race are clear:

- Competitive advantage is short-lived.

- Today's competitive advantage becomes tomorrow's competitive requirement.

- Companies without a competitive advantage should expect, at best, zero return.

Traditionally, companies have looked to marketing and product development for sources of competitive advantage. In today's information-intensive environment, however, these advantages can soon be replicated and converted into competitive requirements. *Consider, instead, customer service as a source of competitive advantage.*

Delivering superior customer service is hard. This is why it can be an enduring source of competitive advantage and the key to a breakthrough business strategy. Once a company gets out in front with superior service and puts in place processes of continuous improvement, competitors will have great difficulty catching up.

In other words, if an organization's business strategy is founded on the concept "Customer service is a strategic source of competitive advantage," it will succeed in achieving breakthrough customer service. But building customer service into the plan is more than putting the words "customer service" into the mission statement that hangs on the wall. And it is more than just saying that everybody must put the customer first. An organization must develop, in a methodical manner, a customer-focused strategy that is based on thorough research. In this article, we discuss how this can be done.

But first we need to understand what "strategy" and "breakthrough" mean.

WHAT IS STRATEGY?

Strategy is whatever a company does to sustain and grow its business value.

"Does" is the key word: a strategy must be implemented quickly to be of value. Strategy is made up of decisions and actions, not plans and reports ("credenza-ware"). Strategy is rapidly creating and sustaining value, not just thinking about it.

A strategic plan takes the most attractive opportunities for creating value and combines them into a coherent implementation process. In developing strategy, organizations should carefully assess—from both a customer service and a business perspective—the complete array of approaches for creating sustained value. Here are some approaches that can be taken:

- Market focus (segmentation and targeting, global as well as domestic).
- Customer loyalty and sales strategy (leading to greater retention, frequency, and margins).
- Product focus (portfolio mix analysis with potential for rationalization and/or targeted new investment).
- Quick "time to market" for new products and other marketing initiatives to enable a product leadership or a fast-follower strategy.

- Strong brand equity with customers and marketing strategy, which justifies a price or volume premium.
- "Total customer management" sales approaches in business-to-business marketing.
- Excellent customer service, using the process to differentiate a commodity product.
- Product and service flexibility (based on core processes with low cycle times and high-quality yields).
- Dramatic operations performance improvement (from months and weeks for throughput to days and hours; from high rework to high first-run yields; from dollars to cents in cost).
- Strategic use of financial structure (for example, leveraged investments, licensing, joint ventures, local country capital sourcing, and dividend repatriation).
- Strategic use of information and communications technology to enable business processes to create disproportionate value.

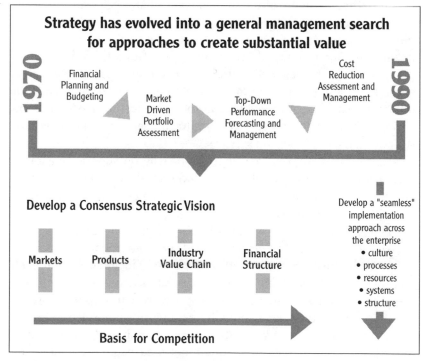

FIGURE 1: The Evolution of Strategy Development

As you can see, a combined customer service and business focus is required. Discovering and validating that focus take a more comprehensive approach, as shown in Figure 1.

This broad-based view of value reflects the new approach to strategy development in the 1990s. Between 1970 and 1990 strategy development for corporations and related strategic consulting moved rapidly from a financial planning and budgeting exercise to an assessment and strategic modification of corporate portfolios, then to a forecasting and future projection assessment, then to aggressive cost reduction and asset management in the mid to late 1980s (generally closely integrated with business process reengineering). Traditionally, companies undergoing a strategic review and identifying sources of value would tend to focus on market assessment (new markets to enter, better market segmentation, perhaps global strategies), and product assessment (product mix and portfolio, new technologies, better product positioning in the market). While these two areas of value creation are still very important, our experience is that the greatest opportunities for creating value may lie elsewhere.

In particular, many of the most advanced strategies focus heavily on the *processes that "touch" customers*. Customer service is regarded quite literally as part of the product—what the customer is paying for. In these companies, market segmentation is done from a customer process perspective as well as from a customer product-needs perspective. Customer-contact processes are then designed differently for different segments. And every customer contact is treasured as an opportunity to increase a customer's value perceptions and to perhaps sell additional products and services.

Designing a strategy that depends heavily on superior customer service is not trivial; but implementing one is truly difficult. In fact, successful strategy implementation usually starts on day one of the strategy development process.

During a strategic review, it is important that the executive committee members (at the enterprise level) or the general management team (at the business unit level) works closely together so that each member, regardless of functional responsibility, develops the same broad-based general management perspective on the opportunities for creating value. Strategies cannot be rapidly and completely implemented unless each member of the team understands the broad issues and how his or her particular functional area helps implement the strategy for the business as a whole. Most strategy implementation fails because functional management and staff do not develop this broad-based perspective.

These failures result from the lack of general management talent in most U.S. corporations today—that is, general managers who have competency and understanding in the broad strategic and tactical issues in each of the functional areas and who can implement strategies based upon creating value from cross-cutting processes. Throughout the seventies and eighties companies focused increasingly on functional specialization for executives who might have developed general management skills and perspective. An effective strategy development process begins to re-create this general management perspective and builds a general management learning competency among the top executives at the business and enterprise levels.

A strategy development process that systematically selects value-creating opportunities and develops an implementation plan is generally able to anticipate implementation difficulties, modify the strategies accordingly, and take management through a seamless implementation. This is the essence of "change management" based upon strategic understanding and general management competency

WHAT IS BREAKTHROUGH?

A breakthrough strategy occurs when a company wins by changing the rules of the industry in which it competes and is rewarded by a disproportionate increase in sustained value.

Consider three grades of strategic change: incremental, substantial, and transformational (see Figure 2). Incremental change involves better "blocking and tackling." Substantial change involves calling new plays, perhaps with new players. Transformational change redefines the game, both the company and its industry. The company breaks through the conventional wisdom of competitive parity to capture and then to sustain an advantage.

What is needed is a systematic approach for thinking through a company's situation and strategic alternatives. Such an approach will follow orderly steps, supported by fact-based analysis:

- Understand the current state of the company and industry.

- Forecast the future state of the industry.

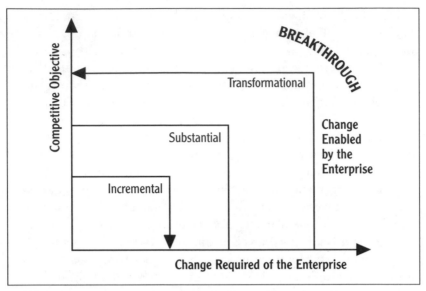

FIGURE 2: How Breakthrough Is Achieved

- Perform detailed gap analysis to identify incremental, substantial, and transformational strategic opportunities.
- Agree on the best external strategy for the company.
- Specify the key internal changes needed to implement the strategy.

The first critical step is to understand external and internal issues from both the company's perspective and the industry's perspective (in particular customers, customers' customers, end-users, competitors, suppliers, and possible new entrants). Fact-based insights gained from a comprehensive understanding can form the basis for good strategic thinking.

This is especially true for customer service. A company that is developing a strategy needs to understand the drivers of customers' value perceptions with respect to service, and then segment customers into groups that perceive value differently. This segmentation will often be quite independent of a segmentation based on product needs. The company also needs to understand best practices in customer service in its own industry and in other industries.

A comprehensive understanding can be organized into four categories, specifying the current and future state of each, as illustrated by the chart in Figure 3.

CURRENT STATE

	Industry	Company
External	Market, product, channel, supplier and competitor trends	Company market/ product focus channels, suppliers, financial strategy
Internal	Best practices and innovations in this and similar industries	Company culture, processes, resources, systems, structure

FIGURE 3: The Four Categories of the Breakthrough Framework

The breakthrough framework is more than just a convenient way to ensure a thorough review of the company's competitive situation. The power of the framework lies in exploring the space between the quadrants. See Figure 4.

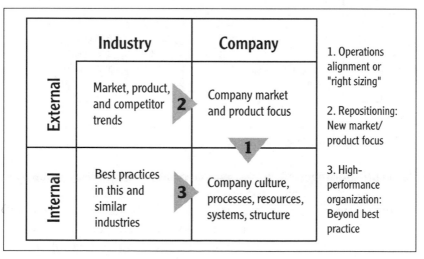

FIGURE 4: Using the Framework to Identify Potential Strategic Directions

This framework suggests four types of strategies, the three shown here and breakthrough. Note that customer service can play a key role in any one of the four types of business strategy indicated below.

1. **Operations alignment** involves incremental change. This strategy is appropriate by itself only for companies who have not kept operations current with market realities. Many, if not most, U.S. companies employed this strategy sometime during the last 10 years under the guise of "right-sizing" or "reengineering," but with the primary objective of cost reduction. Only some of these companies have also learned to keep operations aligned with market/product focus.

   Repositioning market/product focus and becoming a high-performance organization require substantial change.

PRODUCTS

		Current	New
MARKETS	**New**	Build market reach along geographic, demographic, needs-based, or other segmentation dimension	Create a new venture; can best be accomplished quickly by acquisition
	Current	Reposition current products with current customers through product differentiation, pricing, distribution, and promotion	Expand product categories sold to current customers, using e.g., brand extensions, bundling, channel strength

FIGURE 5: Traditional Repositioning Strategies

2. **Repositioning** is what most people mean when they say "strategy." The classic two-by-two matrix shown in Figure 5 illustrates three repositioning options. The three repositioning strategies keep markets or products, or both, relatively constant. They are not mutually exclusive, although most companies focus on getting one right. Each of the three alone implies substantial change.

The fourth strategy shown (new markets and new products) is not really repositioning. Rather, it implies a new business. Experience has shown that trying to do this organically has a low probability of success. Acquisitions fare somewhat better although the burden of proof is heavy: a strategic fit and economic payback. Given that the acquired markets and products are new to the company, the strategic fit is often tenuous, while the economic projections vary widely on shaky assumptions.

Repositioning as a strategy will also drive operations alignment, with a renewed focus on the customer. Indeed, when repositioning strategies fail, it is more often an implementation error than a factual, analytical, or conceptual error in strategy development.

3. Becoming a **high-performance organization** also requires substantial change. The well-documented failure of a substantial majority of TQM (total quality management) and BPR (business process reengineering) efforts testifies to the difficulty of implementing this type of strategy.

   Operations alignment, market/product repositioning, and becoming high-performance organizations can, by themselves or in combination, be value-creating strategies. It depends on the particular company at a particular point in its life; not every occasion calls for a breakthrough strategy. Substantial change can lead to substantial value creation.

4. **Breakthrough** (Figure 6) is transformational. In the other three strategies, competitive conditions in the industry are more or less assumed to be fixed. The strategies involve understanding and responding well to these conditions (to the point of being able to anticipate them). A breakthrough strategy combines the other three and adds a dose of entrepreneurial zeal with the intent of changing the rules and hence the competitive conditions of the industry.

   Breakthrough strategies are often "resource-based" in that the company builds a core competence that transcends current industry practice and thus creates new and attractive market/product/customer service opportunities. Famous examples include:

   - Toyota: the lean production system.
   - Frito-Lay: end-to-end supply chain management and the use of advanced technology.

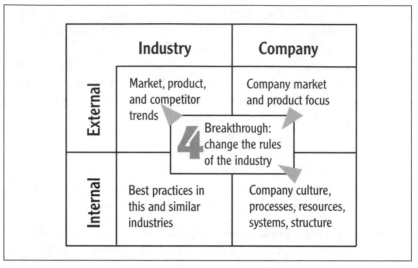

	Industry	Company
External	Market, product, and competitor trends	Company market and product focus
Internal	Best practices in this and similar industries	Company culture, processes, resources, systems, structure

Breakthrough: change the rules of the industry

FIGURE 6: The Meaning of Breakthrough

- Intel: high velocity product development.

Other examples, based on customer service, are described in other chapters of this book. They include

- AlliedSignal: a cultural revolution (later in Part One).

- mbanx: harnessing technology to get closer to the customer (Part Six).

- British Airways: setting new standards for customer excellence (Part Six).

In each of these organizations, resources were developed with a clear vision and intent for breakthrough customer service, resulting in improved economic performance.

Having agreed on an incremental, a substantial, or a transformational external strategic objective is not even half the battle. There are usually several viable alternative routes to achieving an objective. The strategic management team needs to identify, evaluate, and select the implementation route, enabling detailed planning, pilot, and roll out.

The key initial challenge in implementing strategy is to develop a shared strategic vision among the management team members, with customer service at its core.

HOW DOES STRATEGY WORK?

A strategy that works can be articulated in a very precise and coherent vision of how the company will sustain and grow itself. This vision is understood and shared by the management team, which makes it work.

A useful strategic vision statement is a thorough description of the future state of the company; it paints a picture in words and numbers of the business at a certain point in the future (for example, in five years). It includes a measurable financial target that, when attained, assures strategic success by generating sufficient economic value for the company to remain a desirable business entity (compared to what investors could achieve by investing in something else).

The vision statement fundamentally describes what it will take to win. The following outline for a vision statement is based on the breakthrough framework. It can be used for incremental, substantial, and transformational strategies.

Outline of a Vision Statement

A good strategic vision statement can be long or short, as long as it is specific with respect to the following:

Economic Objectives

- Time frame (for example, "In 2001, we will be . . .").
- Financial goals (for example, "Return 20 percent annually on shareholders' equity").

Competitive Positioning

- Markets (customer segmentation and targeting, market share targets).
- Products (especially portfolio life cycle management and margin targets).
- Industry value chain (supplier strategy, company domain, channel strategy).
- Financial structure (cash flow strategy).

Internal Capabilities

- Culture (set of beliefs held by the people of the company about the company).

- Core processes (central set of linked work activities performed by the company to create value).

- People, capital, technology (the company's fundamental resources).

- Systems (especially customer understanding, decision support, performance measurement, and other information-based systems).

- Organizational structure.

Specifying a winning strategic vision is not trivial; implementing it is truly difficult. Both steps must be well considered at the same time. In our experience, successfully implementing a strategy starts with the selection of the strategy team. The team should include key decision-makers, the implementing staff, the people who have significant influence over strategy direction, and those who are driven to improved performance through customer service. In addition, management must promote intensive communication of the vision to all others who influence business performance across the corporation. This communication builds understanding, develops consensus, and encourages commitment.

As the vision is developed and communicated, the process involves key implementation players at all levels of the organization in developing operating targets and action plans. People come together in cross-functional project teams to specify what the company must do daily to succeed with the new strategy. They are then positioned to implement their plans using operating measures and targets to manage according to the strategy that they helped create.

In successful strategies, these front-line plans are integrated into an economic model of the strategy and a business plan that outlines the investments and payoffs expected from the strategy over the next five years.

At the same time, successful companies recognize that because competitor and market conditions can change rapidly, strategy development must also include the reengineering of the general management processes to provide the capability to quickly understand changes and the flexibility to rapidly adapt to them. A solid strategy development process should lead to continuous strategic management of the company.

WHERE DOES THE MAGIC OCCUR?

The magic occurs during rapid implementation. Failed attempts at breakthrough strategy result not from lack of good ideas, but usually from failure to get the good ideas recognized and implemented.

Correct strategic thinking and implementation success should not be independent events. Good strategic thinking requires implementation experience (and thus foresight). Success in implementation depends on key issues being solved early in the strategy development process. A breakthrough strategy is typically based on transformational changes in the enterprise. Some of the key enablers have inconveniently long development cycles. Developing and implementing a major new information system, for example, takes time and significant investment. If strategy is to be "instant" then any advance notice is appreciated.

Implementing strategic change means getting people across the company to change their behaviour. Successful companies will identify early on key performance indicators (KPIs) by which management can measure and reward behaviour. KPIs must be operational and controllable day-to-day by people in the line organizations and, at the same time, linked to the company's competitive objectives and financial results.

BREAKTHROUGH CUSTOMER SERVICE

The ironic part of all of this is that when companies think about breakthrough strategies, they typically think along the market (which customers to serve?) and product (what to sell them?) dimensions. An understanding of how customers want to be served is often missing, and therefore also the breakthrough opportunities therein.

This lack of understanding is most clearly seen in the way that most marketing departments do customer research. Their objectives almost always focus on a needs-based segmentation scheme, whereby needs are defined in terms of products. But often customers care as much (more perhaps) about *how* they are served. Progressive, customer-driven enterprises will recognize at least two dimensions for customer segmentation and product/service offering development: the traditional needs-based customer dimension and a process-based, customer service dimension.

And here lies the great opportunity: if all else is equal with respect to market segmentation and product development, customer service is a wonderful opportunity for competitive differentiation and, perhaps, a breakthrough strategy. This turns out to be the key to integrating customer service into a company's strategic plan. It must factually demonstrate that customer service can be an enduring source of competitive advantage. Only then will customer service be recognized as a strategically important function and given its due in the strategic planning process.

About the author

MICHAEL HANLEY

Michael Hanley is a partner with Coopers & Lybrand Consulting's Integrated Strategic Services in Chicago and the co-author of the firm's *Methodology for Business Strategy Development.*

The Secrets of Improvement-Driven Organizations

INITIATING AND SUSTAINING QUALITY IMPROVEMENT[1]

Stephen L. Yearout,
Coopers & Lybrand, Arlington, VA

WHAT'S KEY TO creating a truly successful, improvement-driven business organization today? How do you ensure that in the quest to initiate and sustain continuous improvement, you have the right infrastructure and metrics to build momentum toward achieving those objectives? Equally important, how do you engage and elicit the ongoing energy and involvement of your organization's employees in this critical process?

Building a truly improvement-driven organization is often an elusive goal for companies—a goal that they strive toward for years without sustained success or a true sense of how to get there. In the eighties, for example, companies focused almost exclusively on improving the quality and performance of internal operations as a way to differentiate themselves in the marketplace. Today, while operational excellence is still a vital component of organizational performance, it is not the sole criterion for determining it. Other factors need to be part of the performance equation. These factors include:

- Responsiveness to customer requirements.

- The quality, cost, and time characteristics of key business processes.

---

[1] Adapted with permission from the American Society for Quality Control, 1996.

- The nature of executive leadership.
- The degree of employee commitment to improvement goals.
- The ability to foster innovation and rapidly manage change.

Understanding the critical roles and interrelationships of these factors is essential if a company is to truly become improvement-driven over time.

No magic formula exists for creating an improvement-driven organization—that is, an organization that consistently meets or exceeds quality-improvement goals and that creates an organizational culture for continuing growth, renewal, and business vitality. Managing any business involves the craft of leadership, the art of empowerment, and the science of business management. But a recent survey reveals that high-performing organizations (those that consistently improve their marketplace, financial, and operating performance) do share certain characteristics. Moreover, these characteristics suggest a model of best practices that are excellent predictors of organizational performance. The survey, which was conducted in the summer of 1994 by Coopers & Lybrand L.L.P. (C&L) in conjunction with the American Society for Quality Control (ASQC), the Rutgers University Center for Public Productivity, and the National Quality Institute of Canada, examined 300 leading organizations across 15 industry sectors. It documents the management practices used by organizations to improve quality, customer satisfaction, and financial performance, and it reveals how practices in one area of a company affect initiatives elsewhere in the organization. Further, it provides interesting insights into the emerging role of senior-level quality managers (see the sidebar, "The Emerging Role of the Quality Officer" on the next page).

The following details those aspects of the survey's findings that relate to customer service and the conclusions that can be drawn about what organizations can do to emulate these best practices.

THE SURVEY'S SCOPE

Organizations that were deemed leading performers by industry analysts and business and trade associations were selected for the survey. In addition, organizations that had received quality awards from both business and government entities were selected. In most cases, the survey targeted the senior improvement officer in the organization.

The Emerging Role of the Quality Officer

How important is the role of the quality officer in leading organizations? As the science of quality management becomes more exacting and demanding, and as organizations make greater efforts to systematically reinforce the importance of quality initiatives, it is apparent that the role of quality officers in organizations is growing.

Survey respondents were asked several questions relating to the role of quality in their organizations and, specifically, to the function of the quality officer. Here are the results:

- Nearly 60 percent of those surveyed indicated that the senior quality officer in the organization reports directly to the organization's senior leader.

- Thirty-seven percent of the respondents said they expect the quality staff in their organizations to take on greater strategic responsibilities in the next three years, specifically in the areas of strategic planning, business process reengineering, and change management.

- Thirty-four percent of the respondents expect the quality function to become fully integrated in the organization's natural work groups and activities.

Out of the 585 organizations that surveys were mailed to, 300 responded. The survey respondents included a wide variety of organizations from both the private and public sectors in the United States and Canada. Among the 300 organizations taking part in the survey were about 20 government agencies, including the Internal Revenue Service, the National Aeronautics and Space Administration (NASA), the Naval Air Warfare Center, and the Office of Naval Intelligence. The following companies also participated:

AlliedSignal	IBM
American Express	Kodak
AT&T Bell Laboratories	Marriott Corporation
Bristol-Myers Squibb Company	McDonnell Douglas
Digital Equipment Corporation	Motorola

Duke Power Company   Ritz-Carlton Hotels
Ford Motor Company   Shell Oil
General Motors   Texas Instruments
Hydro Quebec   TRW
USX Corporation

To gather consistent and meaningful data, C&L organized the survey questions into the seven key areas of customer focus, leadership, employee involvement, innovation, process improvement, improvement measurement, and change management.

For example, respondents were asked the following:

- Whom they considered to be the principal driver of change and quality initiatives in their organizations.

- How frequently and consistently their organizations collected and utilized customer satisfaction data to change or reengineer work processes.

- Whether they believed employees in their organizations were empowered to improve their work processes.

- Whether a strategy was in place to ensure that process improvements occurred regularly.

In addition to collecting data on management practices, C&L gathered information on key performance measures (such as customer satisfaction, improvement results, and innovation) from each respondent. On the basis of these reported performance measures, the entire database was stratified to identify the top 50 (high) performers and bottom 50 (lower) performers. Follow-up research on the high performers was then conducted to verify that their revenue growth, return on investment, and market share performance over the past three years had surpassed that of other organizations in their industries. Thus, the following analysis compares the best practices used by the 50 top performers with those used by the 50 lower performers.

FINDINGS: DISCERNING INTERCONNECTIONS

As mentioned earlier, the purpose of conducting the survey was not only to identify the best practices of improvement-driven organizations but also to discern the critical interrelationships that exist among practices in different parts of an organization. For example, how does commitment to a strong customer focus affect practices in the areas of improving processes, managing change, and involving employees? What kinds of links exist between an organization's commitment to continuous process improvement and the way it communicates the importance of change to employees?

The results of the survey suggest a true line of demarcation between the high-performing and lower-performing organizations. The top performers had the following characteristics.

Cascading leadership.

An area of great interest to C&L was understanding the role of the chief executive officer (CEO), both as a visionary in the organization and as an advocate for the achievement of quality objectives. Although C&L knew that strong leadership is a strong determinant of organizational success, it wanted to know how strong a determinant it is and whether the relationship between strong leadership and success can be quantifiably verified.

The survey found that in high-performing organizations, strong, hands-on leadership by the CEO is indeed a critical predictor of success in gaining measurable performance improvement. But it is not a silver bullet. Other factors are also critically important, most notably the active, hands-on involvement of first-level supervisors in helping employees perform their jobs more effectively. For example, respondents in the top-performing organizations, for the most part, agreed that their "supervisors helped employees to improve work performance" in their organizations. In contrast, respondents from lower-performing organizations were less in agreement about the prevalence of this practice in their organizations. This finding indicates that in high-performing organizations, leadership of improvement initiatives, while driven by the CEO, cascades down to levels below the CEO. The role of first-line supervisors at the department or work-group level becomes critical to seeing that improvement objectives are consistently pursued and achieved.

A stronger, more consistent customer focus.

Conventional business thinking about having a customer focus involves the notion of a company capturing the voice of its customers when opportunities arise and using several vehicles to capture this information in the manufacturing, sales, and distribution processes. Conventional thinking also prescribes that this information be used to guide improvement efforts in the organization.

Best-in-class organizations, however, take these principles a step further. The survey found that top-performing organizations not only pay close attention to capturing customer satisfaction data, they also analyze and use the data to improve, redesign, or otherwise change work processes. As Figure 1 indicates, there is a clear breakpoint delineating what high and lower performers do when it comes to the second of these practices. Respondents from the top-performing organizations strongly agreed (6.24 on a 7-point scale) that they frequently "use customer feedback to improve the way work is performed." But respondents from the lower-performing organizations generally disagreed that this occurs in their organizations (3.56).

How well do the survey respondents understand their customers? Because they are more disciplined and consistent in collecting and using customer information, the top-performing organizations tend to have a clear understanding of their customers' needs and desires.

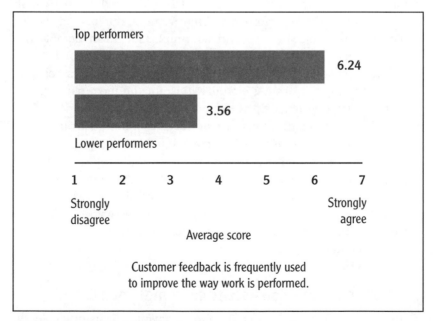

FIGURE 1: Best Customer Focus Practices

Respondents from the top-performing organizations nearly unanimously agreed that their organizations have a clear understanding of customer needs and desires (6.54), whereas respondents from the lower-performing organizations generally did not agree (3.69).

Overall, the survey findings indicate that high performers regularly collect and use customer satisfaction data to improve how work is done. As a result, they have a much better grasp of their customers' needs and desires than do lower performers.

Greater alignment between employee and organizational goals.

Most organizations say that their employees are their greatest asset and that empowered employees are the ones who get the job done. That's good corporate rhetoric in an annual report, but how well does that statement stand up to statistical and analytical examination? How thoroughly do organizations actually follow through to ensure that their employees understand the link between their own jobs and the achievement of larger, corporate goals?

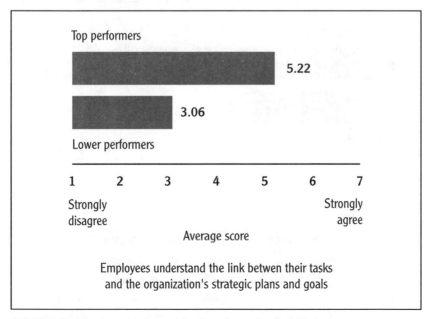

FIGURE 2: Best Employee Involvement Practices Concerning Goal Alignment

The survey asked respondents about employee roles and responsibilities in their organizations. In the top-performing organizations, the respondents generally agreed (5.22) that "employees understand the link between their tasks and the organization's strategic plans and goals" (see Figure 2). Respondents from the lower-performing organizations, however, generally disagreed with this statement (3.06).

When organizations were asked to respond to the statement "Employees recognize and act on their responsibility to continuously improve their work process," the difference between the high and lower performers was even more pronounced (see Figure 3). Overall, respondents from the top-performing organizations agreed with this statement (5.54), whereas respondents from the lower-performing organizations generally disagreed with it (3.13).

Finally, when asked whether quality-improvement accomplishments are typically included in employee performance evaluations, respondents from the top-performing organizations generally agreed that they are (5.37); respondents from the lower-performing organizations generally said they are not (3.42).

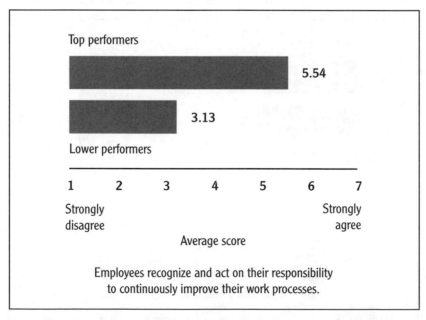

FIGURE 3: Best Employee Involvement Practices Concerning Improvement Responsibilities

These findings suggest that in high-performing organizations, employees' goals are well aligned with those of the organization. Employees understand the connection between their own job function and the larger, strategic plans of the organization. What's more, they take active ownership of their work, acting on their responsibility to continuously improve the way they get work done. To reinforce these behaviours, top-performing organizations frequently include quality-improvement accomplishments in employee performance evaluations.

In lower-performing organizations, there is less linkage between the employees' and the organization's goals, less ownership of job responsibilities to improve work processes, and less organizational reinforcement of work performance around achievement of specific quality goals.

An unequivocal commitment to continuous improvement.

How do high performers treat the practice of process improvement? Although most businesses proclaim that they continuously improve their work and business processes, the top-performing organizations surveyed actually do—again with more consistency than the lower performers. Moreover, the top performers don't do it on the basis of guesswork but rather on external data (including customer feedback) and external organizational comparisons.

High performers establish a clear and compelling link between practices in the area of customer focus and those in the area of process improvement. As Figure 4 indicates, respondents from the top-performing organizations consistently agreed (5.85) that their organizations "use customer satisfaction data to drive process improvements." Respondents from the lower-performing organizations generally disagreed with this statement (3.25). At the same time, top performers are much more likely to use benchmarking to improve their key business processes.

The survey found that in high-performing companies, commitment to continuous process improvement transcends the transactional level (the level at which work is actually performed) and is, in fact, a core operating tenet in the organization. For example, high performers generally have strategies to ensure that process improvement takes place at regular intervals. They also have systems and protocols for targeting which processes get selected for improvement. This is generally not the case in lower-performing organizations.

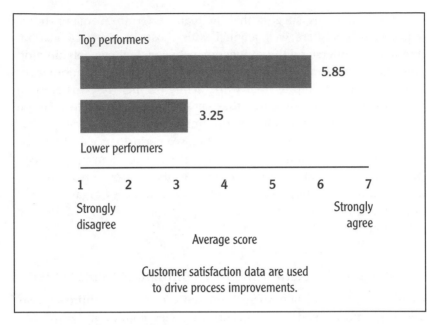

FIGURE 4: Best Process Improvement Practices

The survey's findings on process improvement are significant because they demonstrate that a company's mind-set about ensuring continuous improvement guarantees that mechanisms and systems are put in place to make it happen. This, in turn, leads to the implementation and alignment of employee involvement and customer focus practices to support continuous improvement efforts.

Multiple methods of measuring improvement.

Should organizations measure improvement through a single dimension (such as quality) or through multiple dimensions? In the survey results, the measurement activities of the top-performing organizations clearly stood out from the rest. In fact, the survey yielded some of the most pronounced differences in practices:

- When given the statement "My organization quantifies or measures improvements made in reducing cycle time," respondents from the top-performing organizations generally agreed (5.39), whereas those from the lower-performing organizations did not (2.94) (see Figure 5).

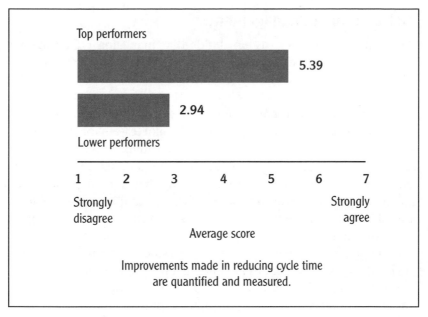

Top performers

5.39

2.94

Lower performers

1   2   3   4   5   6   7

Strongly   Strongly
disagree   agree

Average score

Improvements made in reducing cycle time
are quantified and measured.

FIGURE 5: Best Improvement Measurement Practices

- When given the statement "My organization quantifies or measures improvements made in reducing costs," respondents from the top-performing organizations generally agreed (5.98), whereas those from the lower-performing organizations did not (4.13).

- When given the statement "My organization provides accurate product and service quality performance information to work groups throughout the organization, thereby helping to reinforce the ethic of measuring and communicating quality performance results," respondents from the top-performing organizations generally agreed (5.54), whereas those from the lower-performing organizations did not (3.71).

What do these findings suggest? Simply that high performers are more conscious of the importance of using multiple measurements (specifically, quality, cost, and time measures) to assess organizational performance than lower performers. Top performers recognize that a single measurement focus (e.g., quality) is no longer sufficient as a benchmark for gauging business performance.

Better change management.

Conventional business wisdom holds that managing organizational change is at best an undisciplined process and that managing specific change initiatives is not easily subjected to traditional tracking, monitoring, and assessment mechanisms. Partly for that reason, C&L did not originally plan to incorporate questions about change practices into the survey. But the feedback received from pilot tests of the survey indicated that there is an implicit organizational ability to manage change initiatives in a disciplined, systematic way. For that reason, C&L decided to incorporate specific questions about change management into the survey, not only to elicit data about change management activities, but also to understand the interrelationship of these activities with other business practices.

Again, the survey indicates strong links between change management activities and other business practices. In top-performing organizations, change efforts are strongly linked to and driven by customer needs and expectations (see Figure 6). In addition, the vision and strategy for change is regularly communicated by the CEO, first-line supervisors, and others. Finally, success with change is recognized and publicly reinforced.

For all these reasons, employees in high-performing organizations understand the compelling need for change from the status quo far more clearly than their counterparts in lower-performing organizations (see Figure 7). These employees are much more likely to be given the skills they need to accomplish change objectives—whether in the form of classroom training, on-the-job training, or clear, consistent communication and reinforcement of job expectations from supervisors.

Encouragement of innovation.

Clearly, high performers establish strong cross-connections between their operating practices in the areas of customer focus, employee involvement, and change management. For that reason, it was not surprising to learn that when it comes to innovation, a similar philosophy and operating culture of fostering cross-connections exist.

The survey found that in top-performing organizations, new ideas aren't strictly the domain of creative departments; instead, concepts for new products and services originate at many organizational levels.

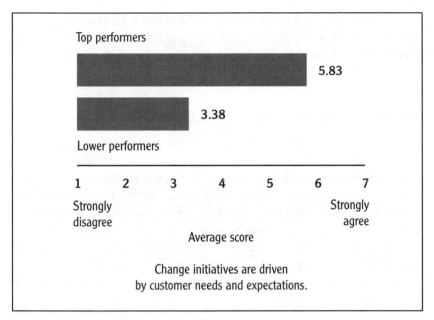

FIGURE 6: Best Change Management Practices Concerning Customers

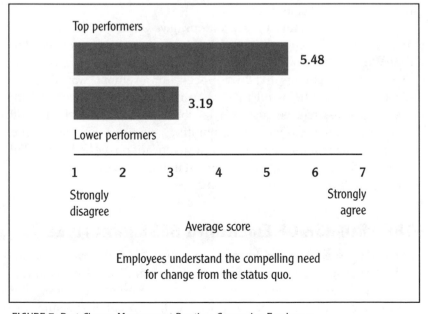

FIGURE 7: Best Change Management Practices Concerning Employees

Innovative ideas from employees are readily accepted by management, which helps to foster an environment in which change is more easily accepted and new ideas can be readily applied to both business problems and practices.

TAKING CHARGE OF CHANGE

Change has clearly become a constant in today's business environment. Yet how effectively do organizations manage change initiatives? One of the survey's most important findings is that an organization's ability to sustain quality improvement ultimately derives from its ability to change. Indeed, change is at the very heart of an organization's resilience and ability to renew itself. Moreover, change cannot be undertaken in an ad hoc fashion. Rather, it must be systematically implemented and managed, and the critical nature and reasons for change must be clearly, consistently, and regularly communicated to employees.

Most organizations face tremendous challenges in these areas. As part of the study, C&L asked the survey respondents to write about the key challenges they face in successfully initiating and sustaining improvement and change efforts.

Many of the surveyed organizations have yet to establish effective, appropriate cross-links between different business practices. For example, one respondent commented that "developing customer-focused measurements that drive process improvement" was of particular concern. Another wrote that "ensuring all employees involved with a given process receive customer feedback" was a critical issue. Still another commented that "incorporating measures of quality into senior management incentives" was a significant obstacle that needed to be dealt with, if, in fact, improvement initiatives were to be driven at the highest levels in the organization.

THE PROMISE OF EMERGING BEST PRACTICES

Some of the organizations surveyed are moving ahead, beyond the initial set of best practices as defined by the seven areas of focus in this survey; they are inaugurating practices that represent another level of organizational discipline being applied to the tasks of driving and sustaining improvement initiatives.

For example, many of the top performers recognize that plans or change must be based on realistic expectations of the organization's ability to change (see Table 1). To successfully sustain change efforts, other top-performing organizations have started to formally align rewards and sanctions to support change objectives and have established metrics with which to measure the progress and pace of change initiatives.

Although the use of these emerging best practices is not as extensive as for the other best practices studied (indicating they are not as universally applied in the top-performing organizations), the differences recorded between the best and the rest within each set of numbers are still noteworthy.

These top-performing organizations are on the cutting edge of organizational growth, renewal, and transformation. They are trailblazers and trend-setters in initiating and sustaining organizational change. If widely adopted, these emerging best practices hold the promise of ultimately helping other organizations to more effectively manage their change and improvement initiatives.

TABLE 1: Emerging Best Management Practices

Practice	Top performers	Lower performers
Plans for change are based on realistic expectations of the organization's ability to change.	4.83	2.81
Rewards and sanctions are used to support the organization's change initiatives.	4.98	3.12
Metrics are established to measure the progress of change initiatives.	4.30	2.92
Employees who are most affected by change understand what is required of them to support changes.	4.96	3.25
Changes are implemented at a pace the organization can assimilate.	4.96	3.31

THE SECRETS OF IMPROVEMENT SUCCESS

The C&L survey of improvement-driven organizations reveals that there are clear and significant differences in the use of management practices by the top- and lower-performing organizations. The research clearly indicates that the profile of a truly improvement-driven organization is one in which the following occur:

- Leaders drive the vision for continuous improvement and change.
- Customer feedback fundamentally shapes the specific nature of changes and the improvements an organization makes in its business processes.
- Employees are informed, engaged, held accountable, and rewarded for their individual contributions to improvement objectives.
- Improvements are systematic and targeted.
- Multiple improvement measures are used to ensure that continuous improvement efforts are appropriately monitored, tracked, and evaluated.

About the author

STEPHEN L. YEAROUT

Stephen L. Yearout is a partner at Coopers & Lybrand L.L.P. in Arlington, VA. He received an MBA from Xavier University in Cincinnati, Ohio. Yearout is a member of the American Society for Quality Control.

CHAPTER THREE

Why Take a Best Practices Approach?

CREATING ADDED VALUE FOR CUSTOMERS

Hugh Bolton, FCA, Coopers & Lybrand,
Toronto, ON

ADDED VALUE…VALUE-ADDED, no matter how you express it, is one of the most elusive yet crucial concepts in business. Customers and clients are constantly asking their suppliers to provide it. Companies always do their best to deliver it. But how do you deliver something that's so difficult to define? How do you measure your success when you're not exactly sure what it is you're measuring?

Unfortunately, there are no easy answers to these questions, no "one size fits all" formula that you can apply, because added value cannot be defined in simplistic terms. There is no single approach that will work in all situations. Rather, what is needed is an approach built from key lessons—a best-practices approach based on the opinions you should value most, those of your clients.

At the same time, however, there's no doubt that the success of most organizations today depends on unlocking not only the secrets of adding value, but also the secrets of delivering that value-added service. In an environment where technology has enabled companies around the world to instantly access huge amounts of knowledge and experience and to perfect their manufacturing processes while decreasing costs, there's very little left to distinguish one product or service from another.

In the end, whether you're providing your customers with a product or service, or your clients with professional advice, the result is the same: it's the organization that learns how to deliver added value consistently that will have an enormous competitive advantage.

DEFINING ADDED VALUE

Before you can make plans to provide value-added service, you must know what it means. But that's exactly where the problem begins—there's no single definition to work with. Added value is a moving target. It means different things to different customers, so you have to let each one of them define it for you:

> Understand what we need. Know our business. Be responsive. I don't want to lie awake at night wondering if you're going to drop the ball—and I don't expect to have to be technically competent enough to understand whether you're doing a good job. I simply want to have the confidence to know that you are.
> —*Bob Phillips, President and CEO, Dreco Energy Services Ltd.*

> Work with us as an extension of our management team. Recognize that we expect you to be extremely competent and to know our business—understanding the issues we face and the deals we make. When you give us advice, do so from the point of view of being a partner in our organization.
> —*Stuart Hartley, Executive Vice-President and CFO,*
> *The Molson Companies*

> Be in tune with the changing marketplace. Be flexible. Make sure you react quickly to what's happening in my industry. Stay on top of legislative and technological changes so that I don't have to. And then let me know how all these things affect my particular needs.
> —*Ken McDougall, Controller and Secretary, Snap-On Tools of*
> *Canada Ltd.*

> Structure assignments so the activities reflect my priorities rather than yours. Just get the necessary stuff done without a lot of fuss and muss and let senior management focus on the strategic future of the business.
> —*David Earthy, President, Woods Canada Ltd.*

To make matters even more complicated, value-added is a moving target not only *between* customers, but *within* customer organizations as well. Even if you think you're meeting your customers' expectations, you simply can't afford to pretend that those expectations won't change. Ten years from now your customers will expect something different—and better. That means you constantly have to aim higher. You have to lead your team into uncharted territory, perhaps with a target that isn't exactly clear. But you have to lead them beyond what your customers currently expect.

Bob Phillips, president and chief executive officer of Dreco Energy Services, an Alberta-based oil and gas engineering and manufacturing firm, agrees. "I want to be satisfied that my suppliers aren't resting on their laurels, because standing still is going backwards. Never stop trying to be better. Things are moving much too quickly."

But how do you hit a moving target? Spend time with your customers. That's the way to do it. If they all define added value differently, the only way you can find their value buttons is by building relationships with each of them. Whether you are providing professional services or manufacturing or business services, technical expertise is no longer enough to win or keep clients. The key today is relationship management, and that's becoming more and more the case in all product and service areas.

In his book *Managing the Professional Service Firm*,[1] David Maister explains why technical expertise alone is a dangerous way to try to win new clients. A number of firms are usually capable of solving client problems, he says. "Unless their skills are truly unique, unmatched by any competitor, professionals are never hired because of their technical capabilities" (p. 112). Instead, clients are looking for someone they can trust. They are being asked to believe a promise. "The act of hiring a professional is, by very definition, *an act of faith*," (p. 114) Maister says. Accordingly, the selling task of all professional advisers is to earn their clients' trust and confidence.

In other words, a professional adviser's task is to sell the relationship, and through that relationship discover what value-added service means to that particular client.

---

[1] Toronto: Maxwell Macmillan Canada, 1993.

PRODUCT VS. PEOPLE

Comments from clients of Coopers & Lybrand Canada confirm the importance of people over product in the professional services environment.

"This is a people business," says Dreco's Bob Phillips. "Service is delivered by an individual for an individual, so the people a firm puts forward must be those who have good communication skills and who can engender confidence."

"A professional services firm is more than just a name," says Stuart Hartley, executive vice-president and chief financial officer of The Molson Companies. "It represents the skilful, experienced people we have confidence in and who work with us as part of our team. We accept audits and tax returns as realities, but they're not why we value Coopers & Lybrand. The value does not come from the product—it comes from the people, from their commitment and dedication."

COMMUNICATION IS PARAMOUNT

The conclusions to be drawn from these comments are obvious. First, the only place where real added value exists is in the minds of clients. Second, you need to build relationships with each one to understand and respond to their definitions of the concept.

This, in turn, leads to another conclusion: You must create an environment with each of your clients that fosters open communication. "It's what you don't know about what's being said about your service that'll kill you," says Bob Phillips. "Make sure you practise straight-from-the-hip, two-way communication."

Open communication helps ensure that each relationship stands the test of time and the onslaught of competition. When you have good communication and a personal relationship with your clients, they are less likely to shop for price. Instead, they'll work with you to resolve any problems.

Asking questions can go a long way in helping to open the lines of communication and find out how your clients define added value. For example, consider asking them about the obstacles that could potentially prevent them from achieving their goals, and then devise a strategy to avoid or overcome those obstacles. Or ask them to envision what they hope will take place: "What must happen to make you consider this transaction or project a success?" Most people don't think that way, so they're intrigued by the idea—and they usually come up with some insightful answers.

PERCEPTION = REALITY

Long-term success for any organization is possible only if its clients perceive that they are receiving a value-added service. Accordingly, the customer's perception of added value—not yours—is the only reality that counts.

Structure your assignment or manufacture your product so that the activities or features reflect your customer's priorities rather than yours. Remember, perception is reality. And the only reality that should matter to you is your customer's.

WHAT ADDED VALUE ISN'T

Though added value can't be discussed in terms that apply to all situations since it can be defined only by individual clients, we can discuss what added value is not.

Added value is not, as some people seem to believe, giving away something for nothing. If clients or customers believe they need help, they're usually willing to pay a premium for it. The secret is to identify what they need help with or what they don't know. If you tell them you're an expert in that area or have a product that will fill their need, they'll pay for the service—and they'll believe they're paying for *value-added* service to boot.

And despite what the management gurus will have us believe, added value cannot be defined simply as "exceeding client expectations."

"I don't think we can ask any more of our professional service advisers," says Ken McDougall, controller and secretary of Snap-On Tools, an Ontario-based organization that sells hand tools, electronic diagnostic equipment, and tool storage units to industrial customers and automotive mechanics. "On the other hand, since we're dealing with a firm that specializes in a particular area, we expect expert advice. We pay for it. Does it exceed our expectations? I don't know. Maybe it's a Catch-22 situation. The better you are, the more people expect from you."

Other individuals say much the same. "I get great service from all of my suppliers," says Bob Phillips. "If I didn't I'd be looking elsewhere. But that doesn't mean that 'great service' exceeds my expectations. I expect each issue I raise with each organization that works with me to be covered one hundred percent. You can't do better than that."

"In my paradigm," says Molson's Stuart Hartley, "people who can meet my very high expectations are the only people I work with." And he says that it's up to the supplier to find out what the client's expectations are.

MANAGING EXPECTATIONS

There may, however, be an argument that expectations can be exceeded if they are managed first. The secret may lie in educating clients as to what they should expect and then delivering a little extra.

The best example of an organization that does this is Disney. Have you ever lined up for a ride at Disney World? At a certain point you reach a sign that says you're 45 minutes away from the beginning of the line, but you're actually only 35 minutes away. When you get there early you're impressed. You forget that you've been waiting for 90 minutes simply because you reach the front of the line 10 minutes earlier than you expected to—and you think it's wonderful!

That's what managing expectations is all about. Some might call it under-promising and over-delivering.

THE CHALLENGE

Managing expectations, opening up lines of communication, allowing clients' and customers' perceptions to define the realities of service, what added value is, and what added value isn't—these are only some of the issues that can arise in a discussion about value-added service.

Do any of these issues provide easy answers? No, because there simply aren't any. What they do provide is proof that added value is a subject worth investigating. And the only way any organization can do that is through communication—among its own people and with each of its clients or customers.

So share stories among your peers. Ask your clients questions. Embrace best practices and learn from the experiences of others. For the organization that gets this right, the pay-off will be incredible.

About the author

HUGH BOLTON, FCA, is chairman and chief executive partner of Coopers & Lybrand Canada, a leading professional services firm that provides solutions for business and government in a wide range of areas, including accounting, auditing, tax, and consulting. He is also a member of the International Executive Committee and Board of Directors of Coopers & Lybrand International.

There Must Be Fire!

THE IMPORTANCE OF
LEADERSHIP AND MANAGEMENT SUPPORT

Jerry L. Fritz, Management Institute,
School of Business, University of Wisconsin–Madison,
Madison, WI

WHEN YOU THINK of the top customer service providers, who comes to mind? Nordstrom, Lands' End, Federal Express, 3M, American Express, The Coleman Company, and S.C. Johnson are the companies usually listed. What do these industry leaders have in common? They believe that:

- It's their people that sets them apart from the competition.

- Investing in the lifelong growth and development of each employee paves the road to success.

- Customer service is not a department, but a philosophy, and should therefore be practised by all employees at every level of the organization.

- Upper management *must lead* the way by believing in it, supporting it, being involved in it, and focusing on it.

A prime example of this focus comes from Mr. H.F. Johnson, of S.C. Johnson fame. In 1927 he said, "The goodwill of the people is the only enduring thing in any business. It is the sole substance. The rest is shadow!" This visionary's words led to the development of his company's mission statement, which still reads today: *With a clear focus on our customers, both internal and external, we strive to be a driving force in providing quality customer support in a rapidly changing environment.*

FUELLING THE FIRE

Does it not make sense that to exceed the expectations of your end-user or external customer, an internal "fire" must first blaze within all employees—a fire that drives everyone in the organization to perform at the highest level and to forge long-term relationships with both internal team members and the end-user? If so how is this fire ignited?

There must be compelling reasons for the flame to ignite. Leading articles on customer service from publications such as the International Customer Service Association's *Service Journal* all lead to one conclusion—*customer satisfaction is your niche*. All products and services can and will be duplicated by your competitors. Your *delivery* of customer service, however, will be your competitive edge. Therefore, every employee must strive to exceed customer expectations. The unique mix of professional employees, supported by an infrastructure that has set customer service standards at all department levels, is the road to success in this highly competitive environment. If you have dramatically increased your employees' level of awareness of the vital importance of customer service, you have taken the first step in the right direction. Now, what's next?

BEARING THE TORCH

Gary Comer, founder of Lands' End, in his 1996 annual report put it simply: "Don't worry about what is best for the company—worry about what is best for the customer." This philosophy, which can provide the spark to light the fire in an organization, must emanate from the organization's leaders. Executives and managers must be role models for the behaviour and performance expected from all employees. Consider the impact Sam Walton had on his organization when he visited the stores and helped customers. Have you ever shopped at a Nordstrom store and been served by a Nordstrom family member? The next time you call customer service at Disneyland or Walt Disney World, don't be surprised if the "cast member" identifies himself by saying, "I'm Michael Eisner. Can I help you?"

The leadership of each of these companies has been developed through team meetings, middle-management caucuses, focus groups, and, yes, even handling a few customer calls. Their "kindling" of the blaze is threefold:

1. Send a clear message to every management level that *all* focus will be on the customer.

2. Empower every employee to do what the customer expects of him or her.

3. Treat internal customers like external customers, since the level of satisfaction of the latter depends on how the former are treated.

Gary Comer positions this very well by saying, "There isn't a part of Lands' End that in some way does not affect how and what a customer thinks of us. They don't judge us by anything I write, or that anyone else writes, but by you [employees]. What you do for our customers, whatever you do, more than anything else, is what we are."

MEETING THE CHALLENGES

In analyzing several leading service providers, we discovered a number of factors that must be dealt with so the flame can continue to burn. Consider how your firm can meet these challenges:

- Improve the level of awareness of customer service in all departments.
- Determine how to instil a positive attitude, pride, and free thinking.
- Remodel the culture, policies, and management structure.
- Maintain consistency throughout the organization.
- Respond to increasing customer expectations.
- Establish performance standards.
- Correct those who suffer from "tunnel vision."

BEGINNING WITH THE END

One component of the Lands' End Customer Service Mission statement may be helpful here. To promote team commitment: *Provide guidance and support by recognizing individuals, encouraging creativity, promoting personal growth, and celebrating successes.*

You may read with great interest the lengthy and detailed Leadership Expectations manual developed by the Lands' End management team. The topics include "Demonstrates initiative," "Exemplifies a role model, "Coaches and develops," "Understands and promotes company culture," and "Promotes teamwork."

What has led to the success of the most highly regarded companies? It is quite obvious—their leadership and management is totally
committed to focusing on customer satisfaction. One of their greatest
strengths is the ability to "begin with the end in mind," as Stephen
Covey suggests in his book *The Seven Habits of Highly Effective People*.[1]
These companies know what the result should be and they employ all
their resources to, first, identify the potential roadblocks and, second,
establish a system or plan to overcome these before they even occur.

LIGHTING THE FIRE

What motivates each employee in your organization? How do employees "recharge their batteries"? What do they need to stay focused? Does
your company's infrastructure support and provide the flexibility
required for offering outstanding customer service? How will you succeed in making customer service a vital component of your organization's marketing strategy? Light a fire and achieve success with the
following suggestions:

- See the workforce as a source of strategic advantage, not just a cost
  to be minimized or avoided.

- Work with people; don't simply replace them or limit the scope of
  their activities.

- Ensure that each individual within the workforce has adequate
  skills.

- Employ leading edge recruitment strategies for front-line employees.

- Use an appropriate coaching process within your management philosophy.

- Develop each person's utmost potential through the application of a
  continuing, lifelong learning growth plan.

Establishing a service ethic within your organization and lighting
an eternal flame of focus among all employees will be the only way to
differentiate your company and survive in your marketplace.

Now, go light that fire!

---

[1] New York: Simon & Schuster, 1989.

About the author

JERRY L. FRITZ

Jerry L. Fritz is director of sales and customer service management programs for the Management Institute, School of Business, University of Wisconsin-Madison. He directs, coordinates, and instructs sales, sales management, and customer service workshops and conferences designed for practising business professionals.

A Leader's Perspective on Becoming Customer-Driven

INTERVIEW WITH JAMES SIERK, ALLIEDSIGNAL SENIOR VP AND BALDRIGE AWARD JUDGE

E.J. Kahn III,
Strategic communications consultant, Boston, MA

BY ALL MEASURES, 1994 would have seemed a banner year for AlliedSignal Corporation, based in Morristown, New Jersey. With $12.8 billion in annual revenues, this manufacturer of aerospace, automotive, and engineered materials had easily maintained its lofty position as a member of the Dow Jones Industrial 30, and was among the top 40 companies of the Fortune 500. Almost a decade had passed since the merger of the Allied and Signal corporations. The transformation from a company whose revenues came exclusively from oil, gas, and chemicals to one whose lines of business ranged from business jet engines and environmental control systems to braking systems, spark plugs, nylon fibres, and polyester was moving forward nicely. For the first time in seven years, annual sales had grown in all three of the company's principal areas of business. Productivity was up too, the highest increase in three years. Yet in that same year, AlliedSignal began a singular effort to make customer satisfaction more of a priority than it ever had been before.

Why would such a dominant industry leader feel compelled to force even more change? Early in 1996, senior vice-president James Sierk was reminding a Houston audience, comprising AlliedSignal managers, of the reason. "When we started our change process in

1991," said Sierk, "we listed our values. The top one read, 'Satisfying our customer is our first priority.'" Three years later, said Sierk, customer satisfaction measures had only slightly improved. The bottom line notwithstanding, AlliedSignal had become too inwardly focused. "Our customers," concluded Sierk, "were telling us that." By listening closely, AlliedSignal was reversing the trend—building revenues by developing "high loyalty" among its key customers.

The road-map for this activity was Jim Sierk's responsibility. Sierk had joined AlliedSignal in 1991 as senior vice-president for quality. He'd made his mark in the quality arena with Xerox, where he capped a 26-year career by leading the team assembled at that company to compete for—and eventually earn—the Malcolm Baldrige Award in 1990. Subsequently, Sierk was named a Baldrige judge, and for the past three years has read some 10 applications annually from the best companies in the United States. "One of the advantages of being involved in the Baldrige process," notes Sierk, "is that you learn a lot from good organizations."

Because few executives are similarly exposed to a broad spectrum of leading-edge thinking and activity in the fields of quality and customer excellence, *Knowledge/Knowhow* (published by Coopers & Lybrand Consulting's Government Consulting Practice) asked Sierk to share some of those lessons learned. Their discussion gives us some answers to the question "What are the characteristics of a company steeped in customer excellence?"

Sierk: To begin with, customer-driven companies understand near-term requirements and expectations, and they identify distinct market segments and customer groups. One thing that impressed me was the number of meetings, both formal and informal, these businesses have with their customers. They sit down, agree on mutual goals, and routinely measure their performance against those goals. The biggest companies and their customers will schedule face-to-face discussions between their CEOs every quarter. In one case, a supplier that was larger than its customers generated measures to help its customers measure the supplier's performance.

Knowledge/Knowhow(KK): How do customers perceive performance?

Sierk: One thing that's struck me is how common the terms "delighter" and "satisfier" are becoming. That's the context of perception. The best strategies assume that delighters will become satisfiers before long. For example, a few years ago, our major aerospace customers expected us to deliver goods "near the end" of a given month. Now they've moved to specific days, and the windows are shrinking. In the automobile industry, deliveries are already scheduled three times daily. If that's a delighter now, it'll be a satisfier in the near future, because every supplier will have to offer it.

KK: Are satisfiers enough to guarantee customer repurchases?

Sierk: No, but I'm limited in what specific examples I can point to, because of confidentiality agreements. One company, however—Ritz-Carlton Hotels—has stated publicly that its studies indicate a substantial difference between people who said they were satisfied with the hotel's performance and people who stated they would return to the Ritz as guests. Customer satisfaction, the Ritz's inquiry showed, wasn't the key metric in identifying those who would return.

KK: Do Baldrige applicants commonly collect and analyze customer knowledge, and seek feedback for improvement?

Sierk: Yes, they have good processes for both collecting and listening. I've noted several best practices here: the use of an e-mail system that's universally accessible; focus groups that include the customers' customers; senior-level reviews—called "presidential" in Japan—after each major win or loss to improve processes; close examination of errors on customer orders and analysis of why they occurred; resolution of customer complaints at the first point of contact; surveys that include former customers and target customers; and training in customer listening for all associates who have customer contact.

KK: Don't customers need to have access to information from your company, too?

Sierk: Yes. Providing easy access to enable customers to seek information, to comment, and to complain is another characteristic of customer-driven companies. Best practices include actively soliciting complaints from customers—not setting goals for complaint reduction; having good software to track resolution of problems; tight deadlines for resolving problems; and treating complaints as symptoms.

You need to put in place problem action teams that prioritize the root causes of these symptoms and resolve them each week. Statistical data suggest only one out of nine dissatisfied customers complain, so you must get information from the other eight.

KK: This sounds as if the organization's listening skills have to be well-developed.

Sierk: They do. The Baldrige applicants spend time and effort training customer-contact employees in both listening and relationship-management techniques. Among the best practices that I've encountered are mapping everyone who contacts a customer—in person, in writing, by telephone, or through e-mail—and understanding the measures and satisfiers at each contact point. There's a northern California Baldrige winner, Granite Rocks, which delivers crushed stone. Every truck driver is trained in selling techniques. They have more contact with the customer than virtually any other Granite employees, and that training has had a positive impact on the business.

KK: Should these employees also have the power to resolve customer issues?

Sierk: Of course. And the dollar limit that a customer-contact person has in resolving a complaint is a typical Baldrige examiner's question. If a sales rep says he has to get management approval for every adjustment in a customer's favour, he's not very empowered. At L.L. Bean, a few years ago, telephone reps had a dollar limit on adjustments. If you called to say you wanted to exchange, or return, or have replaced any item worth less than the dollar limit, the rep couldn't say "No" without a manager's approval. "Yes" was an answer she could give on her own. I tested that one day, telling the phone rep, "I've been a good customer for years. You can see that from past purchases on your computer screen. Give me a free pair of socks, the ones on page 64 of the catalog." They cost eight dollars, as I recall. And the rep couldn't say, "No." Instead, she responded, "I'm sorry. I have to talk to my manager about this." I knew I was not going to get a pair.

KK: You've been on the leading edge of this theory of customer intimacy, and its importance, for more than a decade. How would you describe its development?

Sierk: It's been initiated by the customer. Fifteen years ago, a few American businesses looked at their supplier bases and concluded that there were too many suppliers, and that none of the relationships were particularly close. By the late eighties, closer relationships had developed. Relationships among the bigger suppliers and customers moved toward partnerships. Within organizations, barriers broke down, allowing suppliers to design systems for customers that permitted seamless logistics practices. Quality levels moved from the norm of two percent rejects to a much stricter 100 parts per million. This was driven by the customers and by the competition. At AlliedSignal, where our primary customers aren't consumers but other companies, it was critical to build close relationships.

KK: How has that manifested itself?

Sierk: All our measures are customer measures. The customer becomes visible throughout the organization, even on the factory floors, where our folks are seeing customer information. But we're still moving toward full partnering with the customer.

KK: To return to the Baldrige applications, are there any other characteristics we haven't covered?

Sierk: Several. One is having a clear understanding of competitors' competencies—that is, considering competitors' strategies in your own [strategies], using reverse engineering of major competitors' products to understand technology and cost performance, and having an accessible database maintained by the account team with key competitive information. Another characteristic of Baldrige applicants is having linkages between customer-satisfaction goals and goals for improved operational performance. Yet another one is using measures developed by customers as a first priority. And finally, sharing knowledge of customer-satisfaction results with all employees in the organization.

KK: Is striving for excellence in customer relationships as much of a challenge today as it was when you were at Xerox?

Sierk: We're doing things twice as fast as Xerox did because we have an advantage. It's the blueprint left behind by companies like Xerox. We can see the path. And we're not walking cautiously. We're racing.

About the author

E.J. KAHN III

E.J. Kahn III is a strategic communications consultant, author, and editor, based in Boston.

This article was written for Coopers & Lybrand's bi-monthly publication *Knowledge/Knowhow.*

Part Two

Best Practices in Creating and Using Measurements and Standards to Achieve Excellence in Customer Service

O V E R V I E W

Achieving breakthrough customer service requires more than strategy and good intentions. An organization needs the proper support mechanism to bring strategy to life, so that it becomes more than a poster on the wall. A support mechanism comprises standards of performance and dedication to measurement, internal and external. Standards are guideposts, but care must be taken to create the right guideposts and the right mechanisms to measure performance.

Best-practices organizations survey their customers regularly to determine their needs and the extent to which the company is meeting—or exceeding—them. Successful companies are more likely to survey customers on a variety of areas, including the effectiveness of complaint handling, customer satisfaction, conformance to standards, customer needs, and new product ideas. But best-practices organizations don't stop there. Not only do they measure their actual performance against standards they have established for themselves, but they also compare themselves against their competition.

Organizations that achieve breakthrough customer service know that a commitment to customer satisfaction must be backed up by a complete understanding of their customers (internal and external), the competition, and the marketplace, as well as by an ability to identify and respond to areas where change is needed.

The authors of the articles in Part Two discuss four of the measurement concepts identified above: internal/corporate measurement, external customer measurement, customer complaints, and benchmarking. In Chapter 6, Peter Lawton provides a perspective on the first concept—internal customer measurement. He deals with the role of corporate performance management and performance indicators as important components of an effective management system. He also provides a process for establishing and measuring these mission critical indicators. In Chapter 7, David Wilkerson offers a step-by-step approach to create an effective external customer measurement system. But you will find his approach slightly different from that of most organizations. The author argues that organizations must have internal measures that are process-oriented, measured and managed by process operators, and linked directly to measures designed for customer satisfaction.

Another effective listening tool that was identified earlier is the comment/complaint system. In Chapter 8, Chris Daffy provides brief case studies and a message: Never be complacent; be constantly on the alert and prepared to change and react. The direction will come from listening to the voice of the customer. In Chapter 9 Joel Rosen writes, "Customer complaints represent more than just customers venting frustration; they are wake-up calls and a key to enhance our revenue." Rosen goes on to examine a number of lessons learned and the process tools to use. In Chapter 10, the last article in the measurement concept series, the Eastman Kodak Company's benchmarking success story, is founded on a simple premise: "No matter how good we think we are, there must be somebody out there performing similar tasks, but in a different way—perhaps a better way. Kodak has made a significant investment in the principles and practices supporting benchmarking. In this article, the authors share with us Kodak's methodology for success.

How do organizations use measurement principles? And have these helped them succeed? You will find the answers to these questions in the case studies that follow and tie these concepts together. The case study of Bell Canada, in Chapter 11, offers insight on how the tools described above were used to tap into the voice of the customer and to change the processes that touch the customer.

As you read the contributions in Part Two, think of the tortoise, which can move forward only when it sticks its neck out. It must come out of its shell, and look around and beyond itself to progress. Take a lesson from the tortoise. Look outside your organizations, talk to your customers (both internal and external), and learn from the best practices of others.

S.A.B.

Mission Critical Measurement

DEVELOPING AND USING
CORPORATE PERFORMANCE INDICATORS

Peter Lawton, Coopers & Lybrand,
Toronto, ON

CORPORATE PERFORMANCE MANAGEMENT and performance indicators are clearly becoming important components of an effective management system. In an era of constant organizational change and upheaval, performance indicators are the organizational anchors and touchstones—providing direction, stability, and guidance.

All organizations are experiencing significant shifts in managing and measuring. Cost pressures and declining revenues are creating an environment that is becoming less forgiving and more demanding; there is more pressure to perform and an increasing intolerance of underutilized assets. Business imperatives require well-developed and focused performance indicators.

THE IMPORTANCE OF MEASURING PERFORMANCE

Many good reasons exist for developing effective performance measures. One reason, according to Peter Drucker, is that you can't manage what you don't measure. Here are what some indicators can provide:

- Performance indicators give organizational leaders an immediate but comprehensive view of the organization and its key performance areas.

- They focus attention on the most critical areas needing management action.

- They also communicate priorities and direction, and translate that direction into results.

- They can be used as a lever to support appropriate behaviour, linking individual and team performance measures as well as linking today's actions and tomorrow's goals.

- Key performance indicators also directly highlight the barriers that are blocking the implementation of goals and performance improvements, and the introduction of effective organizational change.

- Used properly, these indicators can enhance the existing planning process, budgeting and resource allocation, personnel motivation, and incentive and employee performance management systems.

- They can also improve personal goal setting and the monitoring and decision-making systems.

- Finally, they can provide reliable evaluation criteria that are applicable to different organizational units.

We believe that well-conceived and well-communicated corporate performance measures put strategy and vision—not rules and control—at the centre of the organization. They pull people toward the overall vision. As such, they help organizations become employee-centred, customer-centred, and purpose-centred. The focus is on collective goals and results, not on individuals, processes, or systems. Once corporate indicators have been established, employees can then develop appropriate behaviours and processes that will move the organization toward these goals and results.

Best-practices organizations are also developing performance indicators as a principal means of decentralizing authority in the organization. Delegating resource control and authority to lower levels in the organization requires clear lines of accountability and clear expectations. Performance indicators clarify in measurable terms the accountability relationship between successive levels in the organization, and provide a common frame of reference for direction and priority setting.

In short, effective performance measurement enables an organization to align its management processes and to focus on implementing a long-term strategy. A performance measurement program also gauges the operating effectiveness of the organization, sets standards for expected behaviour and performance requirements, and provides guidelines for managing performance, developing skills, and helping employees to build pride into their work and their team.

We generally use the concept of the "balanced scorecard," which is now being widely applied in developing performance measures in many different types of organizations. The balanced scorecard facilitates the development of the distinct categories of measurement that are most appropriate for the challenges facing the organization.

Using the balanced scorecard approach, we have developed a "spider web" format to display and present these measures to management. A key advantage of this presentation format is that the balance between the measures is easily seen and demonstrated to management. As a result of resource allocation decisions, one of the measures is often increased at the expense of another, creating an imbalance. The power of the Spider Web format lies in locating the imbalances among the cohort measures within each category. The consequences can be seen simply and sometimes quite dramatically.

DEVELOPING MISSION CRITICAL PERFORMANCE INDICATORS

The six-step process for establishing mission critical indicators is as follows:

Step 1: Establish a senior team to develop the indicators.

Step 2: Develop corporate mission critical performance indicators.

Step 3: Develop functional mission critical performance indicators.

Step 4: Build the indicators into the management system.

Step 5: Drive the indicators down through the organization.

Step 6: Ensure that the value added by the indicators is sustained.

Step 1: Establish a senior team to develop the indicators.

Not everything that counts can be counted,
and not everything that can be counted counts.
—Albert Einstein

The first step is to bring together a team of the senior managers or organizational leaders to develop the indicators. Present and discuss with this team a measurement system that will provide them with a workable but comprehensive framework to translate the strategic objectives into a coherent set of performance measures.

Step 2: Develop corporate mission critical performance indicators.

The key component of this step is a workshop with the senior management group to identify the distinct categories of measurement that are most appropriate for the organization, its situation, and the purpose of the measurements. At the corporate level, these will most likely relate to strategic imperatives, corporate change initiatives, or corporate performance in relation to the key stakeholder groups of employees, customers, owners, and the community. You may need to review the organizational direction and strategy prior to this workshop. At the

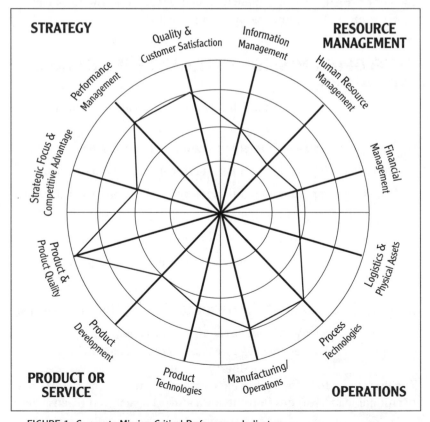

FIGURE 1: Corporate Mission Critical Performance Indicators

workshop, designate individuals on the team as champions to be responsible for developing the measurement information for each indicator.

Figure 1 shows corporate mission critical performance indicators for an organization at the highest corporate level. In this case, the organization is clearly focusing on supporting product and product quality; the resource management activities are not performing as well, perhaps neglected as a result of overemphasis in the product area. The diagram shows the need for investment in resource management.

Step 3: Develop functional mission critical performance indicators.

This step goes beyond the corporate level to identify and measure mission critical indicators at the next level down, typically the strategic business unit (SBU), divisional, or functional level to support the

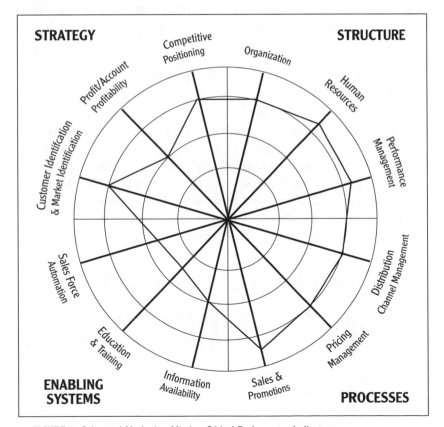

FIGURE 2: Sales and Marketing Mission Critical Performance Indicators

overall corporate measures. A follow-up workshop is typically organized for the champions to bring forward and present their indicators.

Figure 2 shows the mission critical performance indicators of a sales
and marketing function. In this case, the enabling systems, although mission critical, are not performing as well as the other components.

Step 4: Build the indicators into the management system.

Develop a process for using and responding to these indicators regularly
as a key component of the management system. These indicators should
be built into the management agenda as a regular item so the managers
can use them to assess current performance and then drive improvements and change initiatives. Clearly, some measures need to be
reviewed frequently and others less so; however, a "Facts Book" or briefing update at the monthly senior management meeting can be a very
valuable tool to guide management decisions and resource allocation.

Step 5: Drive the indicators down through the organization.

Present these measures to the lower levels of the organization, where
individual goals and performance measures can be set in order to support the corporate measures. Communicating these measures down
through the organization is important in enabling all individuals to see
how their work fits into the mission critical activities of the company.

Develop workshops for middle management and other staff where
the indicators can be presented to them and translated into supportive
but more specific and appropriate measures within the organization.

Step 6: Ensure that the value added by the indicators is sustained.

As with all management initiatives, this process, not just the measures
themselves, needs to be reviewed regularly to maintain and modify the
measures, as appropriate. This is particularly important when a number of different senior manager champions are responsible for different
components of the scorecard.

CASE STUDY
Measuring the Mission Critical Performance of a Distribution Company

The case of a company that we, at Coopers & Lybrand, are currently working with demonstrates our approach and methodology. We began by organizing a workshop with the senior management team to set the corporate performance indicators at a broad level.

Developing the Corporate Mission Critical Indicators

During the workshop we developed the categories of measurement that were most appropriate for the organization, its situation, challenges, and issues. We also clarified and referred directly to the corporate strategy, the vision, values, and critical success factors, as well as the other strategic imperatives. Figure 3 shows the corporate mission critical indicator categories that were identified.

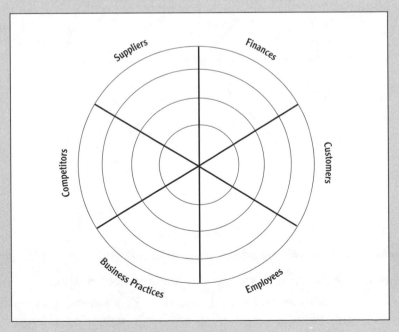

FIGURE 3: Corporate Mission Critical Indicator Categories

Developing the Mission Critical Indicators for the Customer Category

At a subsequent workshop, we developed specific measures within each of the categories. The operational measures developed were directly linked to the drivers of future organizational performance. Individuals were then designated as champions to work with the consultants, to be responsible for the development of the measurement information for each indicator, and to bring them back to the team for review and approval.

Figure 4 shows the mission critical indicators for the customers category.

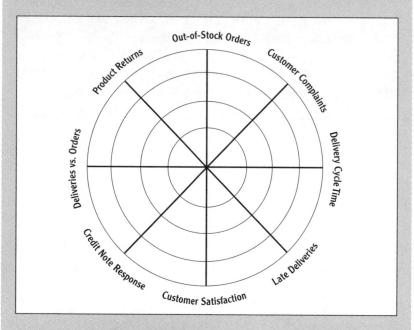

FIGURE 4: Customer Mission Critical Indicators

Building the Indicators into the Management System

After these workshops, we continued to work with the team to support the task of collecting, formatting, and presenting the information, and then interpreting what it meant. The organization is now in the process of setting goals and performance improvement targets based on the analysis of the data. When this is completed, the other components of the management system and decision-making processes will be reviewed to ensure that the necessary performance indicator follow-up and supports are in place—for example, strategic planning, executive decision-making, budgeting, performance management, and incentive systems.

CONCLUSION

Developing mission critical performance measures and creating key indicators are challenging tasks requiring creativity and initiative. Once these indicators have been developed, effort and discipline are required to maintain and support them on a regular basis, and to consistently use them to guide corporate decision-making. These measures can, however, be important sea anchors in a time of organizational change. They guide and direct strategy and change efforts, providing some firm ground and stability when it is needed. We believe that the process of developing key corporate performance measures is itself mission critical.

> *If you don't measure it, you can't understand it.*
> *If you can't understand it, you can't control it.*
> *And if you can't control it, you can't improve it.*
> —James Harrington

About the author

PETER LAWTON

Peter Lawton is a principal in Coopers & Lybrand Consulting's Human Capital Management Practice. He is based in the Toronto office. His fields of expertise include performance measurement, strategic issues management, corporate transition and change management, organizational and management development, executive group effectiveness improvement, and process management reengineering program design and implementation.

Measuring Customer Satisfaction Effectively

David Wilkerson, DBA,
Coopers & Lybrand, Arlington, VA

Most organizations have internal measures of performance. Many organizations these days have a mechanism for gathering customer-satisfaction feedback. Few organizations, however, measure the effectiveness of their internal processes and link these measures to quality and customer satisfaction.

INTRODUCING QUALITY MEASUREMENT

Fred Smith, chief executive officer of Federal Express, said, "Quality is defined as performance to the standard expected by the customer." When your organization focuses on service quality, it becomes devoted to meeting and exceeding customer expectations. To achieve this, you must implement an objective measurement system. Effective measurement systems are critical to quality organizations. They will allow you not only to track and collect performance data, but more important, to analyze the data and use this information to make decisions.

There are practical methods that all organizations can use to develop objective indicators of quality—for example, number of defects, operating performance, and conformance to specification. By measuring performance against these indicators, you can get hard data about the customer's perception of your quality. This information can help you both focus improvement efforts where they will make a difference in customer satisfaction and allocate organizational resources most effectively. By tying process performance and process measures directly to customer satisfaction measures, the measurement system creates a critical link to quality as defined by your customers.

Consider the following. Every organization has processes—a billing process, an order process, a manufacturing process, to name a few. Each process is made up of a number of activities that ultimately lead to, say, a bill or invoice. By measuring both the customer's degree of satisfaction with the process and the factors that affect that satisfaction (for example, billing accuracy, timeliness of bill, clarity of bill), you can identify the specific action that must be taken to increase customer satisfaction.

Measuring quality and performance will help you improve the products and services you deliver to your customers. This article will show you how to create a quality measurement system that enables you to find out what your customers want, measure your performance against those standards, and change your work processes to increase customer satisfaction. You will also learn about practical applications of the quality measurement system in a variety of organizations.

A good performance measurement system will:

- Be driven by customer needs.
- Be flexible and adaptable to the changing imperatives of the organization.
- Be effective, yet simple to understand.
- Provide a scoreboard to evaluate, motivate, and provide accountability.
- Be rooted to the organization's strategic plan and critical success factors.
- Be credible, with real measures—not manipulated ones.
- Provide early indications of performance variation.
- Allow for process operators to get immediate feedback on performance.

WHAT HAPPENS WHEN YOU DON'T MEASURE QUALITY?

The greatest danger in not measuring quality lies in the potential failure of your organization to provide what the customer needs when he or she needs it. The obvious consequences of this for you are the loss of respect and ultimately loss of business from the people necessary for your survival. If you do not know what your customers expect from you and, further, how well you are meeting those expectations, you will not know where improvement efforts are needed. You risk focusing your attention on areas that your customers do not value—a serious waste of both time and resources. David Osborne and Ted Gaebler, authors of *Reinventing Government*,[1] see performance measurement as the key strategy for developing results-oriented government. They make three points relevant to all organizations.

1. If you don't measure results, you can't tell success from failure.

2. If you can't see success, you can't reward it—and if you can't reward success, you are probably rewarding failure.

3. If you can't recognize failure, you can't correct it.

By measuring quality as defined by your customers, you will direct your efforts and resources where they will add the most value: to the issues most important to your customers. In addition, you will be able to recognize trends in performance outcomes that affect customer satisfaction, allowing you to attend to problems before customers become disgruntled. You can track your performance with regard to customer satisfaction and plan strategic objectives accordingly.

MEASURING SERVICE QUALITY

Organizations should measure the aspects of their processes that are related to customer satisfaction. To create a true link between customer satisfaction and process improvement, you should see a cause and effect relationship among the results of these measures. If you don't see this relationship, it does not necessarily mean that you have improved the wrong things. You may have improved an outcome that wasn't as

---

[1] Reading, MA: Addison-Wesley Publishing Company, 1992.

important to customers as you had anticipated. Trying again is a critical part of this approach. Your goal is to improve quality as the customer defines it. So you must go back and improve other aspects of your performance until you see greater satisfaction. *You are looking for that link between cause and effect.*

The link between customer satisfaction and process performance can be determined scientifically. This link is not mysterious, but the relationship is complex. The following four-step process will link customer satisfaction and process improvement.

The Four-Step Quality Measurement System

1. Identify your customers.

2. Conduct research on customer expectations and satisfaction.

3. Identify and measure the process outcomes or deliverables that lead to customer satisfaction.

4. Improve your performance of factors that drive the quality of those deliverables.

The remainder of this chapter describes how to take these steps. Along the way, you'll see examples of the challenges you can face in developing measurement systems, and how others have dealt with them.

THE FOUR-STEP PROCESS

Step 1: Identify Your Customers.

The first step in our process, identifying customers, is the foundation for customer-driven quality improvements. Answering "Who are our customers?" means both listing and describing them. This description guides the entire measurement strategy. It also helps categorize customers into logical subgroups. This is a useful practice since each subgroup may have different expectations or use services in different ways. It is important to distinguish the difference between customers and stakeholders. Customers are those who use your products or services; stakeholders are those who have a vested interest in your operations and results. The focus of this book is on your customers, although the concepts may apply to stakeholders as well.

To define and meet customer expectations, you first have to know who your *most important* customers are. You might think this step would be the easiest part of measuring quality, but the opposite is usually true: identifying customers can be the hardest part.

How Do You Identify Customers?

Understanding who your customers are and what products and services they receive is critical to assessing their specific demands and expectations. Your customers are the people who receive and use the output of your process. One of the best ways to start identifying customers is to use a simple worksheet like the one shown in Figure 1.

Customer Identification Worksheet

Process Name Group	Customer	Output Received
_____	_____	_____
	_____	_____
	_____	_____
_____	_____	_____
	_____	_____
	_____	_____
_____	_____	_____
	_____	_____
	_____	_____

FIGURE 1: Customer Identification Worksheet

To identify all customers, examine *who uses or has interest in your products and/or services*. When you organize your customer base, keep in mind that similar customers tend to have similar demands and expectations. Logical customer categories may include product, service, location, industry, size, etc. On the other hand, these may be characteristics and the important categories may be loyalty or job function.

An example of how to identify customers by function comes from the U.S. General Services Administration's Federal Supply Service (FSS). The FSS is a government "department store" for office supplies, tools, furniture, etc. Federal agencies can get their supplies through FSS, but they also have the option of using private sector suppliers. When FSS went through the process of identifying its customers, it came up with five distinct groups.

1. Top management for all user agencies—for example, secretary of the interior or congressional committee leaders (if government supply operations became subject to scrutiny). Customer concerns at this level would be general: Are people getting what they need within budget? Are costs comparable to private sector alternatives?

2. Operating management—managers of served agencies. Their concerns would likely relate to cost advantage and timeliness of delivery.

3. The governing office—made up of agency procurement officers. Their main quality concern would be whether the rules have been followed, proper authorizations obtained, and paperwork filled out correctly. The bills for FSS purchases go through these officers for payment, so fulfilling their expectations is clearly important.

4. Clients—the key customers in each government unit who order the supplies for their departments and who could just go down to their local office supply centre for their needs. If it is cheaper, easier, and/or quicker to go to a local shop, or if supplies are unavailable through the government store, the supply staff will choose that option. So the FSS managers have good reason to learn about these customers' needs.

5. The end-user. These are the folks who needed the supplies to begin with and who have the least control over whether they get the right materials to do the job. The end-users sometimes get overlooked. They are inconvenienced and can't serve their customers (the public) properly if the wrong kind of flip charts arrive for the meeting.

They can't buy supplies themselves, but they certainly experience frustration when things go wrong. In complex government agencies, end-users may have no idea where their complaints should go.

In addition to those categories of customers listed for FSS above, two other customer groups can also be important: (1) Internal customers—the people who are part of the work process that produce the goods and services. By better serving internal customers, an organization may also be improving service to external customers. (2) Those with whom the FSS has a regulatory, supervisory, or adversarial relationship. Measuring and improving those relationships can be crucial to delivering quality services and allocating resources appropriately.

Once you have a comprehensive picture of your organization's customers, you must gather information on their expectations and levels of satisfaction. You will use this information later to set priorities for areas of process improvement efforts. But first you need to prioritize customer groups, because customer service quality must be specifically focused and multifaceted.

Identifying customers and placing them in priority order is a very important aspect of quality and performance measurement. You cannot do everything at once. So this step helps you focus your resources where they will add the most value.

Within an organization, it is probably best for a team, rather than any one individual, to be responsible for this step. Leadership focus and vision must drive the activity. But the team should include employees who deliver the services. Since the purpose of customer service measurement is improvement, the people who produce your products or services should be fully involved so that they feel ownership of the improvement process and contribute ideas for improvements.

Don't be concerned if you do not have crystal clear, well-defined customer groups at this point—press on. Use what you have to guide the next step. Once you have collected data from customers, you may want to redefine your customer groups.

Summary of Step 1: Identify Your Customers

You now have a complete description of your goals and an organized and useful listing of customers. You will return to this information often when developing your measurement system and making process improvements. Also, you will find that these customer profiles identify issues, problems, and improvement opportunities you can address immediately or as a future task. This information will not have been so obvious before; now it is organized for effective decision-making. At the same time, be sure to obtain agreement from those involved.

All the information you have collected will be used in the next step of this process.

Step 2: Conduct Research on Customer Expectations and Satisfaction.

Once you have your list of customers in priority order, you are ready to move on to Step 2 in our four-part system—gathering information on customers' expectations and level of satisfaction. The keys to measuring customer expectations and satisfaction are planning, setting clear objectives for your research, and implementing your plan effectively for valid results. This can be quite simple with the right approach. You must find out two things:

1. What do your customers expect from you?

2. How well are you currently satisfying these expectations?

A good way to determine the relative importance of customer expectations is to use a quality grid like the one shown in Figure 2. Satisfaction Loyalty is mapped horizontally and importance mapped vertically; data points correspond to your performance according to your customers. If customer research is well-planned and well-executed, you will be operating in the upper right-hand quadrant: You're doing the *right things right*. This ensures that you are applying resources exactly where they'll benefit customers most. Proper planning will avoid random information that has no clear applicability, and will ensure that your research will tell you what you need to know.

Executing your plan properly is the second part of doing the right things right. This means producing research results that measure the factors targeted and that are reliable, consistent across all measurements taken, valid, and accurate. This is critical to the manager who is going to use this information to make important decisions and track progress over time. At a minimum, you should conduct a pilot test of your measurement tools with a small group of customers. This will help you refine and validate your methods.

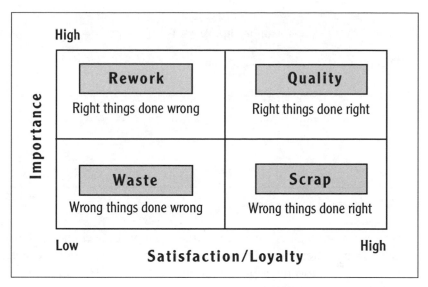

FIGURE 2: Quality Grid

While many research methods can measure customer satisfaction, we believe that surveys that are properly designed and conducted are the most effective and efficient way for you to get consistent, reliable information on a multitude of clients. A customer survey is necessary to gather relevant information, but this is not an "off-the-shelf" product. Every research tool must be customized to an organization's research goals and business environment in order to produce useful information. You need to get the *right information* from the *right customers* based on your organization's *current needs.* Don't overwhelm customers with requests for information you don't really need. Surveys can also be repeated to measure changes over time. Before developing your survey you may want to explore key issues by talking to customers, either through personal interviews or through focus groups of six to eight customers. This pre-survey information can help you decide where to focus your survey questions. It may also point out problem areas you hadn't been aware of. The customer interview form shown in Figure 3 would be a useful tool.

Let me emphasize that measuring customer service requires repeated assessments of customer satisfaction. *You must be sure that you're getting it right, keeping it right, and continuing to focus on the right things.* Customer priorities often shift over time, as external situations

Customer Interview Form

Importance (1–5)	Expectation	Satisfaction (1–5)
_____	_____	_____
_____	_____	_____
_____	_____	_____
_____	_____	_____

FIGURE 3: Customer Interview Form

or customers' strategies change. You must monitor these changes. How often you survey depends on the cycle time of service delivery, the cycle time of your improvement plan, and your resources. At a minimum, however, you will want to repeat surveys at least annually. Otherwise you may miss developing trends.

Remember, too, that every time you measure, the results of customer-satisfaction research can have immediate uses and benefits. Results may reveal a problem that has an obvious and easy solution that can be carried out immediately—a quick fix.

Information about customer satisfaction can also be a useful tool for managers and employees. At Dunlop Tire Company, management performance evaluations are tied to customer satisfaction levels. Other organizations could do the same—in effect making customer satisfaction a part of everyone's job.

Summary of Step 2: Customer Research

When your customer research is complete, you're halfway there. You've identified your customers and learned what's important to them. Now it's time to link these results to process improvement, which brings us to Steps 3 and 4 in the quality measurement system

Step 3: Identify and Measure Work Process Outcomes.

Throughout the measuring process, keep in mind that your goal is to create a cause and effect relationship between each type of measurement you take. When your measures show you have improved a critical aspect of a work process, you should also see an improvement in your work process outcomes—and then in your customer satisfaction ratings. When this linkage exists, as depicted in Figure 4, you know your work processes are creating value for your customers.

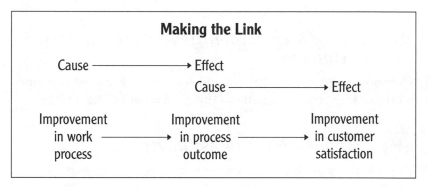

FIGURE 4: Making the Link

To create this link, first translate your customer expectations into quantifiable work process terms. This involves defining and measuring the *work process outcomes* that cause customer satisfaction. (Work process outcomes are sometimes called *service levels* or *service standards*).

Let's say, for example, that you are the manager of a cafeteria, and your customers expect a clean environment. How can you express this subjective expectation—*cleanliness*—in terms of your work process outcomes? Cleanliness usually relates to a number of work process outcomes, including setting up and arranging the seats and maintaining the cafeteria area. What quantifiable indicators could you use to measure your performance in these areas? How about the time it takes customers to find a clean table, the number of clean tables available at 15-minute intervals, the number of times the tables are bussed and wiped clean per day, or how often floors are swept, mopped, and polished? All these are measurable results of process performance that go into meeting the customer's expectation for a clean environment. We sometimes call these the "bosses' measures," because bosses want specific information about work process results.

It is best to approach this task as a team, just as you did for identifying customers and as you will certainly do in developing process improvement later on. The time spent on team activities here will pay off well when the time comes to make process changes. When a team is involved in gathering hard facts, these become the basis for decisions about what to change and how. Without this foundation, you have teams making a leap of faith and basing process changes on intuition. This defeats the purpose of measuring quality.

Summary of Step 3: Identify and Measure Work Process Outcomes

Once you have completed Step 3 and defined work process outcomes, you have answered the question, "How well is our process doing?"

Step 4: Improve Your Process Drivers.

Step 4 is where process improvement takes place. This step identifies and tracks "workers' measures," and helps answer the question, "What do we need to change in the way we do the job, and how?" At this point, we use measurement tools, statistical process control techniques, process improvement team approaches, and performance management tools to make necessary improvements.

"Process drivers" are the factors within a process that cause quality performance to vary, to get better or worse. The performance of the process characteristic "drives" the quality characteristic.

One quality result may have many process drivers, each representing some task or operation within a process. Only a few, however, will cause the problems you may be experiencing in your performance results. Aim your search at finding these causes. They will have the following attributes:

- Their performance accounts for most of the variation in a process outcome, and the reasons for this are known.

- They measure process operations known to have major problems or opportunities for improvement.

Finding these causes will lead you to identify and eliminate the root causes of problems that affect performance. This is the key to major process improvement, increased process performance, and higher customer satisfaction.

Developing Process Drivers and Measurements

You already may have a good idea of the process drivers you need. If so, you can begin to define and develop measurements for them. At this point, you will be moving from simply measuring process performance to the first stages of process improvement. So consider getting your measures defined and captured before making process improvements.

You need to select a specific process outcome identified in Step 3. Focus the search on measurable causes that, if removed, will achieve major improvements in the process outcome. If you have a good idea where these causes occur in the process, say so; if not, list possible factors. Using techniques and tools such as brainstorming and cause and effect diagrams, the team develops a list of potential causes that affect the quality result. They eliminate those thought to have little or no effect, and arrive at a short list of three to five candidates.

Summary of Step 4: Improve Your Process Drivers

Process driver data are like the gauges in an aircraft instrument panel. They show how critical parts of a process are performing and give early warning of potentially serious problems. They also measure process improvement and help managers decide where to focus improvement efforts. Over the years, you will be regularly changing the process drivers you measure. This is part of a long-term strategy of continuous improvement in which you deal with problems and opportunities in order of their importance. What is this order? Ultimately, your customers define it.

BRINGING IT ALL TOGETHER: LINKING QUALITY MEASUREMENT AND PROCESS IMPROVEMENT

You can have the world's best instrument panel in your cockpit, but still crash if you ignore what the instruments tell you. Likewise, the world's best quality measurement system is worthless without process improvement. If you do not use measurement to improve your process, you are better off without it. Why? Because you will just be documenting your lack of progress.

A quality measurement system helps you identify where to make process improvements. Then it tells you if improvements result in increased performance in areas important to the customer. If the system does not do this, work on it until you and the people in your process get the right information.

IN CONCLUSION

Measuring quality documents success, not just problems. To complete the process you must show your results to customers, superiors, and staff. Everybody wants to be part of a winning team. These results help build customer loyalty, organizational support for demonstrating improved performance, and morale. When you combine measurement with improvement action, you will have quite a success story. Where does this success story begin? *Just ask your customers!*

About the author

DAVID WILKERSON

David Wilkerson is an educator, manager, and consultant who has developed, implemented, and taught managers how to apply measurement systems in government organizations for more than 20 years. He has provided consulting services to organizations throughout the world and has written numerous articles on cultural benchmarking and organizational assessment. He directed the development of the Organizational Assessment Process, which is used by Coopers & Lybrand affiliates worldwide. He has written a variety of articles on measuring both the "hard" and "soft" aspects of quality management. In 1993, David Wilkerson presented a live nationwide telecast for the U.S. Chamber of Commerce on measuring customer service.

Beware! Success Often Breeds Failure[1]

HOW TO CELEBRATE SUCCESS

Chris Daffy, Consultant and author,
London, UK

Success creates arrogance, arrogance creates complacency,
complacency leads to failure.
—Tom Peters

I first heard Tom Peters make that statement at one of his seminars. It really made me think at the time, and has stuck with me ever since because it's so true. He went on to say that the old saying "Success breeds success" has been proved wrong by so many businesses that it perhaps should be rewritten as "Success breeds failure."

I think he's right. There are so many companies that once had reputations for being leaders in service delivery that have been overtaken by competitors or are under such severe attack that they are likely to be beaten soon. It was interesting to read in *Customer Service Management* (November 1996) how Lexus, a division of Toyota, which for five years had been at the top of the J.D. Power Customer Satisfaction Index in the United States, is now in the number two slot; while Nissan's Infiniti is now on top. This obviously does not mean that Lexus is now failing (there were only 2 points out of 168 between it and Infiniti) but it does show how in the current highly competitive markets, being today's winner can so easily lead to becoming tomorrow's loser.

---

[1] Adapted with permission from *Customer Service Management*, London, England.

Here are a few more examples.

Marks and Spencer. Marks and Spencer (M&S) has for many years been thought of as the top service provider in UK retail clothing with perhaps the best returned-goods policy in the United Kingdom. However, there now appears to be an ever-increasing number of people who say M&S is not as good as it used to be, or maybe that it doesn't seem to be as good. Yet the M&S policy hasn't substantially changed for the worse over the past few years—but that's possibly the key reason for the change in people's perceptions. While M&S has stood relatively still, other retailers have developed ways to provide even better service levels with superior returned-goods policies. So by comparison, M&S now seems worse than it used to be.

IBM. There was a time when IBM was considered to be the world's top company for service in computers. It once even ran advertisements that suggested "nobody ever lost their job for ordering an IBM." I'm sure the company still provides excellent service but it doesn't seem to have retained that top slot for service in people's minds. It appears now to have lost that position to new companies such as Dell who have won numerous awards for being the world's best service provider in computer supplies and services.

AT&T Universal Card Service. The AT&T Universal Card, which was unveiled in March 1990 and had one million account holders just 78 days later, won the Malcolm Baldrige National Quality Award in 1992. It then went on to become the second most popular card in the United States in just two and a half years on the market. This is another example of how success can easily breed failure. The incredible success of the card became one of its main problems.

The management team was keen to continue tackling new challenges and move into other financial services. But when AT&T said no to these plans, team members got bored and most of the original team had left by mid-1993. Without AT&T making continual improvements, competitors were able to copy many of the features that had made the card so attractive. Now it is struggling with a declining market share and a rising delinquent accounts problem.

Sainsburys. For many years Sainsburys was considered the UK's best food retailer for service. But now companies such as Asda, Safeway, and Tesco have driven up customer service and improved returned-goods policies. They have really listened to their customers' needs and so found ways to provide drastically improved customer service levels. This has resulted in substantial growth in their turnovers and profits, to the point that Tesco has taken over from Sainsburys as the UK's most profitable food retailer.

So the road that once led to success can also lead to failure. It is therefore important to ensure that the Success⇨Arrogance⇨Complacency⇨Failure cycle is not allowed to run in your organization. And the best way to prevent the cycle from beginning is to never let success create arrogance. One indication that you are on that path to arrogance, or have gone beyond it and reached complacency, is hearing yourself or your colleagues using phrases like those shown in "The Verbal Signs of Corporate Arrogance and Complacency box."

The Verbal Signs of Corporate Arrogance and Complacency

"We get by."
"We survive."
"We're doing all right."
"We have our own little niche."
"We just keep going from day to day."
"We are doing as well as anyone else."
"We cannot see what more can be done."
"We are of course the world leaders in this field."
"We are very successful so we must be doing things right."
"We have nothing to learn from others, they could learn from us."
"We'd take some convincing that we should
be doing things differently."

If phrases like these are common in your business they indicate that you could be allowing arrogance and complacency to exist. The business may then slip into a slow drift and decline, where potential is unused and opportunities are missed. The result is often failure.

You therefore need to take the kind of actions listed below—probably swiftly—to get yourself off this path. For those that don't think they're on it, these same actions can also ensure that you never are.

Never let things settle.

Don't let things get too organized or rigid. Once they get that way, people tend to assume that they have reached the ultimate goal and therefore cannot get any better. If you keep things moving, constantly changing, and forever improving, people realize that there is no end to the path of continuous improvement. As many people have said, it is a journey with no destination. There is always a way of improving everything. Every step that is taken moves you to a new position from which you have a new perspective that enables you to see fresh opportunities for the next improvements. So keep stirring the pot.

Instigate a continuous learning program for every employee.

Don't ever allow any employee to think that he or she knows enough. Help employees to recognize that they can always get better and that you expect and will help them to do so. Make it core in your business that every employee is constantly involved in a personal, continuous improvement program. Help them find ways to improve themselves and their performance at work.

It's really important that you lead this kind of program by example. Let everyone see that you are constantly improving your own knowledge and skill, through reading, attending seminars, going on training courses, engaging in study visits to other companies and industries, etc. Your example will show that you consider it important enough to do yourself. They will then more readily accept how important it is for them.

Keep comparing yourself (benchmarking) with other companies that have a reputation for delivering high service levels.

This exercise is called "benchmarking"—studying other organizations in your industry and others to see how you compare against them, what you can learn from them, and which of their best practices you can adopt in your business. It is a practice that should never end.

It is also something that should engage the whole company. This is not an exercise just for managers and directors; it is an exercise for everyone. Turn your whole workforce into a team of researchers, analysts, and consultants. Get them all engaged in the activity of studying and learning from other companies' best practices. Teach your people how to analyze what they see and how to incorporate other people's best ideas in your business.

This constant striving for new and better ways of doing things helps to ensure that arrogance never takes root.

Bring in lots of outsiders.

Keep getting fresh and objective views of the business and its different parts. Use external consultants, business schools, students, friends in other businesses, customers, suppliers, people from other departments, etc. All these new and objective views, with different perspectives, help you to see things in a different way. New perspectives reveal things that have previously been missed. This can open people's eyes to new opportunities for improvements.

And don't ever let yourself or your colleagues believe that somebody who isn't trained in, say, engineering can't see a better way of engineering something. The best ideas often come from non-specialists. So bring in the amateurs and expect some great new ideas to result.

Have plenty of people around who don't always agree with you.

If you surround yourself with enough people who refuse to be "yes merchants," but will disagree with you, often and strongly, you will be forced to keep reassessing all that you are doing and so should keep finding ways to improve. This may be a lot more uncomfortable than having a team that always sees things the same way as you do, but it is essential if you want to avoid collective complacency through group thinking. The following quotation expresses this idea rather well:

When two men in business always agree, one of them is unnecessary.
—William Wrigley Jr

Set goals for creativity and innovation.

If people are given targets and goals to create new and better ideas, they are more likely to do so. You should have various rewards for these innovation programs to encourage people to take part. These rewards could be financial but often the best ones are psychological. So don't just pay people for good ideas, praise them as well. The following organizations do this:

3M Corporation. All divisions in the 3M Corporation are mandated to have at least 30 percent of all the products that are sold at any one time to be products that were created within the previous five years. This requirement guarantees that there is a constant regeneration of old products and ideas, and a constant creation of new ones so that the business is continually renewing itself.

Milliken. At Milliken, the textile manufacturer that won the European Quality Award in 1993, the average employee generates 24 suggestions for product or process improvements per year—that is 2 per month, per employee, on average. I don't know what the current UK average is but I'm sure of one thing—it's a lot less! Just imagine if every one of your employees were generating 2 ideas per month to improve the business. What a difference that would surely make to your performance and results.

Leyland Trucks. Another excellent example of a great suggestion scheme is the one operated by Leyland Trucks. It is now the major source of product improvement and cost savings for the business. Every suggestion from the staff earns a £1.00 voucher. They believe that is all that's needed to say thank you. The most important reward people get for their suggestion is the opportunity to quickly try it out for themselves. The best five each month then also win a night out for two at a local restaurant.

The number of suggestions this scheme generates has been steadily growing since its introduction and is now around 16 per employee per year. John Oliver, Leyland's chief executive, says, "It's the quantity of suggestions the scheme generates that counts. So long as we're getting plenty of suggestions coming in we know that amongst them there will be some that will have a great impact on the business. We're therefore happy to pay for them all."

John admits that they did once try to measure the cost-effectiveness of the scheme. But once they'd got as far as calculating that suggestions costing about £3,500 had created improvements and savings worth over £300,000 they decided that was all they needed to know and have never wasted time doing similar calculations since.

These are just a few ideas that you can use to break the success-to-failure cycle. You can probably think of others that would suit your particular organization. The key is to have lots of new thinking and a general attitude that no matter how good you may become, you can always get better!

About the author

CHRIS DAFFY

Chris Daffy is one of Europe's top specialists in customer service. He spends much of his time learning about customer service best practices in organizations of all types and sizes throughout the world. He is the author of *Once a Customer—Always a Customer* (London: Oak Tree Press, 1996).

Customer Service Management, from which this article has been adapted, is published quarterly for executives and managers wishing to attain quality and service excellence (see reference in Appendix I).

Customer Complaints

ARE YOU GETTING ENOUGH?

Joel Rosen, CMC, Horwath Consultants Canada, Toronto, ON

CUSTOMERS ARE THE BOTTOM LINE

"Customers! Who needs 'em? All they do is complain. Nothing is ever good enough. They complain that the service is slow, that the displays are hard to read, that sales people are rude, that they have to stand in line, that it is difficult to return goods or make exchanges, and on and on and on."

Sound familiar? If it doesn't, then you are not looking for complaints. As a result, you are missing out on one of the greatest opportunities to improve your business and enhance your bottom line. Customer complaints represent more than just customers venting frustration; they are wake-up calls and a key to enhance our revenue.

Customers are our most important asset. Without their continued patronage, we would not have any reason to be in business, and surely we would not be profitable. In this article, we examine the customer cycle and put a quantitative value on customer loyalty. In addition, we describe how to manage customer complaints, measure customer satisfaction and dissatisfaction, and build a customer-satisfaction measurement model. While the case study used is from the hospitality industry, it applies to many other industry segments.

THE CUSTOMER CYCLE

Expectations, **acquisition**, **trial**, and **retention**. These are the four fundamental tenets of marketing to customers.

1. It all starts with expectations, customer **expectations**. What are they? What do customers really want? If you ask enough of them, they'll probably all give you the same answer: recognition, excellent service, quality products, great value, and satisfaction.

   All we have to do is deliver on these expectations, day in and day out—always easier said than done. I don't know of one business that exceeds the expectations of all their customers, all the time. But what is important is that we try, because every time we don't meet or exceed our customer's expectations, we run the risk of losing not only that customer, but potential customers, their families and friends, through negative word of mouth. The result is an erosion of the bottom line, profit. And after investing in a customer, it's truly a shame to never see them return.

2. Profit doesn't come without costs. The **acquisition** of customers means that we will incur costs. We spend countless hours and dollars figuring out ways to identify and target the right customer. We develop strategies and tactics to acquire their business. We invent new ways to reach them. Those are the real costs of doing business. Those acquisition costs need to be factored in when we measure the impact of losing a customer.

3. Once we have acquired the customer's attention, we move into the **trial** phase. This phase involves offering incentives and discounts, creating rewards, and looking for ways to add value.

4. Customer **retention** is extremely important and so during the trial phase, costs continue to grow as we continue to service customers in an effort to retain their business. If we lose the customer at this point, all the costs we have incurred are wasted—it's money down the drain. We should seek to continually meet and exceed the expectations of our customers. In doing so, we not only retain the customer, we retain the opportunity to turn our costs into profit. Our satisfied customer returns, tells his or her family and friends to return, and the cycle ensures that we will have those customers for as long as we're in business.

MANAGING THE CUSTOMER'S ENTIRE EXPERIENCE

Managing our customer's experience is an integral part of our business. It's our responsibility to ensure that our customers leave with a lasting positive impression. A recent case illustrates how importance this is.

One of my clients is a major international hotel company. Its success is due in large part to its ability to manage customer relationships. The largest component of the company's business is the corporate market. Virtually all its corporate customers negotiate room rates on the basis of committing to book a minimum number of rooms each year. In addition to getting preferential rates, some corporate customers get benefit packages that can include continental breakfast, guarantees of room availability (during peak periods), and late checkout for their most frequent travellers. Recently, one of this hotel company's largest customers, which books more than 10,000 room nights annually, at a daily rate of $145 ($1.45 million in room revenue alone, excluding food, beverage, telephone, mini-bar sales, in-room movies, etc.), and whose executives have been staying at the hotel for 10 years, complained to the senior sales associate, in the national sales office, who manages the account. The customer indicated that one of the hotels in the chain was not delivering the services promised. The sales associate informed the hotel's general manager and, assuming that the problems would be rectified immediately, so advised the customer.

Several months later, when the contract was up for renewal, the sales associate approached the corporate customer and was informed that the company's hotel chain of choice, for the next year, would be a competitor. Shocked, the sales associate inquired why this decision had been made. The customer politely stated that when he complained about the problems earlier in the year, all the company received was lip service. There was no follow-up to ensure that the outstanding issues had been resolved. Therefore, not only would the individual hotel lose the business, but the whole chain would as well.

Bent on rescuing this customer, the sales associate sprang into action. A call to the hotel's general manager confirmed that in fact something had slipped through the cracks and that the problems were still occurring. Threatened with losing such a valuable piece of business forever, the sales associate created a three-month recovery plan to woo back the customer. This plan included a written apology from the hotel company's president, a personal call and visit to the customer by the hotel's general manager to clarify the problems and propose solutions.

The plan also asked for a grace period of 90 days to rectify the problems, some of which were technical and related directly to the hotel's ability to provide services as guaranteed. Because the relationship was built on years of trust, the corporate customer acceded to the sales associate's request and gave the hotel chain three months in which to convince it to remain a customer. Today that corporate customer is providing even more room nights at a higher room rate, and the sales associate learned the importance of thoroughly managing customer experiences.

When customers complain, we should be thankful. Those customers are saying that they like us, our products, and our service, but we've let them down. They are letting us know that they want us to fix the problem so they can keep buying from us. It's impossible to win back every customer, but if you don't know about the dissatisfaction or if you don't respond to it, you'll lose that customer and that potential profit forever.

VALUING CUSTOMER FIDELITY

Customer relationships are built on trust. Those relationships can become so strong that a company stands to gain all a customer's business for an extended period of time, perhaps a lifetime. As with a marriage, the consumer/vendor relationship needs to be nurtured. The stronger the nurturing, the greater the trust, and the more the customer values the company. The result is increased purchases of the products or services. The moment the company breaches that trust, whether through poor service, an inability to create new products or services to meet its customers' needs, or just not communicating with its customers frequently, it runs the risk of customer infidelity and a resulting loss of profit.

How important is customer fidelity? How do we determine the value of customer fidelity? There are many ways, but I believe the most important measure is through customer defections. It is virtually impossible to determine how many customers leave and never come back. But with today's technology, even the smallest business can monitor and track customer behaviour and use that data to predict how successful it is in preventing customer defections.

The first step is to establish a customer feedback system that will allow you to measure customer satisfaction. This system can be a simple comment card that the customer completes at the point of purchase; or it can be a detailed survey that is mailed to a sample of customers.

This feedback allows a business to keep a constant pulse on its customers, their concerns, needs, wants, recommendations and, most important, the likelihood of their continuing patronage. This information is invaluable and provides the data required to build a simple predictive model to place a value on customer fidelity.

Let's return to the hotel company and examine its situation more closely. Ten thousand room nights were generated by about 520 individuals each averaging 19 nights per year at the company's various hotels. As it turned out, 15 of these travellers (or less than 3 percent) had voiced complaints to their company about the lapses in service. Not very many and not material—right? Wrong! These complaints represented a significant amount of revenue and profit to the company. Not only was the $145 per night room revenue in jeopardy, but so was the additional $65 per stay in incidental revenue (food, beverage, telephone, etc.). The cost of defection was $210 per stay for each of the 15 travellers.

Table 1 illustrates the revenue that would have been lost if just those 15 customers had defected, for the next year and for another 10 years, assuming only a 2 percent inflationary increase in revenue. In all likelihood, revenue would increase at a pace well above inflation.

TABLE 1: Revenue Lost on 15 Individuals

	Total Revenue
Room revenue lost over 1 year	$41,325
Incidental revenue over 1 year	$18,525
Total lost revenue over 1 year	$59,850
Total lost revenue over 10 years	$598,500
Total lost revenue over 10 years (with 2% annual inflation)	**$729,568**

Those 15 people alone represent nearly three-quarters of a million dollars in revenue to the hotel chain over the next decade.

Table 2 shows the impact of losing the entire corporate account (consisting of approximately 250 people).

TABLE 2: Revenue Lost on 250 Individuals

	Total Revenue
Room revenue over 1 year	$1,432,600
Incidental revenue over 1 year	$642,200
Total lost revenue over 1 year	$2,074,800
Total lost revenue over 10 years	$20,748,000
Total lost revenue over 10 years (with 2% annual inflation)	**$25,291,692**

This one corporate account represents more than $25 million in revenue for the hotel company over the next 10 years. Assuming a profit of 15 percent on this revenue, the fidelity of this corporate customer has a value to the hotel company of about $311,000 a year or potentially $3.8 million over the next decade. If the relationship is maintained, that potential revenue generated by the corporate customer may translate into profit. But if the relationship is not maintained, that potential revenue will become lost or forgone profit. And it may not be easy to replace that customer's business.

To protect this potential profit, the hotel company, in conjunction with this corporate customer, must implement a customer-satisfaction tool that will allow them to measure satisfaction on a monthly basis—for example, giving travellers in this company a simple monthly evaluation form on which to record their evaluation of their travel experiences and hotel stays for that month. The corporate customer would summarize these evaluations and forward the results to the hotel company's national sales associate responsible for the account. Specific concerns would be made clear, and the issues dealt with immediately. Hotels would respond with solutions and timetables for the customer.

This approach has successfully been introduced with several other customers of this hotel chain and has resulted in the strengthening of those relationships. While there's no guarantee that the company will keep the business forever, it shows customers that it values their business and will go to great lengths to keep it.

The satisfaction monitor tool also provides the basis for predicting customer behaviour and the potential loss of profit. By tracking the results each month, the hotels know exactly how many customers are dissatisfied and what issues and concerns need to be dealt with.

Virtually all hotel companies track customer comments and monitor guest satisfaction from individual guests; however, not many go to the extent of implementing a system for specific companies or groups. The incremental cost of implementing and maintaining this system is minimal, and the benefits have ensured a strong customer relationship that has exceeded their expectations.

CUSTOMER DEFECTIONS

Why do customers walk away? According to research published by TARP:

- 3 percent move away
- 5 percent develop relationships with other companies
- 9 percent leave for competitive reasons
- 14 percent are dissatisfied with the product or service
- 68 percent quit because of indifference by the owner, manager, or some employee toward the customer
- 1 percent die

What's really revealing in these numbers is that systems can be implemented to minimize 96 percent of these defections.

What's the Cost of Dissatisfied Customers?

Research suggests that only 4 percent of dissatisfied customers complain, and that they will tell 8 to 10 people about their dissatisfaction. In the hotel customer example, if the person responsible for negotiating hotel contracts belongs to an association of corporate travel buyers and tells 8 to 10 other buyers about the problems encountered with that hotel chain, the impact could be devastating. But let's look at another side of the hotel's relationships with its customers. Table 3 provides a profile of the hotel company discussed earlier.

TABLE 3: Hotel Profile

Number of Hotels	Average Size of Hotel	Number of Customers Annually	4% Complain	Annual Revenue per Customer
100	250 rooms	8.3 million	332,000	$200

The hotel has a simple guest comment card that is featured promi-nently in each guest room, at each hotel's front desk, on each table in their restaurants, and in meeting rooms. Comment cards can either be left at the hotel or mailed to the company's corporate office (the card folds into a pre-addressed, postage-paid, self-sealing mailer). Each com-ment card is reviewed and the data entered into a relatively simple data-base. Monthly reports are produced, rating each of the categories on the card, and each card is responded to by each hotel's general manager.

Assuming that 4 percent of hotel guests express their complaints through comment cards, this hotel company has 332,000 guests who are at risk of defecting. Now, not all of these guests will take their busi-ness elsewhere, but they are potential casualties. Some may be infre-quent travellers, some may never travel again; however, the model provides a framework for evaluating potential lost profits. If we assume that each of these customers generates an average of about $200 in annual revenue, they represent total revenue of $66.4 million for the company. At 15 percent profit, these complaining guests have a value of $9.9 million annually.

MEASURING CUSTOMER SATISFACTION

No model can definitively predict lost profit. Whatever model you build will reflect only an order of magnitude. What is really important, how-ever, is not the model or the potentially lost profit, but the solutions implemented to retain customers. The projected lost profit highlights the impact on the business of losing customers

Measuring customer satisfaction is a continuing process. It pro-vides you with not only continuous feedback on your businesses per-formance, but also the mechanism to learn more about customer needs, wants, and expectations. Developing a customer-satisfaction index is as important a measuring tool as a financial statement. The lat-ter tells you where you stand in terms of profitability, while the former tells you how you got there and how you can improve.

Building a customer-satisfaction model is relatively easy. The list on the following page shows the 10 basic steps that are required. What's most important is not collecting the data, but what you do with it. The key is to use the information in a proactive manner that will serve to eliminate annoyance factors, improve products and services, and meet the expectations of customers. It is essential to respond to *all* customer complaints because only 4 percent of *all* dissatisfied customers complain. Remember, they complain because they care. Show them that you care enough to respond. Often, a response alone is sufficient to win back a customer.

Ten Steps to Building a Customer-Satisfaction Model

1. Set standards for providing customer service.
2. Communicate standards to management and employees.
3. Collect customer feedback.
4. Realize you can never reach 100 percent satisfaction.
5. Respond to *all* customer complaints and develop ongoing dialogue with dissatisfied customers to win them back.
6. Analyze results monthly.
7. Compare results with those of the previous month and year to measure improvements.
8. Share results with management and employees.
9. Tie results to performance reviews.
10. Reward employees for excellence.

Constant dialogue with your customers is fundamental to retaining their business. The list below offers 10 tools that you can use to measure customer satisfaction.

Ten Customer Measuring Sticks

1. Comment cards
2. One-on-one interviews with customers
3. Focus groups
4. Direct sales calls
5. Employee feedback
6. Customer advisory panels
7. Third party research
8. 1-800 customer service line
9. Interactive Internet site
10. Quarterly surveys of customers.

Remember, *encourage your customers to complain,* because what we don't know will hurt us.

About the author

JOEL ROSEN, CMC

Joel Rosen is a certified management consultant and managing partner of Horwath Consultants (Canada). He has designed and managed customer-satisfaction, loyalty, and frequency programs for both hospitality and retail industry clients and is a frequent speaker at conferences on these subjects.

The Eastman Kodak Company

BENCHMARKING FOR SUCCESS

A. Turgud (Turk) Enustun,
Eastman Kodak, Rochester, NY
and Karri E. Givens,
Coopers & Lybrand, Toronto, ON

No matter how good we think we are,
there must be somebody out there performing similar tasks,
but in a different way—perhaps a better way.

—Turk Enustun, Director, Corporate Benchmarking,
Eastman Kodak Company

Benchmarking is not just another buzz word to executives at Eastman Kodak. In fact, we, at Kodak, are so committed to the benchmarking process that in 1992, we established a Corporate Benchmarking Office within our Corporate Quality Organization. This enables us to offer support and guidance for benchmarking activities to all divisions within Kodak. One of our primary responsibilities is to reduce the potential for redundancies. As such, we act as a central resource point for all the various divisions within Kodak. Without it, different areas within Kodak could be performing similar benchmarking activities simultaneously and be completely unaware of it. Kodak has saved time, money, and people resources just by having the benchmarking activities coordinated centrally.

As part of our ongoing commitment to support the "Kodak community" worldwide, we offer the following:

- **Training**—for individuals who would like to expand their understanding of the basic concepts and purpose of benchmarking.

- **Consultative support**—for those who require guidance through the benchmarking steps.

- **Increased awareness**—through staff meetings, various Kodak publications, and other forums that proactively raise awareness of the value of benchmarking.

- **Online databases**—to avoid duplication of effort. The database is accessible worldwide and was designed to be user-friendly. It identifies all benchmarking activities within Kodak. It specifically indicates the individuals involved in the activity, the process being benchmarked, and the benchmarking partners.

- **Communication**—through "all points bulletins," which advise the worldwide Kodak community about the benchmarking activities being planned, including visits to other companies.

- **Recognition of excellence**—which rewards individuals or divisions that have used the Kodak benchmarking model to create or add value to the company. We have found that such recognition encourages others within the company to take a more active role in benchmarking initiatives.

At Kodak, we view benchmarking as a constant learning process that consists of a number of elements, such as the following:

- Understanding and measuring our own operations.

- Comparing Kodak operations with other organizations, internal or external, that are recognized as world-class.

- Identifying performance gaps.

- Implementing changes.

- Finding new ways to meet and surpass world-class practices.

In 1992, the worldwide benchmarking focus team adopted a benchmarking philosophy, undertaking to implement the following:

> *A continuous learning process for understanding and measuring our own operations, comparing them to other organizations which are recognized as having superior practices, and implementing plans to adapt and change our operations, to meet and surpass those practices.*

To improve our own benchmarking abilities we have developed an award-winning 11-step benchmarking model, which has proven to be successful many times over. We wanted to make sure the process was easy to follow and comprehensive. Therefore, we created a checklist that clearly identifies "things to do" before, during, and after the benchmarking process. This document ensures that people are aware of all the steps involved and provides guidance where appropriate.

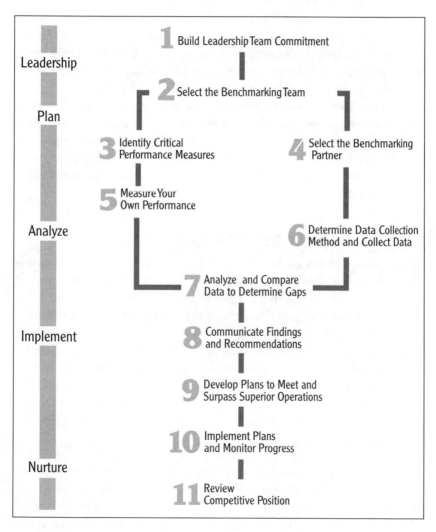

FIGURE 1: The Eastman Kodak Company Benchmarking Process

We believe that benchmarking is about sharing knowledge and learning from the successes of others. Therefore, it is appropriate for us to share with you the specific steps involved in Eastman Kodak's 11-step benchmarking model. We have achieved success on a consistent basis by following these specific steps.

Step 1: Build leadership team commitment.

The first thing you should do is identify the clients and sponsors of the benchmarking activity. You may need to provide more information if further awareness of the benchmarking process is required. Define and prioritize major improvement opportunities, and review your corporate strategy or plans and verify that the proposed changes are in line with them. Then define the scope for the benchmarking study, ensuring expectations are realistic. Also identify any possible interferences that would create problems later. Determine the necessary resources and the level of commitment required to implement the changes as a result of the study, clearly outlining the level of involvement, support, and direction that would be necessary from management.

Step 2: Select the benchmarking team.

Kodak has achieved the best results when benchmarking activities are done as a team. This allows for brainstorming sessions, ensures varied input, and maintains overall perspectives on a continuous basis.

We suggest that you contact potential team members to discuss the scope of the study and clearly outline the objectives. The benchmarking team should include those individuals who are critical to the implementation of the proposed changes, and it is particularly important that management is represented on the team. Team members should also be aware of their level of empowerment and what type of support they will receive for decision-making and for the final implementation.

Once the team has been selected, formally establish the goals, milestones, and timelines for your study. Schedule team meetings to review and monitor progress. In assisting the team to adhere to the original plans, appoint someone on the team to be specifically responsible for monitoring the resources and the costs incurred as the study progresses.

At this point, it is important to develop a clear understanding of the relationships that exist between your operations and others. Gaining insight into your own processes will allow you to examine your current activities and determine where improvements can be made. Using process maps and other appropriate diagrams will ensure that this process is accurate and objective. This activity is best done as a team.

Step 3: Identify critical performance measures.

This step involves outlining the key tasks that are critical to your operation and the associated performance measures for each. Define each measure and decide how the data should be collected. These critical success measures (CSMs) should be well-balanced, and should include leading and lagging indicators. In addition, these should also be directly related to key result areas for your business. To keep this manageable, try to keep your measures to fewer than 20.

Determine how to chart and display data from your operation's current performance, from those of comparative operations, and from those of your own operation's performance over a period of time. Using bar charts or other control charts may be helpful.

Step 4: Select the benchmarking partner.

This is a critical step and should be done carefully. Develop a set of specific criteria for selecting your benchmarking partner. Choose companies that perform the same or similar activities that you do, whose processes are more efficient and effective than yours, and that are known for their world-class standards of performance. The criteria should enable you to judge how well they perform those functions. Before the final decision is made, consider the following questions:

- What do you know about leading operations *within the company (internal)* that perform similar functions?

- What do you know about your *direct competitors (external)* that perform the same functions?

- What do you know about *other companies (external)* within your industry as well as outside your industry that have been identified as having superior operations?

You may find that the companies that have the best processes are not within your industry. This should not pose a problem, because it's the business process rather than the industry that's the key criterion in choosing a benchmarking partner. For example, if you would like to improve your complaint tracking systems, the principles and processes will be virtually the same across various industry segments.

Once you have carefully considered the above, produce a list of potential benchmarking partners. We also suggest that you perform secondary research to examine the external organizations and prioritize them as potential benchmarking partners. Attempt to limit the list to three or four organizations. Then review the list with the leadership team.

It is also important to establish that there will be no difficulty from a legal or business perspective with sharing and exchanging information with the selected organizations. If there are no problems, make preparatory contact with the organizations. Discuss their willingness to take part in the benchmarking initiative and ask them specific questions to determine if an exchange would be of value. Finalize the list of participants and schedule dates and times for the benchmarking visit and information exchange.

Step 5: Measure your own performance.

Clearly define each measure and verify the methods you will use to collect data for each measure. This should be done for your own operation as well as for your benchmarking partners' operations. Ensure that the same measures and definitions are used each time. Collect the data for each of the measures. Determine the practices and behaviours that drive each of the measures. Graphically displaying your operation's current performance is useful.

Step 6: Determine data collection method and collect data.

Finalize the primary methods that will be used for collecting information—that is, via mail, telephone, or personal visits. The team should develop a set of questions that encompasses each of the measures, as well as specific questions about the practices, processes, and behaviours that drive those measures. Evaluate the final data collection plan with the leadership team.

If a site visit is required, arrange a pre-visit to review and clarify the objectives of the study with all participants. Then evaluate your list of specific questions and data collection method, preferably with someone who will provide the required objectivity. Before your on-site visit, it is a good idea to review guidelines on effective visit techniques. In addition, clarify the roles and obligations of each team member. Doing this will help ensure that all the necessary data are collected during the visit.

After the visit, the benchmarking team members should meet to summarize their experiences and review the information collected. If there are any inconsistencies, you need to clarify the accuracy of the data with your benchmarking partner.

Step 7: Analyze and compare data to determine gaps.

Recheck to ensure that the appropriate definitions and methods of data collection were consistent with the original plan. Remember, you cannot achieve an accurate comparison if you are comparing apples with oranges.

At this point you should outline the data and compare them with your own operations. Look for opportunities to implement superior processes quickly, easily, and cost-effectively. Highlight the gaps between what is currently being done and what could be achieved by implementing changes. In addition, forecast the expected future trends in each operation if changes are not implemented.

Align your information with your previously determined major improvement opportunities, and analyze the information to find out if there is an appropriate connection between these and the superior results. Look at the big picture to determine how implementing changes would affect the operation as a whole. Understand the correlation and balance between the measures within an operation.

Step 8: Communicate findings and recommendations.

Communicate and inform others within your company of your benchmarking study via a "Corporate Benchmarking Database" or other communication avenues available within your organization. Ensure you specifically inform project sponsors and any other participating groups, including those that will be affected by any changes.

At this point, your team should define the model and determine the method by which you will present your findings and recommendations. Clearly state your objectives and goals for communication. Provide others with the chance to become involved and offer general feedback. Logically outline the fundamental practices that need to change as a result of the benchmarking study. Highlight the specific events or enablers that will be required to ensure successful implementation.

Once your benchmarking team is ready to officially communicate the findings of the study, it should be prepared to provide the following information:

- The purpose of the study.

- A summary of the benchmarking process that was followed.

- A description of the benchmarking partner and the information collected from the partner.

- Details of how your operation compares with the other operations studied.

- Practices and behaviours that were identified as superior.

- Who will be affected by the changes.

- The next steps, timelines, milestones, and specific enablers.

- Opportunities for additional input.

Step 9: Develop plans to meet and surpass superior operations.

Revisit your original goals and review them to ensure they are in line with your corporate mission, vision, and strategy. Prioritize the practices that need to be changed in your organization. Determine the method in which the progress and results will be tracked. Develop a secondary or backup plan, if enablers cannot be put in place within the original time frames. Illustrate how the implementation will provide the desired return on investment and decide how the return will be measured. It is a good idea to provide a summary report to the participating organizations, but ensure confidentiality of information to protect the relationship between you and your benchmarking partners.

Step 10: Implement plans and monitor progress.

Keep your team together and continue to meet regularly to monitor progress. It is also important to allow management and the groups affected by the changes to review the plans in greater detail. They should assess the situation and make changes if necessary.

During the implementation stage, we contact our benchmarking partners and advise them of the changes that are being implemented. This enhances the relationship and encourages continued dialogue. As changes are being implemented, you may find that additional information is helpful from your benchmarking partners; so it is always a good idea to keep the lines of communication open.

If the implementation is taking place over a long period of time, it may be necessary to provide interim reports to update the progress and status of your activities. During the implementation, you may also collect data from your own operation and make comparisons with your past performance.

Step 11: Review competitive position.

This important step should not be overlooked. Now is the time to compare current performance with those of the benchmarking partners. Remember to ensure that you are comparing apples with apples. Demonstrate how the return on investment and original objectives were achieved as a result of the benchmarking study and communicate this information to the benchmarking team, the affected organizations, and management. Update the results and document the information appropriately.

If, however, there is room for further improvements with the original major improvement opportunity, you should look for alternative organizations that have superior practices but were not involved in the original benchmarking study. As benchmarking is a continuous learning process, continue to look for opportunities for improvements.

SUMMARY

To be the best, you must always look for opportunities to improve. Benchmarking enables organizations to learn from both the successes and the failures of others. Benchmarking allows you to continuously re-evaluate your operations and implement changes that will improve current business practices. Don't be satisfied with the status quo.

Each step of the benchmarking process brings you closer to the next step, which, in turn, brings you closer to achieving your desired goal. To reach your goals, you must formulate a plan, and to be successful, you need to carry out each step of your plan thoroughly.

> *Inventing solutions to problems is difficult in today's world.*
> *Benchmarking provides innovation through observation*
> *of what others do. There's always someone*
> *with a better mousetrap.*
> —Turk Enustun

About the authors

A. TURGUD (TURK) ENUSTUN and KARRI E. GIVENS

A. Turgud (Turk) Enustun is the director of Corporate Benchmarking at Eastman Kodak, Rochester, New York.

Karri E. Givens is a consultant at the Centre of Excellence for Customer Satisfaction at Coopers & Lybrand, Toronto.

Using Benchmarking to Focus on the Customer

BELL CANADA CASE STUDY[1]

Vicki J. Powers,
American Productivity & Quality Center,
Houston, TX

IN A NUMBERS-ORIENTED world, people and organizations pride themselves on achieving the highest possible rating on surveys, test scores, and internal assessments. To be considered average is not desirable—especially when it comes to customer expectations.

But numbers can be deceiving. For example, if you looked at the customer-satisfaction survey results at Bell Canada in 1994, this organization appeared to be handling its customers' needs very successfully. Satisfaction results consistently rated more than 95 percent "yes" on internal processes. But the constant ringing of phones in the Answer Centre contradicted this high score. Customers were not satisfied, and the Answer Centre had to respond to many calls in damage-control mode.

That's when Bell Canada looked beyond the numbers to realize its customer survey process was not capturing accurate information. This process had not changed since 1970, and its collection of data did not lead to specific indicated action. In 1992, Bell Canada concluded that it needed to make significant, incremental, and permanent changes to

---

[1] Adapted with permission from *BENCHMARKING inPRACTICE*, Issue 2, June/July 1996, published by American Productivity & Quality Center.

please its employees and customers. After three years of focusing on this effort, Bell Canada experienced tremendous success throughout the organization. Its focus on the customer, through benchmarking, helped Bell Canada transform its business and change lives.

IN THE BEGINNING

Bell Canada, the largest Canadian telecommunications company, provides both long-distance and local service to more than seven million customers in Ontario and Quebec. As part of its business transformation process, by the end of 1997 it will have reduced its employee base to 35,000 from 45,000 employees.

In June 1992, the Canadian long-distance market opened up to competition, which spurred Bell Canada's customer focus effort through benchmarking. This deregulation affected the Canadian telephone industry more than anyone had originally imagined it would.

"Bell Canada saw a huge loss to market share—and much more rapidly than anyone had anticipated," said Turaj Seyrafiaan, associate director of benchmarking. "We started a three-year transition plan to move from a monopoly organization of 110 years to a market-driven organization focusing on what the customer really needs. We needed a significant improvement that only benchmarking could offer. We couldn't go with a gradual change."

THE BENCHMARKING ROAD TO SUCCESS

In 1988, Bell Canada had started establishing benchmarks in the telecommunications industry. Seyrafiaan said the organization wanted to compare expenses and other criteria with regional Bell operating companies. Since it was positioned as the largest telephone company in Canada, the company realized it had to look outside Canada to the United States for significant change.

"Then individuals at Bell Canada decided that once our expenses were in line, we wanted to break into three or four category lines to examine other companies," Seyrafiaan said. "There were three or four different benchmarking studies done by a consultant. The consultant would collect data, go back to the office, and come up with recommendations. People at Bell Canada were involved only in getting the information."

"Gradually we started to internalize benchmarking, because the consultant needed someone from Bell Canada to translate the data," he continued. "The company started a small benchmarking group, and our role was as a research analyst to help the consultant understand the data."

Bell Canada benchmarked several processes with the consultant's help: maintenance, collection, sales, and cable networks. Seyrafiaan said that these benchmarking studies were more or less successful 50 percent of the time. Yet because they were conducted by an outside consultant, Bell Canada employees didn't feel ownership.

"It was easier for the company to reject than accept the recommendations by the consultants because they were outsiders," Seyrafiaan said. "Employees did not believe what the consultants thought because 'it was not invented here.' And we didn't look at barriers ahead of time to prevent this."

Seyrafiaan said that once Bell Canada joined the Houston-based International Benchmarking Clearinghouse in 1992, it started getting more insight into what benchmarking really was. Its Clearinghouse membership introduced it to other industries—up to that point Bell Canada had focused its benchmarking only on the telecommunications industry.

DEFINING THE RULES

Based on the contradictory numbers—high customer survey ratings and high volume of customer complaints—Bell Canada decided to use benchmarking as a tool to determine what other world-class organizations do to achieve high customer-satisfaction results. In June 1993, Terry Mosey, vice-president—consumer sales and service, formed a benchmarking team to study how Bell Canada could significantly improve customer satisfaction at its Answer Centres. This team included Answer Centre employees (regional managers, front line manager, client representatives who serve customers), the union, the corporate measurement group, and two facilitators from Bell Canada's internal benchmarking group.

One of the first steps to get the team focused on the project was to identify team roles and create a project plan. The timeline called for completing the study in six months. Team members would be responsible for their current jobs as well as for the activities for the benchmarking study.

The benchmarking facilitators, on the other hand, contributed 100 percent of their time to the study.

As one of the two benchmarking facilitators for this study, Seyrafiaan spread his benchmarking philosophy throughout the team: "If you want to be the best, you must play with the best." Seyrafiaan was concerned about the process, while the team was concerned about content. Together they covered it all.

DETERMINING CUSTOMERS' EXPECTATIONS

Early on, the benchmarking team decided to look behind the customer survey results. They set out to find which key service attributes customers valued the most and then built a survey around customer satisfaction, with Bell Canada's performance matched against those attributes.

Bell Canada called more than 200 customers to determine what was most important to them and how the Answer Centres rated in those areas. Daphne Gold, customer service counsellor and team leader of this benchmarking project, said customers identified three general areas of importance:

1. **Access**—accessibility at a time and by a method convenient to customers.

2. **Resolution of service issues**—flexibility of the organization, how knowledgeable, and how willing it was to take the time to listen and resolve a problem.

3. **Treatment**—how friendly and caring Bell Canada was in meeting customers' needs.

Oddly enough, these attributes corresponded to the same areas that employees had identified in employee interviews—five service attributes grouped into the same three categories.

Table 1 identifies the performance ratings for each of these categories, as viewed by customers. These ratings provided the baseline data that would allow Bell Canada to compare itself with other organizations in the study.

TABLE 1: Percent of Customers Rating Bell Canada "Very Good" or "Excellent"

(5 or 6 on a scale of 1–6)	
Access	47.3%
Resolution	70.9%
Treatment	68.6%
Overall Satisfaction	**78.5%**

Gold said originally the team didn't want to collect baseline data, but was urged by the benchmarking facilitators to do so.

"We didn't see the value of collecting data until we got to the site visit interviews down the road," Gold said. "If we collected baseline data, then we could look at their information in the context of our data, and it proved very valuable. We knew that if we could improve our performance by 30 percent in all categories, we could end each day with significantly more satisfied customers."

According to Gold, the customer data confirmed that benchmarking was the appropriate improvement methodology to identify breakthrough enablers to cause significant change. As a result, the team had the full support of Mosey, the executive champion, to begin the benchmarking study.

A RIGOROUS PROCESS

Seyrafiaan said this benchmarking team followed a rigorous process for benchmarking, since it was the first study conducted internally at Bell Canada. A team of four individuals went through five days of benchmarking training at the International Benchmarking Clearinghouse to learn a common methodology. It followed the "Plan, Collect, Analyze, and Adapt" model.

"Because we were new with benchmarking, we didn't cut any corners in the process," Seyrafiaan said. "We trusted the process and knew we would see the benefit down the road."

Before the team could identify its benchmarking study partners, it had to further define key operational issues that related to fulfilling customers' needs.

"We told the team that before they began throwing out company names, we first had to think of our criteria," Seyrafiaan said. "That's why the rigorous process helped."

Seyrafiaan said the team also realized the importance of getting outside the telephone industry. "We wanted to see life outside the telephone industry. Other industries made the process simpler, and we wanted to see how they did it," Seyrafiaan said. "We wanted to see how other industries provided exceptional customer service."

Through secondary research at the Bell Canada library and International Benchmarking Clearinghouse, other benchmarking studies, and customer input, the Answer Centre benchmarking team invited 20 organizations to participate in a high-level metric screening survey. The screening survey, which involved a 45-minute phone call, discussed overall customer satisfaction, customer satisfaction measures, and technology.

Fifteen organizations completed the screening survey—of which two organizations were within Bell Canada. Seyrafiaan said the team then discussed the criteria with the company names blinded. This allowed them to focus on true best practices, and not let company biases creep in. Eight organizations survived this process and were invited to participate as best-practices partners. Only five of these organizations moved on to Phase II—it was bad timing for two organizations, and one company could not participate for competitive reasons.

"Phase II included four hour-long telephone interviews with the best-practices companies to uncover more detail," Seyrafiaan said. "This got into the hows and whys of customer satisfaction. We wanted to identify best practices that related to the operational issues we had identified early on. From this exercise, we had a draft of best practices."

The five best-practices companies were MCI, Chemical Bank, Lands' End , IBM Canada, and Polaroid Corporation. Seyrafiaan said all five organizations helped Bell Canada truly learn best practices in customer satisfaction and discover the factors that led to excellence in the delivery of customer satisfaction. The team selected three companies for site visits, because they were all good in certain areas. These partners had the highest utilization rate of the 21 best practices identified in Phase II and were strong performers where Bell Canada was weak. Table 2 shows the comparison between Bell Canada and three best-practices companies, as determined through primary research.

TABLE 2: Utilization Rates of Best Practices by Partner Companies

	Best Practices Usage Rates
Company A	92.1%
Company B	78.9%
Company C	81.6%
Bell Canada	19.0%

Before the site visits, team members developed questionnaires in small groups specific to each organization. The questions were tailored to the best practices identified for each organization. Six or seven best practices existed for each company. Information was analyzed beforehand to determine if implementation of the best practices at Bell Canada would improve or eliminate some of the customer concerns identified in the planning stage.

ANALYZING DATA

The benchmarking study team analyzed the information in the two weeks following the site visits. Gold said the team normalized performance results using a common metric, Net Satisfaction Index. This allows different rating scales to be compared on equal terms.

From the site visit information, Bell Canada drafted 21 best practices that were linked to the three customer satisfiers: access, resolution, and treatment. Seventeen of the 21 best practices were prioritized for immediate implementation. These included all those that supported resolution and treatment customer satisfiers. As a unique aspect of the benchmarking study, a Customers Come First (CCF) implementation team was created and a leadership team to implement study findings. The 17 best practices would be implemented in Bell Canada during an 18- to 36-month period, from January 1994 to December 1996.

Bell Canada then created goals to direct the implementation effort in four categories: culture, market driven, learning organization, and excellence.

"It was very difficult to see how all of this information related at first," Gold said. "But once we had the goals, it made everything fall together. We were able to stream all 17 of the priority best practices into one of four goals."

FOCUSING ON THE CUSTOMER IN IMPLEMENTATION

The CCF implementation team established five teams to address five specific best practices: a Communication Team, an Education Team, a Customer Care Team, a Process Improvement Team, and Coaches.

In the following paragraphs, the purpose and impact of some of the teams on the organization are briefly described.

Customer Care Team. This team of resolution and information specialists relates to the best practice "Dedicated Customer Relations Team," which handles complex customer issues and executive complaints for three Answer Centres. The goal of this team is to establish customer loyalty. External customers can have access to the team directly or be transferred from a business unit.

"A lot of what we do is recovery and resolution," said team member Trina Doyle. "We want to put Bell in the best light we can and not have the situation go any higher. We take ownership and attempt to delight our customers—without giving away the shop! We have a really positive way of looking at things. We are not a complaint centre."

Doyle believes her team will be around forever, based on the need of satisfying customers. They handle about 300 calls per day just for the vice-president. Although there were always employees to handle the VP line for complaints, the "care" side of the equation is new. The organization has put a special system in place—CARE (Customer Awareness Response Editor) System—to log all information regarding customer calls. Doyle said this database helps employees find the top three to five hot spots among customers and prioritize them right away.

"I think the success of this whole effort goes back to the people who started it several years ago," Doyle said. "They visited companies to see what others are doing and then had to sell that to every person. But once you're sold, you're hooked for life."

Before this team was in place, local offices resolved complaints.

Communication Team. This team, which started in October 1994, relates to the best practice "Commitment to communications." It has established communication channels to ensure "free" two-way flow of information. This helps client representatives have available, or have access to, current information and resources to fully satisfy customers regarding pricing, strategy, products, and services.

"Our purpose is to effectively manage and communicate information that goes out to the client reps, including training and support," said Debbie Clouthier, a team member. "We work as a middle man to get the information out to our client representatives and provide the voice of the customer to our marketing partners."

Each week, the team sends electronic notes to the client representatives through their workstations.

"We have a weekly huddle to address team issues and create our notes," said Belinda Banks, a team member. "We also conduct training sessions for each Answer Centre to support the introduction of new products, services, policies, and procedures."

Clouthier said that before this team was created, there was no consistency in training and communication. "The whole customer focus initiative has been very positive," she said. "Prior to the Communication Team, there was no standard process to manage the flow of information."

Education Team. This dedicated training group, which was formed in November 1995, relates to the best practice "Dedicated training group integrated with call centre operation." It develops and delivers training for all newly hired employees at Bell Canada. The seven-week course trains employees on the workstation, customer service, and selling skills, as well as giving new employees the opportunity to role-play and spend 18 days working with real customers on the phone.

"Once these new employees finish training, they just need support like any other client representative," said team member Michael Corry. "The 18 days online with customers really give the employees a comfort zone. It's amazing how self-sufficient they are after they've completed training. I had a person sit with me as I took customer calls for two months after my training."

Corry believes customer focus is definitely instilled across the company, especially within the training environment that has been created for new employees. "I try to get across to the students that the customer is the most important thing to us," he said.

Coaches. This team offers peer coaching to client representatives who work with customers in the Answer Centre. This team relates to the best practice "Job standards and training verification." Each office has one coach per 20 client representatives. As coaches, these individuals support the client representatives in living Bell Canada's Guiding

Principles. They listen in on phone calls with customers and coach the employee on how to handle the call and the customer. Everything is based on two new customer satisfaction courses: Achieving Extraordinary Customer Relations and Selling Naturally.

"We like to do two coaching sessions per month with each representative and about five calls per session," said Oshawa coach Fran Woods. "We go online ourselves each Monday, so we don't forget what the reps go through."

"Now the client representatives feel they have an advocate and someone who knows what they go through," she continued. "We've become sounding boards and advisers."

Woods' Oshawa location was the site for the pilot roll-out of Customers Come First (CCF). The CCF team spent eight months on site in Oshawa in 1994 to conduct the roll-out. They started listening in on customer calls and helped the client representatives live the Guiding Principles. That was when the idea came about for peer coaching.

"Coaches are hired in every Bell Canada office now," Woods said. "The customer focus is really entrenched. We've had customer focus courses in the past, done with great intentions, but they weren't really supported or followed up. Now we have the commitment of our vice-president."

Before this team was in place, managers were responsible for coaching their own employees.

CULTURE CHANGES

Bell Canada employees can give first-hand accounts about the impact the customer-focused effort has had on the organization. In fact, what was so outstanding about the project was the significant learning and change that extended beyond the scope of the original project. Before that change, in one case, a client representative quit her position; but she came back once the new effort was in place. As a client representative at Bell Canada for five years, Cathy Tisdelle had heard her share of customer complaints and praises in the Answer Centre. But two years ago, customer complaints seemed to dominate.

"I was so burned that out I went to a lower-paying job within Bell Canada to get away from crazy customers and the hours," Tisdelle said. "Then last year one of the client reps told me how it was a whole new position. I came back in July—about the same time as the roll-out of CCF. I can't get over how much things have changed. There is no doubt the job has been vastly improved. It's nice to say that I've seen this change. When you're in the middle of it, it might not be as obvious."

Tisdelle said that before Bell Canada was customer-focused, the organization was much more sales/business-oriented. She enjoys the way Bell Canada works with customers now.

"I feel more relaxed and able to deal with customers in the way they need,"she said. "Our calls used to be timed, so the customer might wait 15 minutes, and we'd have to rush off the phone. It means a longer wait now, but if we give good customer service at the end, then the customer doesn't seem to mind the wait. I also feel more empowered in deciding what I can do to satisfy the customer," she said.

Another employee, Paul Cichello, who works in the Mississauga office, has recognized the increase in commendations that client representatives are receiving from customers phoning in.

"As a coach in this office, I have listened in on many phone calls when customers praise our employees," Cichello said. 'Customers who call in seem happy. In fact, one customer told a client rep, "You're the best person I've spoken to. I can tell that Bell Canada is changing.'"

RESULTS

Bell Canada has seen significant changes throughout the entire organization as a result of this benchmarking study. Customers, employees, the culture, and organization have all been affected.

Table 3 illustrates how Bell Canada has improved from May 1993. It presents site visit results compared with Bell Canada's target and pilot site results. Table 4 illustrates some of the major changes to the customer and culture as a result of the implementation plan.

TABLE 3: Customer Results from the New Answer Centre

Customers Rating "Very Good" or "Excellent" for New Answer Centre

	May 1993***	Best Observed**	Target***	Pilot Site*	Bell Ontario*
Access	47.3%	95.0%	80.6%	75.0%	64.0%
Resolution	70.9%	90.0%	93.0%	88.0%	79.0%
Treatment	68.6%	95.0%	93.1%	92.0%	86.0%

* Pilot site and Bell Ontario figures are for March 1996.
** From best practices review
*** Bell Canada

TABLE 4: Impact of Implementation Plan

CUSTOMER

Before:	Transformation to:
Unclear values	Guiding principles
Focus on regulator	Focus on customer satisfiers
Inconsistent standards	Customer-based contact standards
Internal needs drive business	Customer drives business
Objective customer satisfaction	Objective customer delight/first-call resolution

CULTURE

Before:	Transformation to:
Parenting	Partnering
Leadership impeded by administration duties	Management role defined
Focus on performance	Focus on processes and training needs
Unclear selection criteria	Select for core competencies
Mixed messages	Balanced recognition and measurement plans

Bell Canada has also installed a mechanized system to collect data and analyze for root cause. As a result, complaints have increased, providing valuable improvement data.

CHALLENGES

Throughout this benchmarking study, Bell Canada faced several challenges in conducting the study and communicating the results to employees.

"The most challenging part of the study was staying focused and following the steps in the process," Seyrafiaan said. "It's like walking in the woods and seeing lots of flowers along the way. You're tempted to stray to look at the flowers, but you need to stay on the path. Because we had support from top management, it was easier. Everything came together to contribute to the success of this benchmarking project."

Lessons Learned

- It is beneficial to benchmark companies outside your industry.
- Hosting a "Sharing Day" with benchmarking partners was extremely successful.
- Even though it might add time, following the structure for benchmarking really helps. It made other companies realize Bell Canada knew what it was doing.
- It helps to have a subject-matter expert involved. This gives the company the ownership for implementation.
- When you organize around the customer, all processes and interaction with the customer seem to fit.
- You must start making a difference:
  - Do "early wins" first.
  - Continue to measure customer satisfaction.

Gold also described aspects that were challenging in her role as team leader of the Answer Centre benchmarking project. "One of the biggest challenges was keeping momentum after two and a half years," Gold said. "And trying to develop a whole new culture in an organization our size—about 1,200 employees."

FUTURE IN BENCHMARKING

Seyrafiaan said he would not consider Bell Canada the best in benchmarking, but he thinks it is moving in that direction.

"We have pockets where benchmarking has become a big part of the overall direction of the organization," Seyrafiaan said. "In two to three years, benchmarking will be organization-wide. Our culture is obviously changing. We now have members of the Business Transformation team who realize we can't just do something once," he said. "You must continually check yourself against the best-in-class and try to learn from them. Benchmarking is going to happen again and again and again."

Note: Bell Canada was a Gold Award recipient in the International Benchmarking Clearinghouse's 1995 Benchmarking Awards. Judges believed this study was well-planned, managed, and executed.

About the author

VICKI J. POWERS

Vicki J. Powers is a communications specialist and editor at the Houston-based American Productivity & Quality Center. She writes case studies on best-practice organizations for APQC's publication series, *inPractice*.

Part Three

Best Practices in Achieving Process Improvement

O V E R V I E W

You have to have continuous improvement.
If you stand still, no matter how good you are today,
you'll still get run over by the crowd
that once was behind you but is doing better.
—Paul Vita, Wallace Co. Inc.

The global marketplace. The information highway. The online, paperless society. We live in a technological age where keeping up is virtually impossible. Nevertheless, if you want to be taken seriously in today's business world and develop an organization that is easy to do business with, you've got to be constantly learning, adapting, and improving with technology at your side—and nowhere is that more important than in the delivery of improved customer practices that are *executed through improved processes.*

For businesses competing in global markets, setting themselves apart from their competition has become more and more challenging. Many organizations turn to technology to help them achieve that critical edge, only to discover that technology alone doesn't guarantee success. In the last few years there has been a marked increase in the number of companies that are focusing on improving customer "touch processes" (processes that affect the customer experience) and on managing customer relationships. What we've also discovered, however, is that many less-than-successful organizations seem to jump on the customer-satisfaction bandwagon without really understanding their specific customers' service needs or where they should be concentrating their efforts.

Similarly, many companies are adopting new technologies—instead of improving their service delivery—simply because they've heard that technology is the future of customer service. They don't want to be left behind—a follow-the-leader approach we call "the central tendency." Organizations operating under this tendency often end up with mismanaged, misdirected customer relationships because they haven't taken the time to understand what their customers need or what elements of the processes satisfy or irritate the customer.

Our research[1] has exposed some of the common myths associated with process improvement in customer care. We have discovered the facts, as well as some best practices of the organizations that are most successful in improving customer satisfaction.

Our analysis of the data highlighted three categories of organizations that are successful in achieving improved customer satisfaction:

1. Technology-focused organizations

2. Process-focused organizations

3. Customer-needs-focused organizations

It is imperative to understand all three categories because only then can you improve the processes that touch the customer. Organizations in each of the three categories are successful in improving customer satisfaction with their different approaches. However, companies that exhibit characteristics of all three organizational types but that focus primarily on *processes* are by far the most successful.

THE TECHNOLOGY-FOCUSED ORGANIZATION

We define technology-focused organizations as those that have implemented advanced technology in their customer relationships. Successful technology-focused organizations typically offer a number of advanced customer care capabilities designed to make it easy to do business with their customers. (This will be discussed in more detail in Part Four.) While technology-focused companies are successful in improving customer satisfaction and service, as well as their competitiveness, they do not achieve as high a level of customer satisfaction as those that focus on process.

THE PROCESS-FOCUSED ORGANIZATION

Process-focused organizations that have improved customer satisfaction are most likely to have reengineered their customer order fulfilment, customer-relationship management, or marketing processes— processes that touch the customer.

---

[1] *IDEAS* 1995 (Toronto: Coopers & Lybrand, 1995).

Process-focused companies have the highest levels of employee productivity, often due to their reengineering of key customer processes. But these companies usually need to make better use of technology, which can maximize the effectiveness of their customer processes. They also need to improve communication with suppliers and customers, which can fine-tune processes to address specific customer requirements.

CUSTOMER NEEDS-FOCUSED ORGANIZATIONS

Customer-needs-focused organizations are defined as organizations that continuously seek out information on what their customers want, getting closer and closer to understanding what customers value most. These organizations are dedicated to seeking out and listening to their customers, using customer-satisfaction measurement studies, complaints-tracking mechanisms, and employee-satisfaction measurement tools.

Customer-needs-focused companies typically have the most direct, accurate information about what their customers want, but often neglect to implement the changes necessary to increase customer satisfaction. These companies are the least successful of the three types of organizations. They are information seekers, but haven't created an environment in which they can capitalize on that information. They need to become better acquainted with supporting technologies and incorporate customer information into company standards.

PUTTING IT ALL TOGETHER

The *IDEAS* study results show that companies that have achieved the highest customer-satisfaction levels are those that take a holistic approach, combining technology, process, and customer-needs focuses. They have the technology to be responsive to customers, and their use of that technology is guided by customer input. New technologies are introduced to the company with a process focus, allowing the organization to improve customer service and, at the same time, maximize employee productivity.

The key for these companies is strategy—learning how to balance technology selection, process improvement, and timely implementation to fulfil the needs of both internal and external customers. Successful companies choose the right technologies and then pay careful attention to their use, usually enlisting the help of experts from outside the company, who can offer objective analysis and broad experience.

The research suggests that there is a standard progression of activities within the organizations that improve customer satisfaction, retain customers, and enhance revenue. Companies that have applied technology to their advantage have used customer input, first, to help define their key customer touch processes; second, to define the objectives and goals of process improvement—with technology as the enabler; and finally, to measure the success of changes implemented and to guide corrective action when necessary.

Consider the following. Building your organization into one that customers want to do business with is analogous to building a house. What can you do to differentiate it from any other that can be built?

First you start with a strong foundation. That means having a thorough plan based on customer input, but which also takes into consideration external elements such as competitive influences and market needs. Chapter 12, written by Sandip Patel provides you with the foundation. Patel highlights practices found to be effective in customer service design initiatives. Next you build a solid frame, again using customer input, but using technology as the tools and binding that hold the structure together. Chapter 13 outlines a new framework for customer segmentation. With that segmentation strategy as a guide, you may want to consider using technology-based and non-technology-based enablers—for instance, who gets special 1-800 access to the customer service department? And who gets your best salespeople?

Finally, you refine the interior, the true differentiator. This requires well-trained craftspeople, so that you have the right tools (technology), at the right time, in the hands of those who know how to use them effectively. Sometimes these craftspeople may not be within your organization and that is the premise of Chapter 14. Organizations have at least three options, self-provisioning (or insourcing), cosourcing, and outsourcing. Tudor Negrea and Lorne Severs provide you with the information to decide which option to consider. Once that decision is made, proper controls and monitoring are required. Chapter 15 by Suresh Gupta, Jay Singh, and Robert Largey provides that guidance with lessons learned from reviews with organizations that have made the mistake of having too few controls in place.

But the job is not finished when that house is built. Organizations need a common goal to ensure that ongoing maintenance is carried out and that a theme of continuous improvement is alive and well. Best-practices organizations have turned to awards and certification to rally the organization toward a common objective. And ISO certification is a popular route to take. Part Three finishes with Chapter 16, in which Larry Brandt describes in detail the experience of an organization that has won awards of excellence, using ISO certification as a rallying force.

Choose your tools carefully.

S.A.B.

Laying the Groundwork for Successfully Implementing Process Improvement

Sandip Patel, Coopers & Lybrand, Boston, MA

ORGANIZATIONS NEED TO change. The market drivers have changed and for many organizations, the issue is one of survival. Only 12 of the 43 exemplary companies identified in Tom Peters' *In Search of Excellence*[1] remain in good shape today. Many organizations are involved in analyzing and "reengineering" their business processes in an effort to dramatically raise efficiency, cut cycle time, improve customer service, or all of the above. Business process reengineering (BPR) is a high-stakes game: much time and money is invested in transforming the business, and the payback to the organization can be enormous. However, BPR efforts fail more often than they succeed.

A study by McKinsey & Co. concluded that BPR often results in little or no significant impact on the economic performance of a company, even when the cost of reengineered processes are improved by 60 to 80 percent. Mutual Benefit Life reengineered its policy-issuing process to achieve a cycle time efficiency of over 90 percent, and within months filed for Chapter 11 bankruptcy protection. These stories of the failure of reengineered processes to contribute to a company's economic performance illustrate today's process paradox. They are examples of

---

[1] New York: Harper & Row, 1982.

investments in processes that were not the primary source of economic added value to their organizations.

Our experience in working with companies to transform them into customer-focused organizations has established five basic principles for getting started:

1. Define your customers. In our opinion, there are no internal customers—only external customers who are the buyers or consumers of your products and services.

2. Establish a process map that is aligned to the corporate strategy. A process in this context is defined as an end-to-end process that starts with a customer need and has a measurable output, which has value to the customer.

3. Identify the "moments of truth"—customer "touch points," or points in the process that influence, or "touch," the customer.

4. Use an economic value-based framework to make decisions about process treatments—redesign, outsource, commercialize, etc. This serves as the basis for establishing a road-map for transformation.

5. Ensure that key performance indicators (KPIs) are established throughout the priority processes and designed to have a positive impact on the customer's perception at every "moment of truth" and are leading indicators of financial results.

This chapter highlights some practices we have found effective in focusing on customer service design initiatives.

ESTABLISHING THE RIGHT PROCESS MAP AND THE APPROPRIATE MEASURES

Customer care pertains to the combination of actions that an organization must take to retain its customer base and gain new customers, or how it leverages its image as a customer-focused enterprise. In effect, customer care or customer service is not a process but a set of processes and activities throughout the "service value chain," which all contribute to the customers' perception of the quality of service. This set of processes, organized logically, makes up the process map for the customer care function in the organization. It is important to create this map soon after the business processes are prioritized, so that the right focus for customer care is established before starting the transformation effort.

Once the process map is established, process attributes should be specified for each process to ensure that a consistent and focused customer perspective is maintained through the design effort. Each process has its own customer touch points, the moments of truth that affect the customer's perception the regarding the quality of service. And each customer touch point has service aspects that drive the customer's perception of superlative service. These drivers are customer value drivers. Focusing on these value drivers is critical to achieving the target service levels desired by the customers. Specific, quantifiable performance measures can assist in ensuring this focus and encouraging service representatives to perform appropriately.

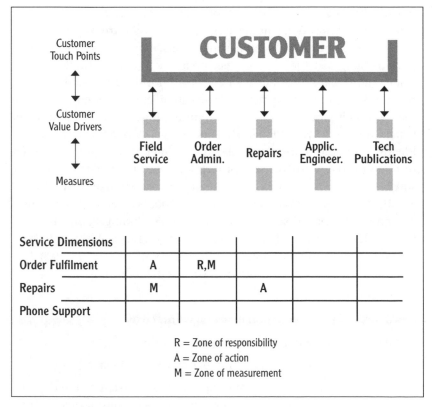

FIGURE 1: Customer Care Function for a Manufacturing Firm

For example, a manufacturer may have a series of processes that constitute the customer care function for its business. Each process plays a role in delivering service. But service to the customer will be adversely affected unless the measures of performance at the process level are aligned to responsibility for implementation. In Figure 1, while the field service staff "act" to fulfil an order, the order administration unit is responsible for logging the completion of the order and is also measured on the timely execution of the order. This is an extreme case of misalignment because the field service staff have no incentive or responsibility for the timely completion of the order. On the other hand, the order administration unit is in the unenviable position of both responding to customer complaints and hounding the field service staff for timely completion of orders so that the administration unit can meet its performance targets.

Another example of this concept comes from a customer service organization of a life insurance company, which redesigned its core processes to improve declining service levels and introduced a new 1-800 line to centralize all its service operations. A process map was developed to categorize the key business processes that made up the service value chain. The process categories were prioritized for redesign, and measurable performance metrics were established to set targets for the redesign. This was accomplished by conducting customer surveys and using Coopers & Lybrand's (C&L's) Service Cycle Workshop approach to identify moments of truth and related customer priorities. The redesign team employed a structured approach for designing the new customer service operation using C&L's proprietary process simulator, SPARKS™. SPARKS™ was used to model the current process, analyze process metrics, and test "what-if" scenarios for redesign, including staffing models, volume fluctuations, and impact of technology. The results included significant improvements in time and costs, with the new 1-800 line tripling the incoming call volume, as well as the following:

- 20 percent improvement in capacity
- 70 to 90 percent reduction in average unit costs
- 40 percent reduction in average elapsed time
- more than 90 percent reduction of department backlog

Moreover, the process of participative work design resulted in the service representatives internalizing the process of continuous learning and improvement to create, assimilate, and proliferate their work processes.

THE BUSINESS PROCESS INVESTMENT^{SM} FRAMEWORK[2]

Successfully reengineering business processes requires an understanding of the difference between excellence in creating efficiency and excellence in creating value. The goal of efficiency is served by getting the process right. The goal of creating value is served by getting the right process right. The value creation goal of reengineering initiatives is often ignored because processes are regarded primarily as sets of activities in an organization, not as invisible assets and liabilities that drive the economic performance of the organization. As customer service, logistics, learning, teamwork, quality, and speed of response—all of which are process-driven—become more and more central to firms' priorities, more and more of their competitive strength rests on both exploiting their process assets and not allowing old assets to become liabilities. This economic view of business processes provides us with the language, techniques, and tools to ensure that process investments are aimed directly at producing process advantage, not just process efficiency. The C&L approach to producing process advantage takes this economic view of business processes, viewing them as either assets or liabilities. We call this the business Process Investment^{SM} framework.

Central to the business Process Investment^{SM} framework is the classification of a process in an "evaluation matrix," shown in Figure 2. This matrix is intended to clarify how important a process is in principle to an organization, and how valuable it is today. The emphasis is on identifying the best opportunity for increasing economic value, where economic value is a combination of customer value, operational efficiency, and future options.

---

[2] The Business Process Investment framework is a concept introduced and discussed in detail by Peter Keen and Lin Knapp in their recent publication *Every Manager's Guide to Business Processes*, Harvard Business School Press, 1996. This section draws on the concepts and approach presented in that publication.

	Value Dimension	
	Assets	**Liabilities**
Identity		
Priority		
Background		
Mandated		

(left vertical label: **Salience Dimension**)

FIGURE 2: The business Process Investment^{SM} framework

The horizontal axis of the matrix—the *value* axis—classifies a process according to its worth to an organization.

- A **process asset** is a process that represents a significant investment in infrastructure, planning, training, and/or information systems, and that provides a distinctive value to the organization in terms of capability, reputation, competitive differentiation, cost, and/or efficiency.

- A **process liability** is a process that diverts organizational capital (in the sense of alternative investment) without providing any asset benefits and/or waste resources.

The vertical axis of the matrix—the *salience* axis—classifies a process asset or liability according to how much it matters in principle to an organization. The distinctions between these four categories can be clarified by regarding them as the dependent to the answer to three questions:

1. Does the process represent what the company stands for, and is it part of the organization's image to its customers?

2. Is the process important and does it matter how well it is executed?

3. Is the process required by government or some governing authority?

According to the answer to these three questions, the process is one of the following: an identity, priority, background, or mandated process, as shown in the matrix in Figure 3.

- An **identity** process represents what a company stands for, who it is, and what its customers think of it.

- A **priority** process is an important element of the company's business, and how well it is executed makes a critical difference.

- A **background** process is a part of what a company does, but something that it does not want to spend a lot of time, attention, or resources on.

- A **mandated** process is executed only because the government or other regulatory bodies mandate that the company do so.

A FRAMEWORK FOR EFFECTIVE DECISION-MAKING

The business Process Investment^{SM} framework serves as a decision-making tool for determining process treatments. Once the process map is established, processes are mapped on the framework. The framework serves as an effective, objective decision-making tool for a senior leadership team to determine future treatment for each process on the basis of strategic intent and leverage points (see Figure 3).

Image		Not Image	
Important	Not Important	Important	Not Important
Identity	N/A	Priority	Background
Identity	N/A	Priority	Mandated

FIGURE 3: Process Classification

In applying this framework, it is important to keep certain points in perspective. First, identity processes may vary by company—even within the same industry. This is based on the premise that the identity process defines the image of the company for its customers. For example, in the insurance industry, customer perception would suggest that while UNUM's identity process is its product pricing process, USAA is identified by its customer service process, and Progressive is recognized by its claims processing (on-the-spot claims adjudication). Second, once established, this tool must be treated as a living framework and periodically evaluated to determine process shifts and changing priorities.

		Value Dimension	
		Assets	Liabilities
Salience Dimension	Identity	ATMs (in late 1970s)	
	Priority	ATMs (in late 1980s)	
	Background		ATMs (in late 1990s)
	Mandated		

FIGURE 4: Evolution of ATMs as a Customer Service Process for a Bank

For example, as Figure 4 shows, in the seventies, when Citibank introduced automated teller machines (ATMs), the process of transaction processing through automated tellers was an identity process for the bank. It established and maintained a brand recognition through the efficient execution of this strategic process. This strategy helped it gain market share. Competitors were known to speculate that ATMs would cause the eventual demise of Citibank. However, we know the rest to be history. By the eighties, the process of transaction processing through ATMs became a priority for banks—something they had to offer to compete. In the nineties, it is more of a background process—a basic requirement to play in the consumer banking market.

CASE STUDY
Applying business Process Investment℠ in a Life Insurance Company

The application of the BPI has proved to be extremely beneficial in prioritizing a corporate-wide transformation effort in a major life insurance company. The company had defined its strategy of becoming a customer-focused, service-led organization by organizing around its key business processes and redesigning the key processes to provide superior customer service in a cost-efficient way. A business process map was established and processes were categorized as adding value (from the customers' perspective), enabling (for the value-adding processes), and governance (administrative) processes.

A quick assessment of the business processes was conducted from various perspectives—customer-satisfaction drivers, current process costs, and supporting infrastructure. The executive management used the results of the assessment to apply the business Process Investment^{SM} framework to the company's existing business processes to establish scope and strategic priorities for the enterprise-wide transformation. The approach used to facilitate decisions about business process priorities is illustrated in Figure 5.

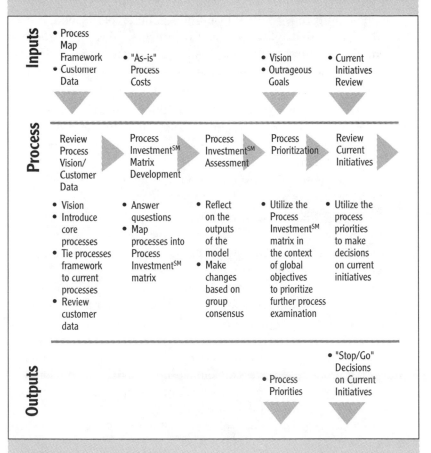

FIGURE 5: Enterprise-Wide Transformation: A Road Map for Getting Started

The results provided some significant insights for prioritizing the investment for the enterprise-wide transformation:

- All its processes, in different degrees, were perceived as liability processes.

- A set of processes that was crucial to achieving the corporate goal of becoming more customer-focused was performed as a background process with a "smoke-stack" mentality that diverted significant organizational capital without providing asset benefits, such as customer loyalty and retention.

- The process of developing new products and establishing the infrastructure for distribution was categorized as an "enabling" process. As a result, it was being performed as a background, liability process. This process, however, needed to be a priority asset process since it defined an important element of the company's business and had a direct impact on customers.

- Over 200 ongoing projects were identified. More than 50 percent of these projects neither contributed to the strategic transformation nor were necessary for maintaining the day-to-day operations and service obligations of the business. These projects were either stopped or put on hold, and committed resources were redirected to support the transformation.

The business Process Investment^{SM} approach assisted the organization in focusing the first wave of transformation and related investment on four key processes that were critical for the company to operationalize its corporate strategy.

The business Process Investment^{SM} framework is a unifying approach that maximizes shareholder value through the process-related services taking place in a company. It provides an economic understanding of business processes. Such understanding, tied to strategic intent, allows the process investments to be aimed directly at producing process advantage, not just process efficiency. This process advantage, which results from tactics aligned to strategy, is key to maximizing shareholder value.

The lessons learned from this case highlight guidelines that are critical to the successful start and execution of any transformation initiative:

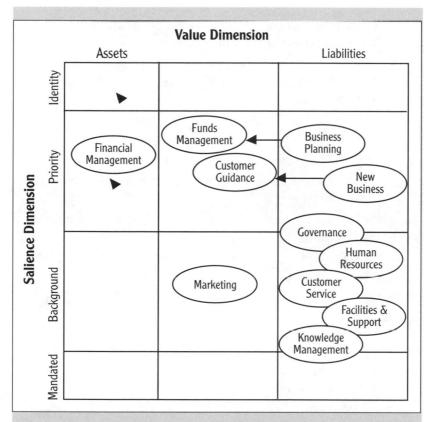

FIGURE 6: Strategic Priority Processes for Transformation

- Strategy must drive the transformation agenda and all investment decisions.

- The approach employed must facilitate fact-based, business-driven decisions quickly.

- A strong fact base and data are important for making meaningful decisions.

- Cost/benefit and customer data provide a sound basis for process decisions.

- Customer desires and touch points are key to assessing value.

- Time commitment and ownership by key decision-makers is vital to the success of the transformation.

- A safe environment and process is critical for constructive debate and effective decision-making.
- The process must allow for conflicting perceptions and thoughts about process priorities. Electronic polling provides such an environment.
- A commitment to action is necessary. Failing to take action sends the wrong message to the organization.
- Actions need to align with strategic objectives.
- Change management must start from day one and become a part of the culture.
- Process priorities must be appropriately communicated to the organization.
- Communication strategies must be devised carefully to avoid misinterpretation.
- Executed correctly, communication can be a powerful agent for mobilizing the organization for change.

About the author

SANDIP PATEL

Sandip Patel is a partner in the Strategy Consulting practice of Coopers & Lybrand Consulting in Boston. He has extensive experience in business strategy implementation and the strategic use of technology for effective decision-making. He specializes in leading organizations through strategic transformation and in applying business modelling and simulation to redesign diverse business operations in the financial services, insurance, health care, and telecommunications industries. He is particularly interested in the leverage of intellectual capital in organizations and the deployment of performance measurement systems. Patel has an MS in Management Information Systems and an MBA from Boston University. He is an associate member of the Institute of Chartered Accountants of India.

CHAPTER THIRTEEN

A Differentiated Approach to Customer Service

NOT ALL CUSTOMER SEGMENTS REQUIRE THE SAME SERVICE

Stanley A. Brown and Sharad Verma
Coopers & Lybrand, Toronto, ON

O NE OF THE greatest challenges facing business today is how to balance the desires of management (cost efficiency, productivity, improved performance, control) with the needs of customers (quality customer service, an organization that is easy to do business with, control). Organizations that have been successful in balancing these sometimes conflicting requirements have broken with tradition by delivering different classes of service and different levels of customer support to different customer segments. The result? Improved profitability and, more important, enhanced customer satisfaction.

Organizations today face a number of basic challenges:

1. Can we afford to offer the same level of service to all customers?

2. How can we reduce the costs of service delivery to the customers who are least profitable?

3. How do we retain customers and achieve customer loyalty within our most important customer segments?

4. Which customers should we "fire" and which customers can we take to a higher level of service?

5. How can we stay in control of the customer service process?

Customers also have a number of (sometimes) conflicting needs. They require control as well —they want information when they need it, not just when it is convenient for the organization to provide it. They prefer to deal with an organization that is easy to do business with— that includes ease in placing orders, obtaining pricing information, and checking on the status of orders.

It *is* possible to satisfy both customer and company needs at the same time. All that's required is the ability to recognize who your customers are and provide them with differentiated customer service. Resources, of course, are not unlimited, and "same" service levels obviously cannot be given to all customers. "Best" service levels must be given to the best customers. But you must first determine who they are and what they need.

Let's start with the first requirement: the ability to recognize your customers, their unique needs, and their potential. This will take a bit of work, but customer segmentation offers a starting point. Instead of the traditional definitions of customer segmentation, which use volume or geographical region as the key criterion, consider using customer profitability. Not all customers are equally profitable and not all have the ability to become your most profitable customers. Therefore, do they all deserve the same level of service? As mentioned earlier, your most profitable customers should get the best service. They may not be willing to pay more for it, but they will be more loyal to you if they receive it.

Here's a second consideration. Customers within like segments most likely possess similar needs as well as a similar degree of satisfaction with their current supplier. The questions that must therefore be answered are: Which customers are in which segments? What are their priorities? and once those answers are known, How can we encourage them to "self identify" themselves when they call into the customer service department?

As a starting point, a substantial amount of research and analysis with both customers and your sales force is required. Your salespeople will be able to define the current and potential needs of their customers. Direct customer research is also mandatory. You cannot assume that you have sufficient information about your customers' current and future needs. Consider the following three possible segments (you may have more), as shown in Figure 1.

FIGURE 1: Customer Segmentation/Support Strategy

Tier I: Low profit, low potential. Customers at this level are your least profitable. They offer limited profit potential and low volume, but regular, repeat business. A simple review of your customer list should enable you to identify which customers fall into this category. Most likely, they will be commodity purchasers. They are expensive to serve and should, therefore, be given low-cost service. They generally do not expect a high level of service (limited or no sales calls), only attention when requested. They typically look for an easy way to place commodity orders and receive the lowest price available.

To service the needs of these customers, best-practices organizations have established direct access lines (a form of self-identification) with limited or no customer service representative (CSR) support. Electronic commerce (Internet) applications and service delivered through interactive voice response (IVR) have been found to be very effective. This service delivery tier should consume less than 10 percent of all CSR available time. At the lowest level of service, client expectations are also lowest, which makes this group an ideal early training ground for new customer service representatives.

Tier II: High profit, high potential. The customers in this group have strong potential for growth. You are most likely one of a number of suppliers to this customer group; however, dominant share is possible. These customers require a set of basic services as well as timely hours of operation or localized service access. Periodically, they require answers to questions concerning inventory availability, order status, pricing, and account status.

Customers in this group are typically given direct phone access to the customer service department through a special phone number (again a simple form of self-identification). The CSR at this tier of service is quite competent in handling the needs of this specialized group, and can generally give customers personalized service with respect to order entry, status updates, and returns. The CSR will not, however, provide "one stop" service for all customer needs within this group and may transfer the call to the accounts receivable department, inventory management, or expediting.

There is an opportunity for CSRs to up-sell—that is, sell additional products—and react to the unique needs of this customer base. This group which should consume 50 to 60 percent of available CSR time.

Tier III: Strategic partnership. This segment represents the highest profit potential. You have a strategic partnership with the customers in this segment. You enjoy a dominant market share position or have a high likelihood of achieving one. This customer relationship is often described as a "true partnership," one where the customer has made the supplier a complete and open participant in the detailed, long-term conduct of his or her business. There is a primary need for suppliers who are proactive and knowledgeable in market conditions and who operate as an extension of the customer's sales force.

Customers at this level require extensive, "one and done"customer support when they contact the customer care centre. They need a CSR or team of CSRs who are knowledgeable in a variety of areas (order entry, accounts receivable, inventory management). The CSR functions as a quasi-sales representative, offering both sales and service, and is viewed internally and externally as competent in anticipating the customer's needs and providing a variety of services to keep the customer informed. Customers in this group also require the flexibility to conduct business in a form that is convenient, whether by fax, phone, electronic data interchange (EDI), or the Internet. More sophisticated means of self-identification exist to recognize phone numbers and link them to individuals within a customer organization (more on this in Part Four).

HOW IT WORKED IN PRACTICE

The following is a true case study of a major distribution organization that services a large customer base across the country. Customer service complaints were increasing at an alarming rate and defections had crept in. Knowing that some action had to be taken, the company conducted a high-level review of its customer files. Not surprisingly, the analysis indicated that not all customers contributed equally to the company's profitability.

That knowledge itself did not lead to a solution. The company had no way of differentiating its service to the most profitable and important segments of its existing customer base. All customers calling into its customer service department were treated equally. While the company offered only a limited service (order entry, price quotations, and order status), in many cases, calls still had to be transferred to other more knowledgeable individuals, a major cause of customer dissatisfaction. Recognizing that it must become more efficient and improve customer service while at the same time differentiating its service, the company conducted a more detailed analysis of its customer base, using traditional and non-traditional classification techniques. Its ultimate objectives were simple and straightforward:

1. Redeploy resources (customer service and sales support) in order to optimize profitability by customer segment.

2. Offer optimal service to only those segments requiring it.

The customer analysis suggested that customer profitability, not sales volume or regionality, should be the basis for segmentation. This led the organization to restructure its customer base. It created five (rather than three) classifications. Your classification, as well as the actions you take, may in fact be quite different.

Tier I: Transitional
Tier II: Maintenance
Tier III: Retention
Tier IV: Base
Tier V: Strategic Partners

Here is some additional detail regarding these classifications:

Tier I: Transitional. These customers—negative gross profit accounts—were high-maintenance accounts and were financially limited on a day-to-day basis. They would be better serviced by phone coverage or outsourced to a third-party distributor. These accounts offered low potential and at some point in time were candidates for "firing,"— that is, targets for disengagement.

Tier II: Maintenance. These accounts provided limited or negative gross profit, but with slight additional attention had potential to move to a positive, yet limited, profit potential—the next 40 percent of accounts. They were generally smaller accounts or those resistant to changing market conditions. They were transaction oriented (many small orders) and required hands-on assistance because of their limited sophistication in systems and process. They were also financially strapped. Restrictions placed on this group were as follows:

- No phone orders allowed; mail, fax or e-mail/Internet only.
- Limited call frequency by sales force.
- Limited sales force support activity.

Tier III: Retention. This grouping was represented by accounts that provided a constant gross profit stream, however, substantially lower than the next two segments—about 20 percent of existing accounts. They could be described as barely scraping by and preferring the status quo to growth The objective in servicing this group was to ensure that these customers did not consume inappropriate resources, particularly at the expense of the next two segments. As a result, the following applied to this group:

- Selective resource allocation.
- Education. This was important, both to keep these accounts in business and to advise them in their purchasing habits to allow them to move up in the segmentation grid.

Tier IV: Base. In this tier were accounts that generated strong gross profit, yet had the potential for improvement—the next 10 percent of accounts. These accounts could be described as less progressive, but a stable, solid force in the industry. They had the ability to move to the next level, but were more focused on current market opportunities. These accounts were targets for heavy investment of resources and time by the company. For this segment, the focus was on being good, not best, typified by the following:

- Second-best fill rate, for example, 48 hours, not 24 hours.

- Target invoice accuracy and back-order fill rate slightly below that guaranteed to the strategic partner group.

- A team approach to customer support.

Tier V: Strategic partners. This group was composed of customers offering the highest gross profit, where the potential for strategic partnership was greatest—the top 10 percent of accounts. These accounts were considered market innovators and leaders in the industry. It was felt that they possessed a more progressive partner orientation. These accounts were recognized to be financially sound, with growth and expansion part of their mandate.

To service these accounts, the company's strategy was as follows:

- Provide one-stop shopping. Route calls to a group of select CSR's who could handle or be responsible for all their needs.

- Make best resources available to deal with the customer. Provide a team approach involving sales, sales support, and customer service.

- Plan joint strategies and measurement of goals. Set objectives in concert with the customer.

- Offer best "total" service approach:
  - Best order fill rate on core products. Guaranteed fill rates, defined by mutually developed contract.
  - Best invoice accuracy. Care taken to ensure that pricing on contracts is always current and accurately transposed to the pricing system.
  - Flexibility of delivery times, packaging, and credit terms.
  - Customized services tailored to customer's needs.

Key performance measurements (KPMs) were developed and monitored for each segment, all within the context of recognizing that not all customers are equal, thus not all customers should be treated equally. And the result? Sales and profitability increased by 15 to 20 percent within an 18- to 24-month period.

SUMMARY

Here's the question you must answer: What are my customer segments and what level of service am I prepared to deliver? Most likely they will cluster in different areas. They may differ by region, product offering, and price point. How high or low your customers' needs occur within the hierarchy, together with their level of satisfaction, will affect the service-delivery strategies required to attract and keep those customers.

Customers may migrate to a new level, or you may wish to move your customers to a higher or lower level in a short period of time as their businesses mature, their profitability improves, and/or the competition changes. The key is understanding who your customers are at all times to ensure that whatever their needs are, you're constantly anticipating—and meeting—them with the right service delivery.

About the authors

STANLEY A. BROWN and SHARAD VERMA

Stanley A. Brown is the partner responsible for Coopers & Lybrand Consulting's International Centre of Excellence in Customer Satisfaction, located in Toronto. Stanley Brown is also the author of *What Customers Value Most: How to Achieve Business Transformation by Focusing on Processes That Touch the Customer* (Toronto: John Wiley & Sons Canada, 1995).

Sharad Verma is a senior consultant at the International Centre of Excellence in Customer Satisfaction, specializing in Strategic Marketing and Customer Relationship Management.

Outsourcing Customer Care: Are there Other Alternatives?

Tudor Negrea and Lorne Severs,
Coopers & Lybrand, Toronto, ON

ORGANIZATIONS HAVE TRADITIONALLY worked to streamline and optimize their supply chain for raw materials and finished goods through the use of tools and approaches such as total quality management, business process reengineering, efficient consumer response, and outsourcing.

Now, however, dramatic economic and competitive changes are reshaping public and private sector organizations, making them intensify their focus on the efficient delivery of critical customer services. This focus includes assessing the options and possibilities offered by the use of outsourcing. In addition to efficiencies in cost savings, outsourcing offers organizations the ability to quickly provide customers "best in class" customer services and practices.

The success of outsourcing in the traditional areas of information technology, help desk call centres, distribution and logistics, printing, and mail centre operations have led to its application in other areas, including administrative services, property and facilities management, human resource administration, and more recently, customer care activities, including telemarketing, technical support, and customer assistance.

In the context of an economy that is based increasingly on services, we believe that:

- Outsourcing is a disciplined approach to optimizing the services supply chain.

- The delivery of services is highly sensitive to economies of scale, size, and specialization.

- There is a solid trend toward a dynamic and adaptive service provision model, in sharp contrast with the static self-provision model of the past.

Industry surveys have estimated that approximately 75 percent of organizations expect to consider using a form of alternative service provision in the next three to five years.

Rather than play follow-the-leader, organizations must consider the implications of outsourcing processes and services that directly "touch" their customers, and develop a clear understanding of the benefits and risks involved.

The discussion in this chapter about the use of outsourcing in the context of customer care includes the following:

- The types of services and functions that can be provided by an outsourcing supplier.

- The key criteria to apply in determining whether an activity should be considered for outsourcing.

- The benefits and risks of outsourcing, including ways to mitigate exposure to risks.

Following the discussion of outsourcing, we offer the spectrum of alternative service delivery options available to organizations. This spectrum covers internal and external delivery methods, including self-provision and outsourcing.

WHY CONSIDER OUTSOURCING OF CUSTOMER CARE?

We define outsourcing as "the provision of services through a long-term agreement, with specific scope and a close relationship, that typically translates existing vendor synergies and economies of scale into savings for the beneficiary."

We have identified some key characteristics of outsourcing that help explain its ability to provide services in a cost-efficient, high-quality manner:

- Outsourcing discourages the frivolous use of scarce resources by settling debt with cash not journal entries. We believe that organizations can better focus on delivering efficient services when the cost of those services is clearly identified with a cash charge to the organization's service area, rather than the services being paid through a non-cash corporate charge or deptartmental transfer of funds..

- Outsourcing a particular function to a third party allows you to take advantage of that third party's skill level and, depending on the size and scale of operations, typically costs less than sustaining the same service in-house. An outsourcing supplier provides similar services to several organizations, potentially benefiting the company through enhanced service levels and lower costs due to their synergies from the size and scale of their operations.

- When the services considered for outsourcing are specific to an industry, an outsourcing supplier can assist industries in providing services such as payment reconciliation through its ability to provide the service to all industry participants—for example, account reconciliation activities such as loyalty program reward points accounting and tracking.

- The use of outsourcing allows the costs of a process or activity to shift to a lower cost base industry. For example, when the activity considered for outsourcing is a support activity (administration, technical support), the cost of labour in a specific industry may be higher than that of an outsourcing supplier.

- The use of outsourcing establishes value for services in a real and competitive marketplace. In assessing the applicability of outsourcing specific activities and services, we require there to be a competitive market of suppliers for any services being considered. This fundamental belief helps ensure that companies receive the best possible price for services.

"Customer care" encompasses those activities within an organization that focus on the management of customer relationships. These include order fulfilment, problem and complaint escalation and resolution, information delivery, payment processing, technical support, and after-sales service. An example of the way that best-practices organizations deliver customer care is through centralized locations, sometimes referred to as "call centres."

Call centres combine the use of highly effective and empowered company representatives with a service framework that relies heavily on state-of-the-art communications and information technologies. Call centres have become a key component of customer care strategies. In fact, organizations have invested millions of dollars in call centres as their focus has changed from a cost function to a revenue-generating function. For example, call centres have shifted their emphasis from providing technical and in-house support, such as help desks, to tele-marketing and sales activities.

Organizations have found that in outsourcing their key call centre functions they are improving their competitive advantage. Outsourcing suppliers employ experts who can manage call centre functions, allowing the organization to focus on its own key competencies, such as product or service innovation, while simultaneously maintaining low costs.

Companies have used external suppliers to provide customer service support for other functions and activities, including:

- Information technology technical support for computer operations within organizations.

- Technical product support and warranty support to external customers for computer equipment and peripherals.

- Customer service for existing accounts, and telemarketing activities for new business development in industries such as telecommunications, financial services, and credit card companies.

- Product inquiries and tracking and trace functions in delivery organizations.

DETERMINING THE TYPE OF ACTIVITIES TO CONSIDER FOR OUTSOURCING

You should choose outsourcing over self-provision only after identifying key functions that can be managed less expensively or more effectively by a third party provider, and at the same time allow you to maintain the same or better service levels.

Not all activities are candidates for outsourcing. It is essential to retain key activities that are not provided in the marketplace at the same level of expertise and cost benefit. Unique activities are typically not candidates for outsourcing; nor are activities whose processes cannot be decoupled from the organization, unless they are reengineered to allow for their decoupling. Medium and large organizations that cannot take advantage of outsourcing may benefit from a shared-services delivery arrangement or consolidation and centralization of activities, sharing the generic activities among different divisions or lines of business, and thus creating internal synergies and the resultant savings.

There is a great deal of discussion regarding the strategic differences in outsourcing core and non-core activities. An examination of recent publicly announced arrangements as well as our own work in this area lead us to conclude that organizations assess the potential for activities for outsourcing according to whether they are unique or generic, not whether they are core or non-core activities. Examples of activities by industry that have recently been outsourced include the following:

- Retailers outsourcing logistics and distribution activities.

- Investment and mutual funds outsourcing the accounting and bookkeeping of the funds while retaining the marketing, selling, and fund management functions.

- Small and large banks in the United States and Canada outsourcing their cheque processing functions, telemarketing, and customer service.

- Information technology companies outsourcing their technical support for their consumer market products, such as printers and other computer hardware.

We believe that in these examples, the characteristic of the activity that determines its applicability for outsourcing is not its criticality but its generic nature. In all cases, the activities are of critical importance to the organization; yet they are being provided by the marketplace efficiently and effectively.

Coopers & Lybrand has identified four criteria for activities to be considered suitable for outsourcing:

1. Routine activities, even if critical or highly technical.

2. Well-delineated activities—that is, they must be capable of being decoupled from the organization's existing structure and processes.

3. Activities that are measurable and manageable at arm's length.

4. Activities that are readily provided by established suppliers operating in a competitive marketplace—that is, there must be several companies available to offer these services, thus ensuring the company always has options available, should it become necessary to change suppliers.

Each activity under consideration for outsourcing is evaluated against each of the above criteria. Any activity that fails to meet any one of the above criteria is excluded from consideration. For example, an activity may be well-defined and measurable, but only provided by one or two suppliers in the marketplace. Therefore, the non-competitive environment does not allow the beneficiary the level of comfort, portability, and options that are required to receive services on a competitive basis. This activity would not be considered suitable for outsourcing. In addition, given the long-term relationship required for outsourcing, competition is essential to maintain the value-price aspect necessary to arrive at a superior provisioning mix of internal and external providers.

It is important to remember that all not activities within a function or process need be considered for outsourcing. Activities can be classified into three areas: planning, reviewing, and doing. A large portion of the planning and reviewing activities are dependent on unique knowledge of the organization and its customers, whereas the activities categorized as "doing" activities are more likely to be generic in nature, and hence can be considered candidates for outsourcing.

BENEFITS OF OUTSOURCING

The effective use of outsourcing can provide organizations with many benefits: higher cost savings, faster access to current technology, availability of highly trained staff, improved service levels, and an overall higher scalability and flexibility of operations.

If you are considering outsourcing call centre activities and functions, you can benefit from the following characteristics of outsourcing:

- **Cost reduction.** Organizations that have outsourced have typically generated cost savings owing to the ability of suppliers to leverage their size, volume, scale, and standardization of activities. The amount of cost savings will differ according to the current costs of self-provision and the uniqueness of the activities. Depending on the activity and the industry context, savings through outsourcing are typically estimated at 10 to 15 percent of self-provision costs.

- **Expertise.** Many organizations do not have the people, technology, methodology, and/or management capability to manage current and proposed operations in-house. Outsourcing allows you to use existing staff strategically to best meet your organization's needs.

- **Technology, investment, and cash flow.** You can gain access to state-of-the-art technology without making large capital expenditures. Depending on the arrangements with the outsourcing vendor, you can take advantage of the vendor's ability to adapt quickly to new technologies as customer service needs change.

- **Scalability.** By outsourcing, you gain the ability to adapt to changes in volume, in the short and long term (seasonal peaks and valleys in volume).

- **Speed and transition.** To meet organizational and competitive demands, companies may have only a short time frame within which to implement a customer service program or offer a new service. Outsourcing may help you speed up the process, by giving you access to the help you need, when you need it. For example, outsourcing can allow you to introduce outbound telemarketing services quickly at the call centre because of the availability of trained telemarketers working with the outsourcing provider.

- **Customer service and access.** This refers to the accessibility of an organization to its customers. Since many organizations operate across time zones and continents, outsourcing can provide customers "7/24" access (seven days a week, 24 hours a day) to customer service.

RISKS OF OUTSOURCING

There are risks associated with outsourcing. Risk factors to be considered include the scope of activities to be outsourced, the fit between the organization and the supplier, and control, pricing and implementation difficulties. We have outlined key risk factors below, including ways to reduce or mitigate the risk:

- **Scope of activities.** It is essential to properly identify the activities and processes that are considered for outsourcing. Improper scope can lead to the duplication of activities performed, difficulties in decoupling the process from the organization, and incorrect financial planning. When identifying the scope, it is important to use a proper level of detail (or granularity), whether this be at the functional level or the activity level.

- **Vendor relations.** There may be a poor fit between the organization and the outsourcing supplier, in terms of organizational culture, values, and beliefs. For example, staff may have different interpretations of effective customer service. To prevent misunderstandings, you may want to interview the vendor's employees and conduct site visits during the preliminary stages of selecting a vendor. These preliminary steps, coupled with meaningful service-level agreements and contracts, can help prevent problems. The contract must also specify the manner in which any disagreements will be resolved.

- **Control and accountability.** You may perceive there to be a loss of control over the activities and functions that are being supplied by an outsourcing provider. The supplier relationship often entails a greater dependence on the supplier to manage the "how" of the process. It is imperative that your organization retain its ability to monitor and control "what" is being performed. These should be detailed with the supplier through the contract and the service level agreement (SLA). The SLA provides the framework for the key service-level targets that the supplier must achieve and forms one of the bases of the main contractual agreement. SLAs include the manner in which these services are measured and the procedure used to remedy unmet customer service targets. SLAs clearly outline expectations, performance levels, monitoring metrics, problem escalation clauses, and associated remedies.

- **Fixed price contract and technology.** A fixed contract removes the competitive nature of outsourcing by eliminating the need for the supplier to benchmark its services against current and future market conditions. A flexible contract allows your organization to reduce or enlarge the scope and volume of activities as required, and improve technology to meet changing market conditions.

- **Resistance to implementation, loss of key staff.** It is imperative that major roadblocks to outsourcing be dealt with before you implement that process. Effective and open communications within your organization can help retain key staff in the organization, and outsourcing suppliers can be encouraged to hire displaced staff during the transition and implementation period. Your organization will have to retain staff both to assist in activities that will continue to be provided internally through self-provision and to monitor the performance of the supplier.

CONCLUSION: ENSURING SAME OR BETTER CUSTOMER SERVICE

The critical issue remains: how can a company effectively outsource key processes and activities, thus allowing a separate supplier to handle the customer relationship? A company spends a great deal of time, effort, and money developing its relationship with customers. A company's ability to service those customers effectively, retain them, and add to its own profitability depends directly on the quality of customer service provided.

The quality and type of customer service must be defined and managed in even greater detail when this service is outsourced. Increased costs, poor service, and a lack of accountability result when a company does not spend sufficient time managing the scope, costs, and service levels required in the outsourcing process.

Your organization would need to resolve the following key issues before completing any outsourcing arrangement:

- Confirm the scope of activities and services to be provided. This includes defining linkage and decoupling points in the customer service process between the company and the outsourcing supplier.

- Formalize and negotiate SLAs with the outsourcing supplier. SLAs, which form one of the bases of the main contractual agreement, provide the framework for the key service-level targets that the supplier must achieve. SLAs also specify how to measure services, and the procedure used to identify and remedy problems from unmet customer service targets.

- Develop a process to evaluate and monitor the outsourcing supplier. Usually a key management position needs to be created in the organization to provide the skills and knowledge necessary for handling the outsourcing relationship. The person occupying this position will have regular contact with the supplier and will participate in all parts of the outsourcing relationship.

Service-level agreements, contractual agreements, definition of scope, problem escalation clauses, penalties, and performance remedies may not seem to be the best way to begin a relationship with a supplier. Yet these will help reduce potential conflicts and misunderstandings in the future.

For a successful outsourcing relationship, each party should clearly understand its respective responsibilities, obligations, and expected service levels before signing a contract. This is critical to ensure that your customers continue to be satisfied in all their dealings with your company.

ALTERNATIVE SERVICE-DELIVERY OPTIONS

Outsourcing, one of the more popular methods of alternative service delivery, has been the focus of this chapter thus far. But over the past few years, the range of service-delivery methods available has expanded from the two options of self-provision and outsourcing to include a broad range of alternative service-delivery options.

These delivery method options are similar to outsourcing in that they shift internal processes and activities to other forms of service provision. Each of these options is, however, differentiated by characteristics of ownership, control, pricing, costs, and the sharing of risks and benefits.

Figure 1 illustrates the spectrum of service-delivery options. As the spectrum shifts from self-provision to privatization, the mix of service delivery shifts from one dominated by internal provisioning to external provisioning. Each method of service delivery is described below.

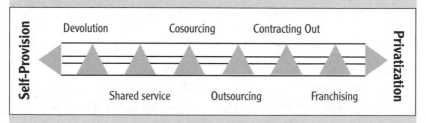

FIGURE 1: Spectrum of Service-Delivery Options

Self-provision: Service is provided through internal facilities managed by full- and part-time staff.

Devolution: Service is provided through the decentralization and transference of responsibilities, obligations, and powers to another internal authority. For example, the head office of an organization will transfer responsibility to provide certain services to the divisions or regional offices. This method is used when a process or activity is directly attributable to these decentralized areas.

Shared services: Two or more related units of the same entity form a joint initiative to create synergy and scale to deliver services. This is increasingly prevalent in large corporations, hospitals, and school boards, which decide to centralize the provision of some activities and share the cost of administrative and technical services.

Cosourcing: Service is provided through a joint-venture arrangement, under which participants share risks and benefits to create new scale and synergy advantages. A third party external vendor is not always involved. These types of joint ventures often operate in perpetuity—that is, there is no defined length in the service contract between the cosourcing entity and the owning organizations.

Cosourcing can exist between competitors—for example, the Bank of Montreal, the Royal Bank of Canada, and the Toronto-Dominion Bank have created a company to handle document processing for all three chartered banks. In this particular case, no Canadian vendors could offer better economies of scale and service levels than the three banks could provide acting together.

Outsourcing: Service is provided through a long-term agreement that has specific scope and a close relationship between provider and principal. Under this arrangement, existing vendor synergy and economies of scale translate into savings for the organization and profits for the provider. This type of service provision is not a joint venture; it is founded on a fee-based contract of fixed duration with options for renewal.

Transformational (transitional): Current service is provided through an outsourcing supplier, but the organization has stated its intention to focus on moving to a new mode of service provision with or without the assistance of the outsourcing provider. The new mode of provision may include the consolidation of activities or adoption of new equipment and technology. Note that since this is a particular type of outsourcing, we have not included it as a distinct point in the spectrum in Figure 1.

Contracting out: Service is provided on the basis of a one-time contract to a supplier, with costs based on hourly rates or completion of project work. In this case, the organization maintains a higher degree of involvement in managing the work, often directly managing the contractor's staff on the project. This includes work in areas ranging from information technology projects to call centre staffing and temporary staffing of administrative and accounting office functions.

Franchising: Service is provided through granting a licence to the selected supplier to provide agreed-upon services within a specified jurisdiction, for a specified amount of time—for example, government ministries franchising organizations to issue driver's licence renewals.

Privatization (divestiture): The obligations of providing service are transferred to a new entity, separate from the organization. Note that in the case of a public sector organization this implies a form of privatization—for example, the privatization of government-controlled utilities and services.

About the authors

TUDOR NEGREA and LORNE SEVERS

Tudor Negrea is the partner in charge of Coopers & Lybrand's Alternative Service Delivery Practice in Toronto, Canada.

Lorne Severs is a senior consultant with the practice.

CHAPTER FIFTEEN

Management Control Systems

HOW TO CONTROL INTERNAL AND OUTSOURCED CUSTOMER CARE

Suresh Gupta, Jay Singh, and Robert Largey,
Coopers & Lybrand, New York, NY

Executing winning strategies is the key to business success.
The best strategy in the world, however, is worthless unless it
can be implemented in changing competitive circumstances.
—Robert Simons[1]

THE GOOD NEWS AND THE BAD NEWS [2]

Corporate expenditures on telemarketing are estimated at around $85 billion annually in the United States, of which about $8 billion is currently outsourced. As the recognition of telemarketing as an effective channel for marketing, sales, and customer care continues to grow, the expenditure in this arena is expected to exceed $100 billion annually before the turn of the century. Furthermore, as corporations continue to restructure around core competencies, the outsourced share of this market will grow at a rate that will allow many telemarketing companies to maintain double-digit growth rates for the foreseeable future.

---

[1] *Levers of Control* (Boston: Harvard Business School Press, 1995).

[2] All numbers are in U.S. dollars and pertain to the United States. No such data are available for the global market.

Not surprisingly, Wall Street is bullish on the telemarketing industry. Many companies have taken advantage through initial public offerings; others are waiting in the wings

That's the good news. The bad news is that this industry is headed for a shake-out. It is full of small entrepreneurial companies whose growth rates are straining their management capabilities. At the same time, the largest telemarketing companies will face tough competitive pressures from savvy, highly capitalized new entrants who are attracted by the industry's long-term potential. With already almost a thousand telemarketing companies in the US alone, and new entrants every year, the marketplace will force a rationalization. The very bullishness of Wall Street will also exact large penalties for small missteps.

THE KEY TO SUCCESS: MANAGEMENT CONTROL SYSTEMS

As the industry grows and matures, what will a successful telemarketing company typically look like? More than likely, it will be a professionally managed, well-capitalized, publicly held company, probably with revenues exceeding $50 million. As telemarketing outsourcing grows, users of the service will be more discriminating and demanding. They will look for partnerships and more risk-sharing with their vendors.

In such an environment, while meeting the technical and technological challenges (including the expansion of telemarketing into "non-voice" media such as the Internet and fax) is critical, perhaps the real differentiator between the winners and losers will be the attention given to management control systems. As companies continue to grow and expand, their ability to control business risks will be sorely tested. For example, one telemarketing company branching out from *non-profit fund-raising* to *commercial work* assumed that there were no significant differences in the operational requirements of the types of work. It stumbled because it failed to anticipate and control the complexity of information requirements, quality assurance protocols, and script changes. Another example is that of an owner-run company that experienced tremendous growth and discovered that delegating decision-making without adequate control systems resulted in things not getting done as intended. Surprises and glitches abounded.

Rapid change stretches the capabilities of any organization: management can be overwhelmed by new and evolving risks, processes and controls can be stretched to breaking point, and the entity may jeopardize its long-term viability while being apparently successful in the short term.

CONTROLS: THE DEFINING CRITERION IN VENDOR SELECTION

In the context of the conditions described above, users of telemarketing services need to realize that the traditional ways of selecting a vendor no longer suffice. Hitherto, *price, service*, and *quality* were often sufficient criteria for selecting the best vendor. However, given the explosive growth, and hence the anticipated shake-out among telemarketing vendors, users must factor in *controls* (necessary to ensure the long-term viability of the vendor) as an additional criterion in their selection process. This may sound obvious and simplistic till you realize that most vendors are straining to keep pace with rapid growth in their businesses. In some cases, their accounting and billing systems are outmoded and cannot accurately capture billing data. In other instances, their capacity to absorb additional volumes and their responsiveness to program changes (including programming and script changes) are significantly diminished because they are operating at peak capacities. It is therefore not unusual to find a lack of congruence between the needs of a user and the priorities of its telemarketing vendor.

Users of telemarketing services should consider adopting a control review methodology for evaluating potential (as well as existing) vendors. This methodology should assess how well these companies are managing their business and process-level risks, and how effective their controls are in ensuring that services are being delivered and billed in accordance with their contractual obligations.

On the other hand, telemarketing companies, themselves, need to take a comprehensive and integrated approach to business-risk management and control so that they can ensure the achievement of their objectives, whether these relate to effectiveness and efficiency of operations, reliability of financial reporting, or compliance with applicable laws, regulations, and contracts.

INTERNAL CONTROL: THE INTEGRATED FRAMEWORK

An approach that can be adapted by both the users of telemarketing services as well as the telemarketing companies themselves is illustrated in *Internal Control: Integrated Framework*,[3] a landmark study authored by Coopers & Lybrand LLP on behalf of the Committee of Sponsoring Organizations of the Treadway Commission (COSO). This approach is widely accepted as the U.S. standard for internal controls. According to the report there are five interrelated components of internal control:

1. Control Environment

The control environment defines the tone of an organization and the way it operates. Factors that make up the control environment include integrity, ethical values, and competence of the people in the organization; the manner in which management assigns authority and responsibility, and the way in which it organizes and develops its human resources; and the attention and direction provided by the board of directors. Robert Simons uses the term "belief system" to define the guiding values, purpose, and direction for an organization: "When problems arise in implementing strategy, a belief system helps participants to determine the types of problems to tackle and the solutions to search for."[4] As such, it is the foundation for all other components of control, providing both discipline and structure. Organizations with effective control environments set a positive "tone at the top," hire and retain competent people, and foster integrity and control-consciousness. They set formalized and clearly communicated policies and procedures, resulting in shared values and teamwork.

2. Risk Assessment

Risk assessment is the process through which management decides how it will deal with risks that pose a threat to achieving its objectives.

---

[3] Jersey City, NJ: Committee of Sponsoring Organizations of the Treadway Commission (COSO), AICPA Publications Division, 1992.

[4] Robert Simons, *Levers of Control* (Boston: Harvard Business School Press, 1995).

Thus while the objective-setting process is not part of the internal control process, it is a necessary prerequisite. Once risks have been identified, sourced, and measured, steps must be taken to avoid, transfer, or otherwise reduce the risks to acceptable levels.[5] Since there is no practical way to eliminate all risks, management must decide how much risk it is willing to tolerate and determine how those tolerance levels must be maintained.

To drive business-risk assessment and control down through the organization, an entity must adopt a horizontal process view in addition to a vertical organization view. Since processes link functions to achieve an objective, control gaps can be overlooked when controls are viewed only from a vertical perspective.

3. Control Activities

Control activities are policies and procedures put into place to assure that management's directives are carried out. They are based on management's evaluation of the control environment, the assessment of risks to the achievement of business and process-level objectives, and the tolerance level for those risks. Such activities permeate the entire organization, at all levels and in all functions, and include a range of activities as diverse as approvals, authorizations, verifications, reconciliations, review of operating performance, security of assets, and segregation of duties.

Essentially, these activities can be grouped into the three categories of objectives to which they relate: operations, financial reporting, and compliance. However, they often overlap and interrelate.

4. Information and Communication

Systems for capturing and communicating relevant information in a timely manner are an essential component of the internal control

---

[5] Simons maintains that an organization must explicitly communicate the risks to be avoided—the "Boundary Systems." The Boundary Systems are essentially negative systems—akin to the Ten Commandments from the Old Testament. By dictating what an employee should not do, an organization can allow individuals to search for ways of creating value within these boundaries (*Levers of Control*, p. 40).

process. These systems are critical to running a company because they produce reports containing operational, financial, and compliance information. They contain internally generated data as well as information about external events, developments, and conditions required for informed decisions.

There must also be clear and open channels of communication that allow information to flow through an organization. These channels must reinforce the message to all personnel that internal control responsibilities are a priority and must be taken seriously. In addition, these channels should make each individual's role in the internal control system clear, as well as provide an understanding of how these activities relate to the work of others in the organization. These systems must provide means for moving important information to the very top of the organization and for receiving inputs from external parties.

5. Monitoring

The rapid pace of change requires evaluating all systems—particularly, internal control systems—to ensure that they are performing as intended. Such monitoring can be accomplished through ongoing monitoring, which occurs during normal operations, and through separate evaluations by management, often with assistance of the internal audit function or outside consultants. When deficiencies in internal control are discovered, they should be reported to senior management and, for very significant matters, to the board of directors, and appropriate remedial action should be taken.

ASSESSING TELEMARKETING COMPANIES USING COSO'S INTEGRATED FRAMEWORK: FIELD RESULTS

Coopers & Lybrand has reviewed the internal controls of several medium to large telemarketing companies, using the COSO framework. Here are some of the findings.

- Ownership of internal control was often vague and occasionally delegated to the controller or the CFO; the CEO seldom acknowledged accountability for it. Over half of the companies we visited had never even considered *internal controls* as a priority.

- Risk assessment across all objectives was not routine, if it existed at all.

- Control activities were, therefore, not consistent with attendant risks.

- Bad news did not travel upstream. For example, one of the companies we visited had a serious outstanding dispute with a large customer over its invoices. But the senior management had never been told of this issue.

- Personnel practices did not support control and compliance; often performance metrics encouraged unintended employee behaviour. In one company, for example, the operations managers' remuneration was directly tied to the number of hours *billed*. Therefore, they tended to overbill customers.

- Business processes were informal and subject to variability. Some companies, for example, had no formal policies regarding pricing. As a result, there was a great variation in pricing similar services to various customers. Often nobody knew whether the company made or lost money in servicing a particular client.

- Great disparity existed between the controls to ensure completeness and accuracy of paid hours and the controls over billed hours.

- Many companies did not have a code of conduct or ethics for their employees.

These findings are not surprising given the state of change in the industry. Many companies are in transition from an owner-operated company to a professionally managed, publicly held company so that management processes have not yet fully evolved. But the main reason for the poor report card is that the rapid growth in the industry appears to have put company management in a reactive mode. Management is preoccupied with bringing in more business and building new call centre capacity. Therein lies the danger. If this drive for growth is not tempered with prudent attention to controls, such growth may not be sustainable and some of these companies may collapse.

The time to pause and take stock is now. Management should ensure that it has built a solid foundation on which to grow. The COSO model of corporate governance can be invaluable in this assessment and can serve as a guide in formulating proactive action plans for improvement.

APPLYING THE INTEGRATED FRAMEWORK OF CONTROL IN TELEMARKETING COMPANIES

Coopers & Lybrand has extended and applied the COSO concepts to the telemarketing industry and developed industry-specific tools and techniques for assessing the various components of control both at the entity level and the process level.

Our top-down methodology starts by evaluating the overall control environment of the entity through gaining a high level understanding of how the various components of control are operating within the company. Some of the issues that need to be probed are shown in the sidebar, in Figure 1.

Evaluating the Control Environment

- What is the attitude toward "internal control" at the company or in a particular business area? For example, does the management have any concerns about "institutional sloppiness" ("always been done that way")?

- How does the company attempt to assure integrity and ethical values among its executives and staff? How are compensation and rewards set? What are senior management's philosophy and operating style? What are management's priorities?

- Are authority and responsibility clearly assigned acroos the organization? Across a particular function? What about accountability?

- How does management organize and develop people to ensure success in their assigned roles?

- Do employees understand their control and compliance responsibilities? How are these responsibilities communicated and reinforced in the organization? Is there an internal control component to employee performance reviews?

- Does the organization's culture and structure encourage or punish employees for reporting problems and concerns?

FIGURE 1: Evaluating the Control Environment

Such an evaluation is best done through one-on-one interviews with every member of the management team. Since the review is intended to solicit candid comments by the interviewee, certain basic principles must be observed:

- The interviews should normally be conducted by an outsider. An internal person can rarely expect a fellow employee to offer objective opinions.

- The interviewee must be assured of complete anonymity of his or her remarks.

- The interviewer should avoid asking leading questions.

	ISSUES	How does the company attempt to assure integrity and ethical values?	How are compensation and rewards set?
INTEGRITY AND ETHICAL VALUES	LEVEL 1	Any overpayments or underbillings are resolved when external parties identify the problems.	Rewards heavily performance-dependent. Bonus plans have upper and lower cutoffs. Pressure on short-term results.
	LEVEL 2	Formal code of conduct exists and is explained to newly hired employees. Related training is included in orientation of new employees. Overpayments or underbillings are tracked and resolved.	Short-term and long-term rewards are balanced. Bonus plans are realistic and open-ended.
	LEVEL 3	Formal code of conduct reviewed, updated, and reissued periodically. It addresses, at least, conflicts of interest, illegal or other improper payments, anti-competitive guidelines, and insider trading by employees. Code of conduct periodically acknowledged. Related training done periodically. Periodic surveys conducted of customers and suppliers regarding employees' business practices. The philosophy that "the customer is likely to be right" pervades the organization. Channels in place for employees to raise questions about improper behaviour.	Rewards balance realism and responsibility/control.
	LEVEL 4	Illustrations of "gray areas" communicated to employees to support policies. Training includes situation analysis and role-playing.	Rewards emphasize owner's perspective, blending individual and overall measurements.

FIGURE 2: Rating Tool for Components of Control: An Illustrative Example

In addition to the interviews, it is also helpful to examine the company's code of conduct, its written policies, and any other means of communicating acceptable or non-acceptable behaviour by its employees. An analysis of the data collected via the interviews and other means is then used to rate the company across the five components of control. Figure 2 illustrates a rating tool for evaluating the integrity and ethical values at a company.

Next, each core process or function is reviewed to determine the process objectives, associated risks, and the relevant controls. Various tools are used to assess how well these processes are controlled. Key tools include the following:

- **Process Mapping.** See Figure 3. The primary purpose of process mapping is to gain a quick understanding of the key activities supporting a process. This knowledge is the key to assessing potential risks associated with the process. For example, what is the risk that the billing process would result in *overbilling* a client?

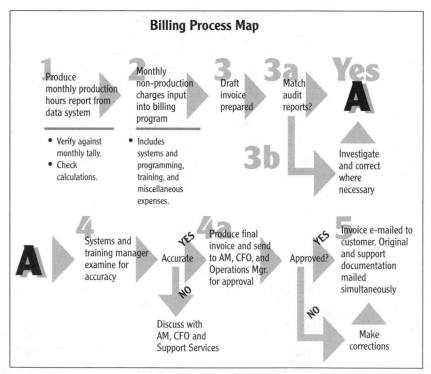

FIGURE 3: Billing Process Map

- **Process Risk Control Matrix.** The process risk control matrix is used to identify mechanisms for alleviating key process risks. For example, the risk of overbilling a client could be minimized by communicating a thorough understanding of client contracts and terms of service.

- **Process Rating Tool.** The information collected during the interviews and through examining shelf data is used to assess each process. See Figure 4 for a sample rating tool prepared from such an analysis.

By analyzing the gaps and disconnections, and linking findings at each level, the overall effectiveness of internal control in the organization is compared to the COSO standard. This allows management to develop comprehensive and integrated action plans for implementing the integrated framework of control.

Users of telemarketing services could use a similar approach in evaluating their vendors. In fact, one of the largest users has adapted this approach to screen new vendors. Following such a review, an action plan could be jointly agreed upon for the vendor to implement improvement recommendations.

Experience indicates that implementing this framework is possible only through the top management's (and the board's) full support and ownership. However, once the new paradigm has been accepted, several tangible benefits accrue from the implementation:

- The board and management have a much greater level of assurance and confirmation that their directives are being carried out as intended throughout the organization.

- Potential problems are proactively identified and resolved, thus minimizing surprises.

- Significant cost savings are realized through eliminating redundant and irrelevant controls and building controls into business processes. Controls thus become business enablers instead of bureaucratic hurdles.

- The integrated framework of control proves sufficiently robust and flexible to adapt to changes (for example, rapid growth, technological changes, regulatory changes, new products and services, and organizational changes).

	PRODUCTION HOURS	**SCRs** (System Change Requests)
ISSUES	How does the vendor capture production hours for billing?	How does the vendor capture SCR hours for billing?
LEVEL 1	Timekeeping is manual. There are multiple hand-offs, and production hours are not reconciled to payroll. The validity of the hours billed cannot be independently ascertained. Audit trails and supporting documentation are lacking.	Timekeeping is manual. Cost of work estimates are sent to customer after the SCR is completed and the estimate is always the final charge. The validity of the SCR charge cannot be independently ascertained. Audit trails and supporting documentation are lacking.
LEVEL 2	Timekeeping is manual. There are multiple hand-offs, and production hours are not reconciled to payroll. However, there are additional controls and independent reconciliations to ensure that the billed hours are correct. Audit trails and supporting documentation exist.	Timekeeping is manual. Cost of work estimates are sent to customer after the SCR is completed and the estimate is always the final charge. However, there are additional controls and independent reconciliations to ensure that SCR charges are correct. Audit trails and supporting documentation exist.
LEVEL 3	Timekeeping is manual but production hours and payroll hours are taken off the same source. Controls exist to ensure the accuracy and integrity of the data. Formal policies and procedures specify the audit trails and documentation required to support the billed hours.	Timekeeping is manual, but cost of work estimates are sent to customer prior to commencing SCR work. In addition, SCRs are billed in accordance with contractual requirements. Controls exist to ensure the accuracy and integrity of the data. Formal policies and procedures specify the audit trails and documentation is required to support the billed hours.
LEVEL 4	Timekeeping is automated and integrated with the production system. Production hours are provided to the invoicing system through an automated feed. System records are archived in accordance with contractual requirements and are auditable.	Timekeeping is automated and integrated with the billing system. SCR hours are provided to the invoicing system through an automated feed. Cost of work estimates are sent to the customer prior to commencing SCR work. SCRs are billed at actual time and expense. System records are archived in accordance with contractual requirements and are auditable.

FIGURE 4: Bill Process Rating Tool

About the authors

DR. SURESH C. GUPTA, MRITUNJAY (JAY) SINGH, and ROBERT D. LARGEY JR.

Dr. Suresh C. Gupta is a partner with Coopers & Lybrand Consulting, where he leads a practice in business process reengineering. His group provides assistance to teleservice companies and their customers in the customer care industry. Over the past two years, Suresh Gupta has led several projects covering a variety of issues faced by the customers of outbound and inbound telemarketing, including process reengineering, best-practices benchmarking, and vendor evaluation and selection methodology.

Mritunjay (Jay) Singh is a director in the in-control services practice of Coopers & Lybrand LLP. He specializes in the areas of business risk assessment and control, business process reengineering, and organizational restructuring. He is a frequent speaker at conferences and seminars on such topics as internal control and corporate governance. He also teaches classes on corporate ethics at the Wharton School of Business at the University of Pennsylvania.

Robert D. Largey Jr. is a senior associate in the commercial and industrial sector of Coopers & Lybrand Consulting. He specializes in the teleservices and customer care industries, where his areas of expertise include business risk assessment, management control systems, business process redesign and operations improvement.

CHAPTER SIXTEEN

The Benefits of
ISO Certification

Larry L. Brandt, CCSE, AMP Incorporated,
Harrisburg, PA

Y OU HAVE HEARD both sides of the ISO certification issue. You have read dozens of articles for and against ISO certification, seen cartoons that malign certification, heard horror stories about companies that went for certification only to find themselves in worse shape or market position after certification. And you have heard stories that seem too good to be true.

Receiving conflicting information is fairly typical when you are deciding whether to pursue ISO certification, Malcolm Baldrige, or other certifications or programs. You become skeptical of what both sides say, but you need realistic information to make an informed business decision for your company. Finally, you ask yourself, "Is ISO certification a benefit or another time-consuming exercise?"

This chapter offers the experience of the Customer Service department of AMP Incorporated in its pursuit of ISO certification. The service department consists of 180 front-line correspondents and 27 managers, supervisors, and administrative personnel. It serves as a liaison between the customer and the manufacturing divisions of AMP Incorporated, quality functions, and distribution centres.

In 1996, correspondents processed some 2.7 million items for orders, change orders, expedites, and quotations with an accuracy rate of 99.98 percent. Twelve-hour coverage and toll-free 1-800 numbers are provided for customers, resulting in 1.37 million telephone calls. This was only 23 percent of inbound communications. The balance was 59 percent fax, 15 percent EDI (electronic data interchange), and 2 percent mail. The department averages three formal customer complaints a month, with a corrective action response of less than two days.

ISO certification can be an excellent match for some organizations. In our case, at AMP Incorporated, we were already familiar with customer audits; we had some documentation and had an established training program with records going back several years; the department was familiar with certifications, awards, contests, etc; and our customers were asking whether we were ISO certified. We were looking for ways to improve our processes, increase productivity, reduce errors, and continue to be a leader in service—worldwide.

The first thing to understand about ISO certification is that it is *not* just another one-time certification, after which you can slide back to the old ways. It is also not just another contest to win or auditors' visits to endure. *The major difference is that you must maintain your level of conformance continually.* There will be surveillance audits every six months and then a reassessment of your entire quality system every three years. This requires an ongoing commitment—ISO certification is not for the faint of heart.

If you are in the process of making the decision whether to go for ISO certification or if you are the person assigned to pursue certification, you need to consider, first, the cost involved, and second, what benefits you expect to realize.

Use ISO Certification as an Improvement Tool

The most important fact to remember when you are deciding about certification is that you can use ISO standards and your own standards and procedures as tools for improving your quality system and daily operations. In our organization, business comes first; ISO certification and ongoing support comes second. By continually using ISO requirements as a tool, they never come into conflict with daily operations or priorities. They function as a resource *not* as a bureaucratic overhead to be served first. Thus, ISO certification can be an endeavour, not an exercise.

COSTS

Costs depend upon several factors, such as:

- The size of the organization to be certified—department, group, division, location, whole company.

- Pre-assessment document review, if applicable.

- Consultants' costs, if applicable.

- ISO training for team members and for employees.

- ISO reference materials.

- Certification assessment session (several days' duration).

- Certificates.

- How much documentation is needed and whether you have any existing documentation.

- Auditors' travel expenses for pre-assessment, certification assessment, and continual surveillance assessments.

- Your travel costs if certification is not for a centralized location.

- Intra-company costs for services of other departments, such as internal auditors, trainers, and technical writers used during the process.

- Whether you have a functioning training system and training records.

- Whether you need to create systems and train people to maintain systems required for ISO certification—for example, a quality system, management review process, design control, document control, product identification and traceability, process control, inspection and testing, test equipment, nonconforming product, corrective and preventive action, records retention, internal audits, service, and statistical processing.

BENEFITS

- **Adherence to procedure and standards—doing the job right!** One of the most important benefits of ISO certification is that it gives you the means to check whether employees are following your standards, specifications, and procedures. At the same time, the standards and documentation you develop aid your employees in doing the job right and prevent inaccurate information from being passed on. Employees now know if they are doing it right because they can confirm it by checking the documentation. They are more confident about their work and make fewer errors. And internal audits, internal and external customer complaints, returned material, and error/accuracy reports show you the non-conformances.

- **Corrective action program**. You can combine all your various processes for error/accuracy reporting, customer complaints, returned material, refused shipments into a focused and proactive program for reporting, resolving, follow-up, and verification.

- **Fewer or no customer audits**. ISO certification along with your own company standards can reduce or even eliminate the need for your customers to do costly and time-consuming on-site audits. So certification saves time and money for *both* your customers and your organization.

- **Better documentation**. Whether you create a function within your group or use services outside your group, controlled documentation ensures the following:

  - Your employees have the latest edition of the documentation they require to do their job—strategically located for their use. Inaccessible documentation is documentation that is *not used!*
  - The documentation meets standards and is professionally done.
  - The standard format and familiar terminology help to ensure use and ease of use.
  - Costs and documents are kept to a minimum.
  - You will not have all sorts of documentation and conflicting information floating around the workplace confusing people and contributing to errors and delays.
  - Managers and supervisors are freed from handling documentation.

  You may find that trust in the documentation leads to trust in the other aspects of the ISO process. Documentation is one thing employees will see more often than any other aspect of the process.

- **Employee buy-in**. Early buy-in to the process is critical to success. It builds momentum, enthusiasm, credibility, *and* participation. Early on, show employees that ISO is not a bureaucratic burden, but rather a tool that can be used for their good. For example, have some members of your ISO team focus on the ISO requirements while the others focus on delivering something employees need. Your employees will begin to see the ISO certification process as a resource to help them and they will judge ISO certification on what it will do for them.

- **Forms control.** "Illegitimate" forms used in your department can be legitimized and redesigned to your standards. Outdated forms can be brought up to your standards. Forms administration is centralized, thus freeing your employees to continue with their work.

- **Weaknesses identified.** Weaknesses in operating processes will be revealed.

- **Improved communications**. All employees are informed of changes in processes and procedures at the same time and with the same information. This information can be used at your work group, department, or staff meetings for discussion and to inform others in your area about procedures or processes now in effect.

- **Improved training**. Training now covers areas not previously covered, such as the quality system, ISO orientation, and procedures review. The review sessions determine whether employees are following procedure and whether they can verify that by locating the documentation that supports the process. Training records are expanded to include the informal on-the-job training—something never done before because no one recognized this informal training as actual training, thus no one bothered to keep records on it. Now, with a simple form, a history of the localized, informal training is maintained.

- **Resolution of internal customer complaints**. Collecting internal customer complaints identifies weaknesses in your performance as perceived by your internal customers. Internal complaints may be every bit as important as those from external customers. To resolve internal problems, you may decide to set up inter-department problem reporting. Remember that internal complaints can have an effect on the final product or service provided to the external customer.

  – *Make complaint-reporting easy* for your internal customers, not a complicated process or one that will scare people off from reporting complaints. Consider setting up an voice message number for customers to report complaints, rather than a laborious and potentially ignored survey.

– *Streamline the process of handling complaints* to make the whole process more efficient and effective, with a quick turnaround time of 48 hours or so. This will encourage use of the system and will show that you are committed to resolving complaints. Respond with brief, concise, and accurate answers to complaints. Follow up with the complainant to see if the concern was successfully resolved.

• **Internal audits**. Some of the most valuable benefits of ISO certification are those derived from internal audits. The audits show conclusively whether (1) your employees are following procedure, (2) the procedure or process is functioning according to the documentation and vice versa, and (3) employees are familiar with the documentation. Internal audits provide an early warning system to identify areas needing attention or those with potential problems or errors.

• **Knowledgeable, confident, and independent workforce**:
  – Employees are more aware of your standards and requirements because of internal audits, documentation, and the continual training they receive as part of the ISO process.
  – Employees know they can handle an unfamiliar or new task because they have access to information about the task.
  – Employees know where to get the information for themselves and are therefore less dependent on supervisors or fellow employees for information and help with problems. This results in fewer interruptions for supervisors or fellow employees, who can thus continue their steady pace.

• **Preventive action**. Preventive action looks at a function, process, or procedure to see if there is a potential problem *before* it occurs. Consider checking on a new process you installed or a long-standing one that you think is running well. Too often a problem does not get any attention until it is critical, which usually makes it more difficult to solve.

• **Easier reassignment of employees**. Employees can be reassigned from one group to another with minimal orientation. They can begin working productively sooner because of your standards, documentation, and training.

• **Records retention**. A departmental records retention schedule can be created for quality records, departmental documents, and customer documents to make them all accessible to everyone, not buried in an employee's drawer or simply lost. Employees know which documents must be retained and where; what the retention period is; and what documents can be maintained locally.

- **Reduced errors**. By tracking errors, you can zero in on the source of your organization's problems. The trends in these errors will help you identify whether the root cause is in training, a process, or documentation. We process 2.7 million items annually, with an accuracy rate of 99.98 percent.

- **Streamlined operations**. Steps that add no value can be removed from processes, as can redundancies. Tasks and responsibilities can be centralized or reassigned.

- **Become a showcase**. You can help other groups or departments evaluate ISO certification or pursue certification by providing factual and realistic information based on your own experience and expertise, not hype; you can show what works and what doesn't, and help them streamline their efforts toward certification. Sharing your experience in certification can save your company money and time.

- **Systematic review**. Every six months we review the vital signs of our operation for indications of negative trends and problem areas so that we can take appropriate action.

- **Unifying force**. Certification can bring together the various groups doing the same or similar work to find a common method or process with benefits for all. And if there can or must be two ways to process something, that is valid as long as both are legitimized and documented. A sense of unity toward a common goal results from employee involvement in the solution.

- **Verification of significant changes made to the quality system**. Verifying whether the changes or improvements you made in a process or system did or did not function as expected is an important benefit and perhaps something new to your organization. We are all familiar with implementing changes, improvements, etc., but often we fall short on verifying the effectiveness. Without this step, you do not know if a change or an improvement is working as designed. You should not consider a change completed and closed until it has been verified for effectiveness. This verification should be built into your complaints, errors, and corrective actions systems.

RECOMMENDATIONS

Here are some of the ways in which we prepared for certification and which worked well for us.

ISO Training

To prepare our employees for ISO certification, we conducted two training sessions. One was a general overview of ISO certification, why we were going for it, expected benefits, etc. The second session, however, was designed to achieve an effect. Members of the ISO team dressed up in baggy Marx Brothers type of attire, complete with horn-rimmed glasses, large noses, and mustaches. The auditor and employee roles were humorously exaggerated to emphasize the wrong things to say and do in an audit. Employees laughed right along with the performance, which hit the desired mark in getting across what to do and what not to do in an audit. We found that this humorous rendition of an audit was the key to making people comfortable with the concept of being audited. We followed this up by publishing a listing of "Dos and Don'ts During an Audit" (see the sidebar on next page).

Retaining What's Good

If you already meet an ISO clause, there is no need to create a more sophisticated process or system than you already have. If you do not meet a clause, create a *simple*—not sophisticated—system or process, and document it. Keep it simple and continue to keep it simple. Remember...*everything you create, you will have to maintain!* Three years after certification, we are focusing on streamlining the processes and documentation we created to meet the ISO and company standards. We now see processes and documentation that can be streamlined or simplified.

Document Dump Day

We all know how difficult it is to get people to part with documentation they trust. But with ISO certification, you cannot permit people to use whatever documents they have. By eliminating those beloved—but uncontrolled—documents, you reduce the chances of those documents being found during an audit.

We set aside the Friday before our document assessment for a contest to see who had the oldest documents. Some days preceding the "dump day," we put up signs all over the place announcing the contest. Other departments thought it funny, but we were serious. Everyone scrambled to find a document they used that was older than someone else's. Prizes went to the five persons who had the oldest documents. And the oldest one was dated 1968 and was still being referenced! Then we filled six large tubs with the documents, manuals, listings, and reports that people had used, loved, and trusted, but that were not current or legitimate.

Preparing Your Employees for Audits

Prior to any actual internal or ISO audits, we conducted trial audits with individual employees to familiarize them with audits. We went through the list of dos and don'ts. By the conclusion of these trial audits, the employee had learned what had been done right and what should have been avoided. Audits are one place where "confession is not good for the soul"! We found that employees wanted to say too much and thus open themselves and the audit up to areas not part of the planned audit. Our auditors have always identified the work groups and subjects or tasks they would be auditing when the date of the ISO audits is finalized.

Dos and Don'ts During an Audit

DO	DON'T
• Answer questions directly and with confidence.	• Elaborate.
• Answer only the question being asked.	• Volunteer any information, whether you think it's relevant or not.
• Ask the auditor to rephrase thequestion if you do not understand it.	• Assume you know the answer.
• Be loyal.	• Complain.
• Be professional, positive, and polite.	• Say you know the answer if you really don't.
• Be honest.	
• Clear your desk and work area of all irrelevant papers.	

Accompanying the Auditor

We recommend that someone from your ISO team always accompany the ISO auditor during the auditing sessions. You will see first hand how the auditor functions (auditors can differ in their interpretations of the standards and your adherence to the standards). You will soon be able to identify a good auditor and a poor one. You can also help the auditor to stay within the boundaries of the audit. You are at hand to support your employees should they be unable to understand and answer a question. And you can also spot non-conformances or potential non-conformances that the auditor does not. We always have two people accompany the auditor. One person is someone very experienced in operations and the other person is the document controller, since audits focus on operations and the supporting documentation.

Rewarding Participants

Always, always reward the people that make success possible! In our case, we had a department picnic to thank everyone for a job well done. It was a chance to relax after nearly a year of hard work. The ISO team did the cooking! Employees loved that. Now, after every surveillance audit, everyone who was audited is singled out and thanked. Everyone in the department is made aware that these people were the ones that made this surveillance audit a success.

SUMMARY

ISO standards along with the Malcolm Baldrige criteria have played a very important role in the success of our quality-improvement processes. These processes together, and even independent of each other, provide valuable resources and a structure for building and maintaining an effective and efficient service organization.

   Three years after certification, we continue to derive the benefits documented here as well as other benefits. Here are some specific examples.

- ISO standards and our own standards and procedures were thought of as a "big deal," but they are now so *thoroughly integrated into the everyday routine* that they are almost transparent to us.

- ISO standards continue to be *a tool and a resource*—not overhead or an impediment to operations.

- There has been *no sliding back* to the way things had been done.

- *Participation remains widespread* because employees have seen the benefits that certification and standards and procedures give them.

- We have a *more unified workforce.* Gone are the various camps of people doing things their own way.

- The ISO certification has contributed to *reducing errors and keeping them down* because the workforce is more informed and alert.

- Our employees are *more confident* in what they are doing.

- If something goes wrong, we have a *resource* (the ISO team) and an established way of resolving it.

- *Other departments have a better understanding* of what we do by obtaining copies of our documentation. It makes it easier for us to explain our processes with supporting documentation. Other departments know that since we are ISO certified what we provide meets company and ISO standards. These departments use our documentation to further educate their people on how work is processed in our department.

- *The ISO reputation carries weight!* We have found that if we need something from an internal department and we even mention its relationship to ISO, we get a prompt response.

Would we do it again? Absolutely! We've received *identifiable benefits* for the money we've spent on it. And isn't that the answer people considering certification want to know?

About the author

LARRY L. BRANDT

Larry L. Brandt, CCSE, is associate director of customer service, AMP Incorporated, the world's leading producer of electrical and electronic connection devices. Its headquarters are in Harrisburg, PA, and the company has 45,000 employees in 215 facilities in the United States and 44 other countries. Larry Brandt has been associated with the customer service department since 1968 when he started his career as a front-line customer service correspondent. Brandt was responsible for introducing EDI to AMP Incorporated in the early 1980s. He developed its Delivery Management Scorecard, has received several AMP Incorporated's Quality Awards, spearheaded AMP's receiving the 1994 ICSA Award of Excellence (manufacturing), and was instrumental in obtaining ISO 9002 certification for the customer service operations at AMP Incorporated in April 1994. The success of the customer service department at AMP Incorporated has been featured in several industry magazines and newsletters since 1992.

Part Four

Best Practices in Using Technology to Achieve Breakthrough Customer Service

Consider two questions. First, can your company afford the cost of poor customer service? Of course not. Your customers are your lifeline to success. Second, if we accept that something should be done, where do you start on the road to keeping your customers happy when they're demanding increasingly faster access to products, services, and information? What follows is the map showing both the starting point and the best practices of others. It's up to you to find the correct route.

THE BENEFITS OF GOOD SERVICE

Your customer care or support centre can provide the solution to poor service—or it can become an impediment to your success. (Note: For purposes of this article, the size of the customer care centre is limitless; it can be staffed by as few as two or three customer service representatives or by hundreds. The concepts described still apply).

According to the well-respected and ongoing PIMS (Profit Impact of Marketing Strategy) study conducted by the Strategic Planning Institute in Cambridge, MA, companies with "superior" service quality enjoy twice the return on sales, twice the return on investment, and an additional 13 points of market share over companies with service quality rated as "inferior." In addition, the study reveals that companies with superior service quality gain market share year to year, whereas companies with inferior service quality lose market share. (See Figure 1.)

But success depends on more than satisfied external customers. It depends on satisfied *internal* customers as well. Satisfied employees are "infectious." They encourage confident, happy customers who are more loyal, which, in turn, improves customer retention and the company's share of pocket (customer's disposable income). In other words, satisfied customers purchase more from the businesses they're happy with rather than from the competition.

Satisfied customers also generate positive word-of-mouth referrals. These three things, increased loyalty, customer retention, and

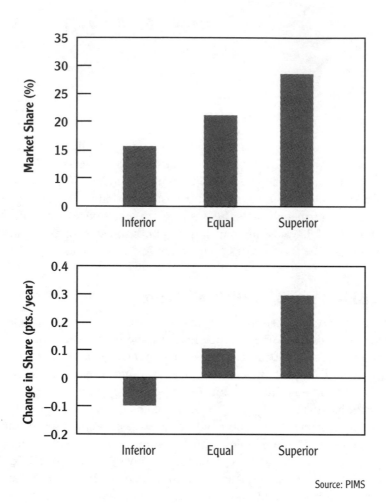

Source: PIMS

FIGURE 1: The Costs of Poor Service

positive word-of-mouth referrals, lead to increased revenue through increased sales and improved profitability.

It's not surprising, therefore, that leading organizations no longer view the customer support centre as a cost centre. Rather, it is now viewed as a profit centre, one that can enhance revenue and improve the profitability of the organization as a whole. To achieve this meta-morphosis, however, a number of changes in organizational structure and practice must take place.

LATEST TRENDS

Let's now deal with the second question. Where do you start? Our review of industry trends (Coopers & Lybrand's 1997 IDEAS Study) and our experience with best-in-class operations suggest that leading organizations exhibit three major characteristics, or pillars, within their customer support centre environments: consolidation, integration, and workforce management (this third factor will be discussed in Part Five). (See Figure 2.)

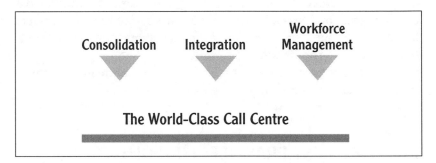

FIGURE 2: Leading Trends in Customer Support

Depending on the size of your organization, some of these may be more applicable than others. But the basic principles underlying each of these characteristics apply to all organizations as they strive to become what customers value most: an organization that's easy to do business with.

In Chapter 17, Christina Luik provides an overview of the first two characteristics and explains how to hear the voice of the customer. She says that to be truly tuned to the voice of the customer, organizations must continually collect information on customer needs, integrate this with the customer care processes, and ensure that this information is communicated to all who come into contact with customers. *Only the right technology can make that happen.*

Microsoft, which has created a prototype system for the high-volume customer support call centre of the future, provides one of the best examples of how consolidation, integration, and workforce management can be used in a customer support centre. The system is based on a simple "hub and spoke" virtual call centre environment. There are no agents in its main centre, but its satellite centres are all networked, with an

Integrated Services Digital Network (ISDN). This web of networked centres functions as a single centre with common databases, reports, and agent management. It has a single switch, which is responsible for routing calls to the appropriate agent at any one of eight satellite centres.

This Microsoft web consists of 4,500 agents managed by 400 supervisors. There is one automatic call distributor (ACD) spread remotely (the ACD distributes the incoming calls to the next available agent or customer service representative). The calls are thus routed more efficiently than they were when several independent switches were handling the load. Not only can the organization use powerful routing to a choice of locations, and add trunks and staff easily, but it also attracts better people, puts smarter people on the phones and, ultimately, boasts happier customers.

The bottom line? Microsoft has structured its centre in such a way that it has put the phone where the experts are rather than bring the experts to the centre.

INDUSTRY BEST PRACTICE: CONSOLIDATION

Conventional wisdom has suggested that as the size of an organization and its customer base increases, so must the number and locations of its help desks. While the logic is correct in that all organizations want to remain close to their customers, advances in technology make this type of decentralization unnecessary.

Today, numerous geographically dispersed call centres are being replaced by fewer centres with a maximum staffing in the order of 250 to 300 full-time-equivalent staff. These centres are logically networked and linked together by common technology and customer database information. The resulting benefits include (1) better customer service, through reduced caller wait times, and (2) lower operating costs, through significantly reduced staff and equipment costs. Such is the case with KeyCorp, as described in Chapter 18.

INDUSTRY BEST PRACTICE: INTEGRATION

The key to integration is technology itself. But according to Joe Kulak, in Chapter 19, organizations must apply technology to achieve their objectives. The choice of technology follows the organization's customer care strategy.

Leading call centre environments incorporate such technology as computer telephony integration (CTI), ACDs, and client-server technology. This technology allows the centre to use agents more effectively by switching them between a variety of business activities as well as between inbound and outbound calls during overflow periods (referred to as "functional blending"). The authors of Chapters 20 and 21 illustrate the best-in-class examples of CTI in action, as well as the challenges facing organizations and the solutions.

The technology used by call centres within organizations is converging, which means that the centres are using increasingly standardized technology components. Standardized operating platforms offer companies economic benefits from size, scale, and volume. Cost savings are also achieved in technological support and agent training.

Through integrated voice response (IVR), call centres offer callers the ability to conduct transactions and complete inquiries electronically without assistance from call centre support staff. Integrated call centres also allow callers to be automatically routed to the most appropriate call centre and group of agents, improving customer service and handling.

Other integrating technologies, such as a centralized telephone number for all call centres, improve the organization's handling of new products and enable the organization to give high-priority, special service to important clients. And let's not forget two other forms that are reshaping the way in which we market ourselves to customers and interact with them, the customer database and the Internet. In Chapter 22 Pat Finerty discusses how to create a customer-focused database, using eight key lessons learned from his work with best-practice companies. The customer database is the heart of the organization. An unfocused database will lead to inefficiency and inferior performance. In Chapter 23, the role of electronic commerce is explored. The authors discuss the latest research on the use of the Internet, offering advice to those who wish to consider it as a means to get close to the customer.

SUMMARY

The cost of poor customer service—for both external and internal customers—can be high for any call centre. In fact, sales lost through dissatisfied customers can be as high as 10 percent, and this doesn't take into account the hiring, firing, and retraining costs associated with unhappy employees. Conversely, companies offering good service achieve a 12 percent return on sales, a higher market share, lower employee turnover, improved products and productivity, and a solid, loyal customer base—definitely goals worth striving for. The chapters that follow will help you achieve these goals.

S.A.B.

CHAPTER SEVENTEEN

How Technology Can Help You Hear the Voice of the Customer

ASSESSING CURRENT AND FUTURE CUSTOMER NEEDS

Christina Luik,
Coopers & Lybrand, Toronto, ON

THE PAST 20 years have seen a paradigm shift in how organizations view their customers and in how they assess current and future customer needs. To be successful in the 21st century, organizations will need to change the way they manage their customer relationships. They will need to look at the technology and underlying processes being used in order to exceed customer expectations and achieve total customer satisfaction.

Many people think the phrase "voice of the customer" equates to information that is gathered from customer focus groups and surveys. Others feel that the customer service departments are the only parts of organizations that have the opportunity to deal with the customers and assess their needs. *Nothing could be further from the truth.*

The voice of the customer is a lot more than conducting annual customer-satisfaction research or listening to complaints. *To be truly tuned* to the voice of the customer, organizations must continually collect information on customer needs, integrate the information with customer care processes and communicate the information throughout the organization to everyone who comes into contact with customers. An example of an organization that has integrated processes is Federal Express. Customers and employees of Federal Express can obtain information on the status of shipments at any time, instantaneously, from customer representatives located anywhere in the organization. Federal Express constantly collects customer feedback on its performance and on customer expectations.

Integrating the voice of the customer into an organization involves two key elements:

1. There must be a comprehensive customer-relationship management process that captures customer information and instantly makes it available to the staff who deal directly with customers. The customer-relationship management process starts with pre-sales marketing activities and communications that a customer receives. It continues with the sales cycle when customers make inquiries related to products and services, and deal with sales representatives. The process is maintained through the post-sales activities of order processing, invoicing, delivery, and ongoing customer service contact, including checking current account status, diagnosing problems, and resolving them. A complete customer-relationship process encompasses all interactions between a customer and your company.

2. The enabling technologies need to be in place. These include the telephone systems, management information systems, and information technology that support the process. The capability to integrate data from diverse sources such as order processing, billing systems, sales and customer surveys into accessible information is essential.

   The technology must also convey the customer information to the customer service, marketing, sales, and management desktops. An example of an enabling technology that does this is Lotus Notes groupware, which has been used to develop a contact management system. The Notes software enables any employee, anywhere in the world, to view customer information in the customer database. Contact management systems typically contain profile information on customers, contact history, and details on past and current purchases.

THE CUSTOMER-RELATIONSHIP MANAGEMENT PROCESS

Traditionally, organizations have interacted with customers through functional silos that deal with specific customer needs as they arise. For example, many organizations have deliberately created silos, or walls, to protect their marketing, sales, and customer service functions from one another. Within each silo separate databases are kept—none of which talk to each other because they were individually developed to meet the unique needs of one silo only. This leads to redundancy in the data and multiple points of customer contact. Now, leading-edge organizations are redefining the functional silos and implementing a process for managing the entire life cycle of the relationship with that customer.

This customer-relationship management process is shown in Figure 1.

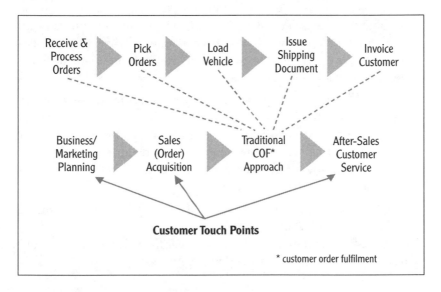

FIGURE 1: Customer-Relationship Management

World-class customer-relationship management processes have the following characteristics:

- **They enable the development of strong customer relationships.** World-class processes support customer contact and communication at the level that is appropriate for each customer. Customer relationships are strengthened by making the customer information accessible quickly and easily.

- **They integrate sales and customer service.** These processes do not disconnect between organizational silos. They offer uninterrupted information transfer and access from pre-sales to after-sales service.

For instance, technology enablers such as computer telephony integration (CTI) allow customer information to be displayed on customer service representatives' screens when a customer calls. Information provided by the customer is input during the call and passed directly to order processing without paper or human intervention. Sales representatives receive updated customer status information in real time. If the customer calls back with a question, the most recent information is again available.

- **They facilitate improved sales and service productivity.** These processes capture sales leads, and allow tracking of sales prospects throughout the sales cycle. Capturing this information requires more than automation—it requires customer service and sales representatives who specialize in customer care and are available to listen to the voice of the customer.

- **They integrate global operations on common communication and operating platforms.** World-class organizations offer the same level of service to customers anywhere in the world through customer care centres that access common customer databases. These databases enable any centre to respond instantaneously to all customer inquiries and resolve them on the first call.

In the following paragraphs, we explore two of the current trends in customer-relationship management and look at how leading organizations are using enabling technologies to hear the voice of the customer and assess customers' current and future needs.

TREND 1: CONSOLIDATION

Today, many organizations are using technology to consolidate their customer care functions to more effectively capture and respond to customer needs. The centralized customer care centres are networked and linked together by common technology and customer database information. The benefits of consolidated customer care include enhanced customer service through better customer responsiveness (because consolidated centres can schedule their staff more effectively and plan to meet the volume of calls) and reduced operating costs (because fewer staff and equipment are needed in a consolidated centre than is the case when many centres provide the same types of service to fewer customers on a regional basis).

Customer representatives use technology such as computer telephony integration (CTI), automatic call distributors (ACD), and client-server technology to more effectively identify which customer is calling, access the account profile, and complete transactions while the customer is on the line. Through integrated voice response (IVR), call centres enable callers to conduct transactions and complete inquiries electronically without assistance from a live agent. Other technologies such as centralized telephone numbers for all call centres enable organizations to better service new product introductions and give high-priority, special service to important clients.

The first organization profiled in this chapter is a manufacturer and distributor of health-care products. The company has undergone several shifts in how they hear the voice of the customer and use technology in the past two decades. In the 1970s, customers were able to request order delivery times and frequencies at their convenience. Any additional costs incurred to meet their needs were passed along to them and, in turn, to the ultimate consumer. Quality was a larger concern than cost in those days.

In the 1980s, cost containment and hospital buying groups made their first appearance, dramatically changing customer expectations of suppliers. Customers had new requirements: large hospitals were demanding daily deliveries, customized surgical kits were ordered by individual specialists for specific procedures, and items were customized for each hospital. This meant that suppliers were required to have custom items available on demand for customers, thus taking on the inventory carrying costs. The supplier faced the need to consolidate their multiple distribution centres and networks, and to centralize both distribution and customer billing.

By the end of the decade and into the 1990s, new technology made it possible for this organization to respond faster and better to changing customer expectations. The company was the first in the industry to implement electronic data interchange (EDI), which allowed customers to have a direct link to ordering and automatic replenishment. In fact, this company developed the first proprietary EDI network in use in North America and, in doing so, set a new standard for the way hospitals dealt with suppliers. It also established centralized call centres for customers to talk directly to customer service representatives and place orders 24 hours a day.

This is one of many organizations that have implemented a

comprehensive process and used technology as an enabler for assessing current and future customer needs, in the following ways:

- Through its centralized call centres and databases, the company captures customer information and is able to proactively contact customers to automatically replenish stock.

- Through online product information that customers can access on their own, the company can inform customers of new products and services.

- By assessing customer purchase information, the company can determine whether the products and services it offers are meeting customer needs.

TREND 2: INTEGRATION

Marketing, sales, and customer service functions all contribute to customer satisfaction. Each has the opportunity to directly capture information about customer needs and communicate this throughout the organization. Organizations that have fragmented processes have multiple points of customer contact for inquiries. As a result, customers' needs are not communicated to the employees who deal with customers.

To capture information on customer needs, world-class organizations are following an emerging trend to integrate information systems in order to provide the sales, customer service, and marketing functions with the following capabilities:

- **Integrated, up-to-date customer historical purchase and profile information.** All information about a customer and its accounts are captured throughout the sales, order entry, invoicing, and complaints-management processes, and maintained on a comprehensive database.

- **Online access to customer database information from anywhere.** Up-to-date, specific customer details are available to customer service and sales representatives at any time, instantaneously.

- **Technology to capture and update customer needs and purchase information from customer premises.** Sales representatives can enter customer order information directly onto laptop computers when they are with the customer. The information is transmitted directly to the corporate databases and confirmation reports are available while the representative is still at the customer's site.

The second organization profiled here is a manufacturer of diagnostic imaging systems and solutions that sells to medical centres around the globe. In April 1996, the company, which was formerly a division of a multinational organization, became independent and had to quickly understand customer needs and expectations in order to succeed in a rapidly changing and mature market sector.

Customer service was heavily dependent on personal intervention by individual sales representatives, regardless of whether the customer was placing orders, needing warranty service, or making general product-related inquiries. This burden on the sales representatives reduced the selling time that was available for generating new business, caused duplication of effort throughout multiple systems and areas, and took away from the sales representatives' time to manage relationships with existing clients.

The company needed to provide the sales force with the appropriate tools to respond to customers quickly and proactively. The sales representatives needed the support of the right technology so that they could have access to customer information and respond to customers without delay. Providing laptop computers and direct electronic links to customer data online was one of the tools considered, but automation could not by itself bring the voice of the customer into the organization.

Integrating the sales, customer service, and customer-interaction processes was critical to ensuring that the voice of the customer permeated all levels of the organization. This was accomplished by implementing three key initiatives:

- **Capturing and tracking all customer data.** Database account profiles were developed that accurately captured both market opportunity and customer needs. Communication processes were aligned to ensure that global strategies and regional plans were in sync with the market and that customer needs could be rapidly met.

- **Elevating customer relationships to a higher business level.** Geographically located teams of customer representatives were formed around customer segments. The teams were responsible for profitably interacting with and increasing the number of customers. Selling in front of new customers and growing existing customers were maximized through a disciplined sales process.

- **Redesigning work roles to position "functional experts" supported by expert systems in front of the customer.** Post-sales support for ordering, routine inquiries, and technical support were redesigned through the development of a "customer satisfaction centre." Experts, supported by integrated technology, now handle complaints, technical assistance, ordering and delivery inquiries. The organization implemented integrated operating platforms and advanced call centre technology globally to allow customer calls to be routed to the appropriate service areas. Centralized telephone numbers were another feature of the integrated process that enabled the organization to provide single point of contact and quick, accurate resolution of inquiries.

The integration of processes, systems, and technology allows this organization to communicate the voice of the customer throughout the organization. Strategy, product line, and service offerings are driven from an accurate assessment of customer needs. Interaction with the customer is facilitated and leads to accurate profitability assessments early in the selling process. Easy-to-access systems with up-to-date information enable the organization to proactively manage the customer relationship.

SUMMARY

Improved customer satisfaction and profitable growth can be achieved only by listening to and hearing the voice of the customer. You cannot accurately capture customer needs and fulfil them if you use only isolated, narrow programs such as annual customer satisfaction measurement or marketing research. A clear strategy aimed at creating customer satisfaction, robust processes, and enabling technology must be in place to allow the voice of the customer to permeate all levels and functions within an organization.

Having comprehensive, consolidated customer-relationship management processes in place facilitates both understanding and acting on customer needs. Successful customer-relationship management ensures that every contact customers have with each person they deal with in the organization leads to customer satisfaction. These relationships are created through understanding and hearing the voice of the customer throughout the organization.

Customer-relationship management processes need to be supported by enabling technology to disseminate the customer information to all the people in the organization who have customer contact or influence customer satisfaction. Technology-supported processes that are integrated to capture customer needs and respond quickly to customer inquiries provide organizations with one of the most powerful competitive advantages—they become easy to deal with.

Technology and process are, however, only tools to help people, who are the real key in bringing the voice of the customer into organizations. Organizations need to do everything they can to enable their employees to make the most of every contact with customers and achieve customer loyalty.

About the author

CHRISTINA LUIK

Christina Luik is a principal in Coopers & Lybrand Consulting's International Centre of Excellence in Customer Satisfaction located in Toronto. She specializes in assisting organizations develop and implement marketing and customer service programs and customer retention strategies. She is an expert in helping clients develop business-process improvement strategies based on the voice of the customer. She has worked with clients in Canada, the United States, Mexico, South America, and the Caribbean in many industry sectors.

Why Fewer Customer Support Centres Are Better

KEYCORP CASE STUDY

Joan Berish and Carolyn Leist,
KeyCorp, Cleveland, OH
and Natasha Milijasevic,
Coopers & Lybrand, Toronto, ON

KEYCORP IS ONE of the largest financial service companies in the United States with assets of over $67 billion. Through three principal lines of business—corporate banking, consumer finance, and community banking—the Cleveland-based company provides retail and wholesale banking, investment, financing, and money management services to individuals and companies across the US. KeyCorp companies have a presence in 44 states from Maine to Alaska, including its network of KeyCenters, 2,000 automated teller machines (ATMs) and affiliated offices, and a Web site (www.keybank.com). Its vision is "To be the first choice of those seeking world-class financial products and services."

But that vision does not come without some challenges, not the least of which is the need to be close to the customer, to give differentiated, exceptional service, and to be cost efficient. Added to that, customers are more savvy, more technologically literate, and have less time on their hands. One of KeyCorp's primary actions in response to these facts had been to focus on establishing world-class call centres (it originally created 14) that would provide excellent customer service.

However, with escalating costs, greater technological advances, and even higher customer service demands, KeyCorp began to recognize the need to change the way it operated its call centres. This chapter is an account of both how it remedied that situation through consolidating its call centres into four strategic locations and how it benefited—through reduced costs, increased customer satisfaction, technology improvements, and economies of scale.

THE CHANGING CUSTOMER

KeyCorp recognized that achieving differentiation in an evolving financial service marketplace was a formidable challenge. Customers were becoming increasingly better educated, more sophisticated, culturally diverse, and technologically literate. Most significantly, they were looking for value-added products and services. KeyCorp's competitive environment was also changing. Competitors, both banks and other financial institutions were using technology as a weapon, emphasizing convenience, service, and speed, and intensifying their focus on niche customer segments. These competitors were increasingly offering their services through easier, more tailored delivery channels. Financial service products were coming to be viewed as essential commodities, leaving little chance for differentiation.

To respond to this changing marketplace, KeyCorp re-evaluated its call centre environment. It realized that its customers and potential customers today want convenience and speed, and that tomorrow they will want even more convenience and even more speed.

A late-1995 survey of the top 100 bank holding companies, found that telephone service centres handled only 10 percent of typical retail transactions. Respondents estimated that this would increase to 15 percent by 1998, against 41 percent for retail branches, 31 percent for ATMs, 6 percent for home banking, and 7 percent for other banking alternatives.

Simply put, it is much easier for customers to pick up a telephone at their homes or offices than get into their cars and drive to their local branches to verify if a cheque has been posted or to transfer funds from one account to another.

CONSOLIDATION IN RESPONSE TO THE CHANGING CUSTOMER

Prior to March 1994, KeyCorp's call centre services functioned in 14 regional centres across the country. After a seamless consolidation, KeyCorp now has four standardized call centres operating 24 hours a day, 7 days a week, 365 days a year. These consolidations have translated into cost savings of over 40 percent with over 25 percent more customers being served. Service levels improved from long waits on hold and high abandonment rates (the percentage of customers on hold who hung up before their call was answered) to an average answer speed of less than 15 seconds and abandonment rates of less than 2 percent of calls (further details of specific improvements are given under "Increased Customer Satisfaction"). Table 1 shows the comparison of pre- and post-consolidation costs and service levels.

TABLE 1: Call Centre Consolidation

Pre-Consolidation 1993

5,000 VRU[1] calls blocked 3,000 CSR[2] calls blocked	4,000 customers go to branch @ $6.00 per transaction 4,500 customers go to a branch @ $6.00 per transaction Total cost: $51,000
5,000 VRU calls abandoned 4,000 CSR calls abandoned	Cost: $0.25 each Cost: $2.45 each Total Cost: $11,050
70,000 VRU calls handled 23,000 CSR calls handled	Cost: $0.25 each Cost: $2.45 each Total Cost: $73,850

Pre-Consolidation: $135,900

Post-Consolidation 1995

0 calls blocked	400 customers go to branch @ $6.00 per transaction Total Cost: $2,400
200 VRU calls abandoned 600 CSR calls abandoned	Cost: $0.25 each Cost: $2.45 each Total Cost: $1,520
79,800 VRU calls handled 29,400 CSR calls handled	Cost: $0.25 each Cost: $2.45 each Total Cost: $91,980

Post-Consolidation: $95,900

Cost Savings: $40,000   **Increase in customers served: 28%**

[1] VRU = Voice Response Units   [2] CSR = Customer Service Representatives

This consolidation effort has produced a win-win situation for all, with improved economies of scale for the corporation and better service levels for KeyCorp's customers. In fact, an independent survey firm conducted a customer-satisfaction survey with 5,000 customers in four market areas, and concluded that current customers overwhelmingly consider KeyCorp the "best bank" and view themselves as "highly loyal." One reason is the reinstated focus on retaining customer relationships.

Today, KeyCorp has one virtual nationwide call centre with four physical sites managed as one logical entity. KeyCorp's call centres handle over 150,000 calls per day, of which 80 percent are handled by an automated system.

But things weren't always this smooth. Prior to the achievement of four integrated call centre locations, KeyCorp had 14 distinct call centres, geographically dispersed across several states; it also maintained several other related telephone activities spread across the corporation. It was not uncommon to find a small bookkeeping department in one of KeyCorp's offices that performed call centre activities. Service levels, hours of operation, and the technology used varied greatly among call centres. In addition, specific products such as credit cards, consumer loans, and retail deposit accounts were serviced by individual departments. With the call centres spread across the company, policies, procedures, and systems were also inconsistent.

MOTIVATION BEHIND CONSOLIDATION

Three primary reasons prompted KeyCorp to merge its 14 call centre locations into 4 call centre locations (Buffalo, NY; Cleveland, OH; Dayton, OH; Auburn, WA). The reasons were (1) to reduce costs, (2) to improve customer satisfaction, and (3) to take advantage of improved technology.

Reducing Costs

Consolidating the call centres could have led to a reduction in the number of customer service professionals and team leaders required to run the centres. However, the actual labour complement increased because each of the centres would now operate 24 hours a day, 7 days a week. If the hours of operation were the same as those in existence before consolidation, wage and benefit expenses would be lower. Other cost savings included a reduction in overhead expenses, such as office space, furniture, and equipment and other technology.

A large expense of any call centre is that of 1-800 telephone numbers. With four consolidated call centres, the quantity of those toll-free numbers could be reduced. KeyCorp now has one primary 1-800 number for its customer service: 1-800-KEY2YOU. This telephone number provides universal inbound access and has become a valuable marketing asset.

Prior to the consolidations, KeyCorp also had several different contracts with long-distance carriers. Consolidations enabled KeyCorp to negotiate the best price with one company, thereby realizing economies of scale. All equipment maintenance contracts (for phone systems, voice response units [VRUs], etc.) were also reviewed in order to renegotiate corporate-wide pricing and master purchase agreements. And with fewer call centres, the acquisition of large capital equipment could be coordinated between call centres to avoid redundancy or the purchase of incompatible hardware and software.

Before consolidation, support departments, such as technical and managerial support, were spread across the country to service the small pockets of call centres. Once the call centres were consolidated, so were the support teams. The call centres now have a dedicated training department that focuses on the needs of new employees and conducts continuous training of customer service professionals. Previously, each customer service centre had a different training program. Now, KeyCorp has dedicated professionals who train new employees consistently and professionally.

So, as expected, the consolidation of call centres has resulted in substantial cost savings to the company.

Improving Customer Satisfaction

Prior to the consolidation, KeyCorp customers called the customer service department, a small bookkeeping department, or a branch to receive account information. Often customers had to be transferred to a different department to receive a full answer to their inquiries. With the consolidated call centres, customers now call only one telephone number—1-800-KEY2YOU—to receive information on their accounts.

Industry surveys indicate that the value of responsive and knowledgeable telephone service from one's financial service provider is becoming more important. As KeyCorp sought to compete with other large commercial banks and financial service providers (mutual funds, brokerage firms, insurance companies, etc.), having cost-efficient, consistently responsive, highly productive, and technologically sophisticated call centres became imperative. The call centre environment also became standardized, creating a "virtual call centre." (Without standards, there was no consistency between the centres. Calls were answered differently in each centre; therefore the centres could not be backups for each other. With standardization, centres could back up, and handle overflow from, one another.) The virtual call centre can be accessed anytime, day or night, by all customers, across business segments.

Customers don't need to know the details or methods that support exceptional customer service. Today, when customers call the one toll-free number, they do not know which location they are calling. Before consolidation, the hours of operation differed for each centre, and a call centre was rarely open on a holiday. Today, with four call centres supporting one another, holiday coverage is possible because they take turns handling customer calls at these times.

Quality scoring was also extremely inconsistent before the consolidation. Each customer service department throughout the country maintained its own method of quality scoring—using different methods. As a result, KeyCorp was unable to truly measure its customer service. Now, consistent monitors are performed. The methods range from mystery shopping programs, customer direct mail surveys, and call observations. The scoring ranges are now consistent from coast to coast, ensuring that quality customer service is delivered.

Another improvement resulting from the consolidations was the elimination of call blockage. Customers may have received a busy signal when trying to call one of KeyCorp's call centres. In the new consolidated environment, call blockage has been eliminated, and customers can now call anytime and get through to the centre. Prior to the consolidations, VRUs and live customer service professionals were not available for all KeyCorp customers all the time. In the consolidation, the VRU systems were upgraded and made consistent, allowing the customers to receive account information 24 hours a day, 7 days a week. Live customer service professionals are now available at all times consistently throughout the country.

With all KeyCorp's calls routed into one of the four call centres, the service levels can be tracked and monitored more efficiently than they could be when more call centres existed. The abandon rate has dropped from an average of 15 percent prior to the consolidation to less than 2 percent. A 10 percent blockage rate also existed, meaning that 10 percent of the incoming calls received a busy signal. Now the blockage rate is 0 percent. The average speed of answer has dropped from between 60 and 90 seconds before the consolidation to less than 15 seconds.

TABLE 2: Key Performance Indicators

Key Performance Indicators	Retail Banking Best-in-Class Goals	KeyCorp Then and Now
Voice-response usage: Percentage of calls handled exclusively by VRU	> 80%	Then: N/A Now: 80%
Average speed of answer	15 seconds	Then: 60–90 seconds Now: Less than 15 seconds
Abandoned calls to customer service professionals	2%	Then: 15% Now: Less than 2%
Blocked calls—busy signals	≤1%	Then: 10% Now: 0%
"Mystery shopper" and silent-call monitoring scores	100%	N/A

The consolidations truly improved customer satisfaction and KeyCorp is now able to measure it accurately and consistently.

Taking Advantage of Improved Technology

The final reason why KeyCorp decided to consolidate call centres was to take advantage of improved technological capabilities.

Prior to the consolidation, the 14 call centres had different telephone systems, which were not compatible. Some systems were antiquated or not user-friendly. For the purpose of establishing the four regional call centres as clones, new AT&T G3V3 PBX/ACDs (private branch exchange/automatic call distributors) were purchased. In addition, advanced call routing became a reality and, with a view to the future, interflow capability was installed. The calls are now automatically routed to the call centre where the volume can be handled. This creates a virtual call centre out of the four call centres. PCs and LANs (local area networks), not used before the consolidation, were installed, allowing the customer service professionals to service the customer better and faster. Also, by establishing fully redundant mirror image call centres, the company is protected from unplanned outages.

CONCLUSION

With the support of top management, KeyCorp has consolidated its call centres, implementing state-of-the-art technology and resources combined with well-trained representatives. With rigorous service standards in place and ongoing benchmarking against the "best in the business," KeyCorp is committed to continuous improvement.

By consolidating its many call centres to a handful of streamlined centres, KeyCorp has reduced costs, improved technology, achieved economies of scale, and most important, enhanced customer satisfaction.

KeyCorp's call centres are an integral part of the corporation's strategic plans and customers can continue to expect consistent quality customer service. Its best-practices efforts in call centre consolidation have brought KeyCorp one step closer to achieving its vision of becoming the first choice of those seeking world-class financial products and services.

About the authors

JOAN BERISH, CAROLYN LEIST, and NATASHA MILIJASEVIC

Joan Berish is the chief administrative officer of Electronic Commerce at KeyCorp.

Carolyn Leist is the manager of Analytic Support of Electronic Commerce, at KeyCorp in Cleveland, OH.

Natasha Milijasevic is a consultant with Coopers & Lybrand's International Centre of Excellence in Customer Satisfaction, Toronto.

CHAPTER NINETEEN

Achieving Your Vision

THE ROLE OF TECHNOLOGY IN ENABLING AND INTEGRATING THE ENTERPRISE

Joe Kulak, New York, NY

BACKGROUND

The effectiveness of customer care may depend on technology, but customer care should not be driven by technology. This chapter will explore several of the enabling technologies that allow world-class companies to achieve their business objectives. Often these companies are trying to solve seemingly opposing objectives such as reducing operational costs and improving customer intimacy (establishing a customer segment of one).

Typically, we see these as mutually exclusive business objectives, as depicted in Figure 1. You will see, however, that these objectives are not incompatible. Rather, it is up to us to restructure the business and apply technology to achieve these objectives. The first step of any customer care or call centre project should be to understand your overall customer care strategy. Is customer care an opportunity or is it a cost

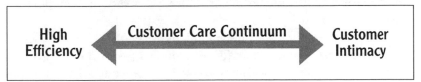

FIGURE 1: The Customer Care Continuum

OLD VIEW		BEST PRACTICES VIEW
Customer Service Deals with Problems	Paradigm Shift	Customer Care Is an Opportunity
• What do we HAVE to do? • "Just Get It Done" mentality		• ANY contact with our customers can produce value • Service is a differentiator

FIGURE 2: Customer Care Approach

factor—a necessary evil that must be performed to sustain the business? Figure 2 illustrates the two views.

Studies performed across multiple industry sectors indicate that your competitors see customer service as an opportunity, as a competitive differentiator.

How do you mobilize yourself to take advantage of this paradigm shift? Which technologies will enable your organization to realize your customer care strategy? This chapter explores several major areas of technology innovation, what the technology enables your organization to do, and how it can help you achieve your business goals and objectives.

CALL CENTRE MODEL

We will use as a model a best-practices call centre infrastructure, which depicts the major technology components of world-class call centres (see Figure 3). Since customer service call centres contain numerous enabling technologies that provide capabilities from the simple to the highly sophisticated, this model correlates each capability to a logical component and provides a framework that shows the interrelationships among the components.

For further simplification we have depicted the major telephony functions in black, and the major information systems functions in grey.

It is most important to understand, however, that in a world-class call centre these are not separate components performing individual jobs. In such centres, these functions are interdependent and integrated to present customer service representatives (CSRs) with a complete

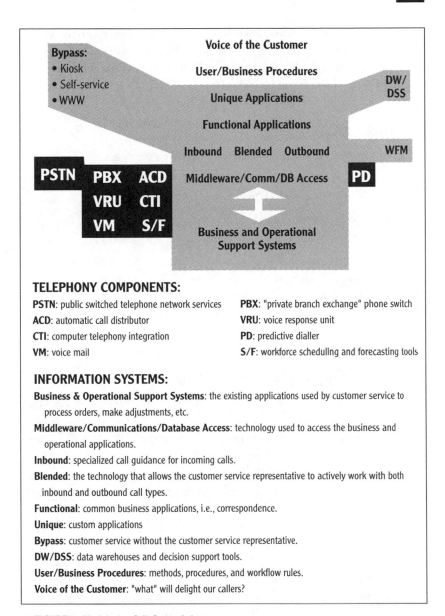

FIGURE 3: Model of a Call Centre Infrastructure

view of the caller (customer) and to provide the representatives with the appropriate tools at the appropriate time to achieve customer satisfaction. Similarly, call centre supervisors and managers are provided with a suite of tools that enable them to manage the resources of the call centre—representatives, telecommunications, workflow, etc.— to maximize efficiency while maintaining high levels of customer satisfaction and representative enrichment.

TECHNOLOGY

Technology enablers can be grouped into three categories:

1. Advanced intelligent network capabilities offered by the telephone/communication companies.
2. Telephony capabilities provided through customer premise (telephone) equipment.
3. Data processing capabilities.

The capabilities provided by categories 1 and 2 overlap, as do the capabilities provided by categories 2 and 3. The following sections discuss the business capabilities of technology enablers independent of the category to which they belong.

Public Switched Telephone Network Services

The Public Switched Telephone Network Services (PSTN) provides the link between the customers and the customer service centre (see Figure 4). It provides information regarding the phone that the caller is calling from (Automatic Number Identification, or ANI), as well as the phone number that the caller dialled (Dialled Number Identification Service, or DNIS). Companies use this information to match phone number with customer and with economic value of each customer in order to improve customer service by, first, routing the caller to the best available representative, and second, determining the level of service they will provide to the caller. In the model in Figure 4, the network telephone services identifies both the caller's phone number and the number the caller dialled and passes this to the PBX or ACD. That phone switch determines the intelligent call routing on the basis of the ANI/DNIS information and the availability of appropriately skilled customer service representatives.

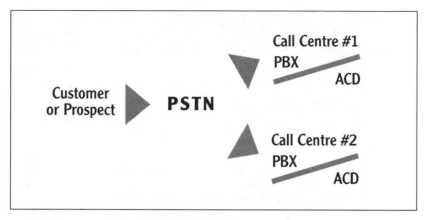

FIGURE 4: Public Switched Telephone Network Services

Trend

Deregulation and privatization are fostering significant changes in the telecommunication industry. It is important that you select telephone service providers, local and long distance, that can support today's business needs and that have a commitment and strategy to supply the infrastructure to meet the needs of the future.

Capability of the PSTN

- Provides Automatic Number Identification (ANI) or Caller Line ID (CLID)—the working telephone number of the originating call.

- Provides Dialled Number Identification Service (DNIS)—the telephone number dialled by the caller. This information can be used to provide specific levels of service based upon the number dialled.

- Redirects calls from one call centre to another, giving your call centre manager the flexibility to reroute calls to other call centre sites. This feature can be activated by predetermined conditions, routing of calls after a certain time of day, or in the event of an emergency at your request.

- Provides least-cost routing. With this feature, calls are received, analyzed and then routed by the PSTN to the customer service call centre with the lowest telephone communications costs.

- Provides variable trunk-line circuits. This feature provides real-time service and termination of trunk lines. With this capability, the telephone-service provider can change the number of trunks or capacity of the trunk lines' real-time according to call volume. This service reduces the call centre's cost (since it is based upon resources consumed and is not a fixed resource allocation required to support peak call volume) and provides greater flexibility to accommodate fluctuations in call volumes.

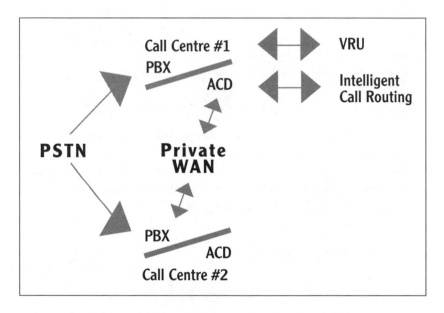

FIGURE 5: Private Branch Exchange or Automatic Call Distributor, the PBX/ACD

Private Branch Exchange or Automatic Call Distributor

The Private Branch Exchange (PBX) or Automatic Call Distributor (ACD) provides the intelligent switching and call routing capability. It links the information about the call, as well as the call itself to the customer service call centre. Figure 5 depicts a multiple call centre environment, with the ACDs in each centre linked to one another creating a "virtual" call centre. Effectively, call loads can be balanced across the call centres as though they were one larger centre. In addition, the model in Figure 5 shows the ACDs supporting Intelligent Call Routing and the interface to the voice response unit (VRU).

Trend

The customer care call centre industry is moving toward megacentres, with 750 to 1,000 representatives per site, and networking two or more call centres together into one virtual call centre. This provides efficient management of human resources and ensures business continuity should one centre be affected by a disaster.

Capability of the PBX/ACD

- Enables multiple ACDs to be networked, or to "talk to one another," sharing information about the availability of CSRs, specifically determining where the next available representative is so that the call can be routed to the first one available.

- Provides for the interflow of calls. This feature enables an ACD receiving a call to determine the best ACD on the network to process the call and route the call to that ACD. The overall effect is one of multiple call centres acting as one virtual call centre.

- Provides for the intraflow of calls. This feature enables an ACD to route calls to specific representative work groups within the call centre on the basis of operational rules supplied by the call centre supervisor. For example, if all representatives are busy in the primary work group, then the calls can be routed to a secondary work group where representatives are available.

- Provides skills-based routing. With this feature, calls are first received and analyzed, and then their characteristics mapped to a rules-based algorithm that determines, then applies, the routing rules to the call. Specifically, a call is routed to the "best available" CSR—for example, billing inquiries would be routed to representatives who can quickly and succinctly respond to and resolve a billing problem.

- Provides last-representative routing, which is the ability to route a repeat call to the same person who handled the first call. If that representative is unavailable, the system will route the call according to predefined rules—for example, the caller can leave a message, request a callback, or be routed to another representative in the same work group or to a supervisor.

- Provides well-defined computer telephony integration (CTI). Information is passed from the PSTN to the PBX to the ACD to the call centre representative application via CTI. This capability requires that the link between the ACD and CTI meet accepted industry standards.

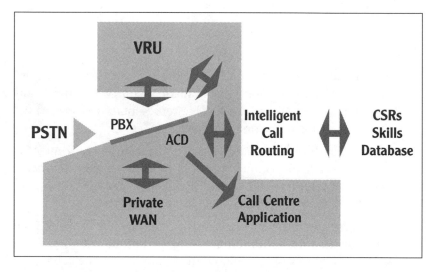

FIGURE 6: Call Centre Management Reporting System

Call Centre Management Reporting System

Managing a call centre efficiently requires timely information on the state of all call centre operations. PBX/ACD vendors provide specialized management reporting systems that provide information about call centre operations. Typically, organizations are dissatisfied with the old stand-by reports of the past. Today's managers need more than just "Average Speed of Answer," "Calls In Queue," group statistics, or representative productivity measures, etc. These present only part of the picture. Today's managers require a comprehensive view of the results.

Trend

Call centre management reporting will be supported by the aggregation of several information sources—namely, the ACD statistics, the representative application, the PBX, and the business and operational support systems. Management will thus be able to achieve the desired result for each customer interaction.

Capability of the Management Reporting System

- Supports a consolidated database of operational performance statistics. This feature will allow statistics from the ACD, the representative application, and other data sources (as they are identified) to be aggregated into one information repository, which will be made available for real-time display or print on demand.

- Enables call centre management to use commercially available forecasting and scheduling tools to perform "what if" analyses and detailed staffing forecasts to optimize production efficiency.

Voice Response Unit

The Voice Response Unit (VRU) can be an integral part of providing high levels of customer service. The VRU depicted in Figure 7 acts as the

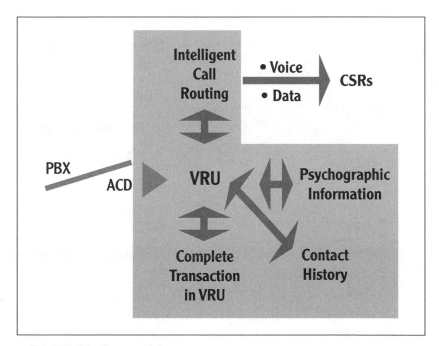

FIGURE 7: Voice Response Unit

catalyst. It receives the "caller-entered digits" from the caller's touch-tone or rotary phone, or recognizes speech to get the information required to access previous contact history, customer profile information, and subscription information. On the basis of this information (also called a "database dip"), either the caller is routed to a live representative or additional functions are performed in the VRU to the caller's satisfaction. At any time, the caller may choose to speak to a customer service representative, at which time, all the information collected to that point (voice and data) will be transferred to a representative.

Capability of the VRU

- Enables the caller to transfer to a live CSR at any time during the call.
- Provides a CTI interface, which supports the transfer of the call and passes along caller-entered digits and any associated information retrieved about the caller. The CSR will receive all information about the call, avoiding the need to request the same information again.

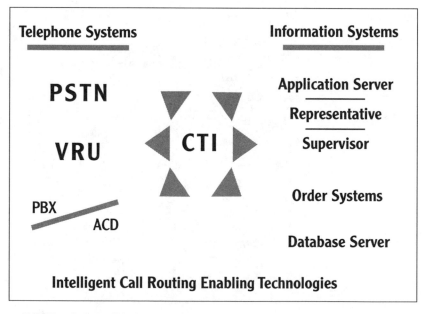

FIGURE 8: Computer Telephony Integration System

Computer Telephony Integration System

In most companies today, the representative spends the initial part of a call identifying the customer and locating the customer records. A Computer Telephony Integration (CTI) system eliminates this by identifying the customer and displaying the appropriate screen to the representative as he or she receives the call; this process is called a "screen pop." It enables the representative to immediately get to the purpose of the call, saving time for both the representative and the customer— time that can be used to take more calls or discuss additional needs of the caller. Moreover, the representative can spend his or her time talking with the customer rather than focusing on how to navigate the business system. CTI technology has the potential to significantly reduce talk time, improve service levels and results, and differentiate your company from the competition.

Computer-to-telephone interface is the glue of modern call centres. Figure 8 depicts the computer telephony integration system at the centre, providing the linkage between the information systems and other call centre applications such as contact management and workflow management, on the one hand, and the telephony systems such as the PBX/ACD, the VRU, and the PSTN, on the other hand. Intelligent call routing is shown in both the telephony and the information systems arenas. This is just one example of potential overlapping solutions, wherein PBX/ACD vendors as well as suppliers of call centre applications are providing different levels of intelligent call routing capability.

Capability of the CTI

- Provides a flexible link between telephone infrastructure and the information systems infrastructure. CTI interprets the language of the PBX/ACD and translates the "telephone" information into computer-understandable instructions. This link must be flexible enough to support multiple computer operating systems to ensure that the solution will support the current computer environment, as well as accommodate changes to it.

- Provides support for industry standard call-control features. Call controls are the telephone capabilities that we are all familiar with— dialling a number, putting a call on hold, transferring a call, etc. In the context of CTI, we are placing these controls in the computer system and allowing the computer to have the same capability as the telephone.

- Supports intelligent call handling (ICH), which is the process of collecting information about the caller, then evaluating the information and providing unique instructions or call guidance aids to the CSR. For example, if we know that a caller is 90 days past due on prior purchases, the call guide would prompt the representative to ask the caller why payment is late, or the call guide could advise the representative to tell the caller that this order will require payment in advance.

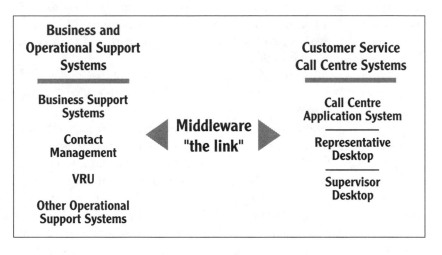

FIGURE 9: Middleware

Middleware

Figure 9 depicts the middleware as the link between the customer service call centre application and the various business and operational support systems. Middleware enables computer systems to talk to one another without the intervention of the customer service representative. In addition middleware can be quite powerful. For example, it can be given instructions to read the entire customer contact history and purchase history records, and display to the customer service representative only the appropriate information. The middleware therefore has a degree of intelligence based on the business rules provided by call centre management.

Capability of Middleware

• Provides an interface to other computing environments. Middle-ware must support access to your current computing environment, as well as provide access to the other systems that will be integrated into the customer call centre computing environment.

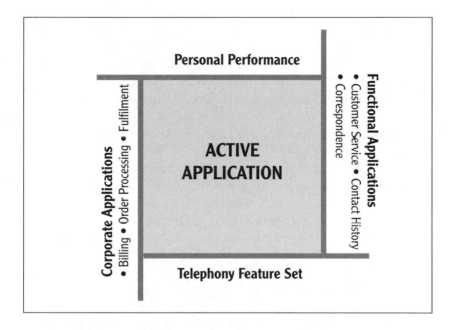

FIGURE 10: Customer Service Representative Control Tower

Customer Service Representative Control Tower

At most call centres, the customer service representative's desktop application is where we see tangible evidence of business and computer-telephony technology innovation. Figure 10 portrays the desktop that best-practices companies are building. They call it the "Dashboard," the "Control Tower," or the "Cockpit." The intent is that each customer service representative has access to the resources of the company at exactly the time when they are needed.

The "active application" of this Control Tower is in the centre of the representative's screen. Surrounding this application are toolbars enabling access to other information and processing sources from throughout the organization. On the bottom is the Telephony Feature Set. This enables the representative to conference, transfer, hang up, or receive a call. It also reports how efficiently the call centre is operating—that is, number of people in queue and average wait times. On the left are icons enabling access to corporate applications. Here the representative can access the order processing system to place an order, access the billing system to inquire or post a credit, or change a billing address. On the top are icons that contain the representative's calendar and daily action item list, as well as the representative's personal and groups performance for the shift. Really good representatives want to know how they're performing. Lastly, on the right are the toolbars representing functional applications. These can access an online directory, the firm's Intranet for new product information, a correspondence system for letter generation, or an imaging system for contracts—whatever is relevant for the needs of the caller.

Many centres use customized customer care applications that provide access to many of these applications through a call guide or verbatim script. At a specific point in the conversation the CSR is prompted toward or delivered to the appropriate application or information repository. The problem with such systems is that they rely on a planned predictability of the call. In the world of the customer care centre, CSRs have to be prepared and be able to go where their customers want them to and when they want them to.

The construct described here supports either approach: for the new CSR, the active application can be the call guide or script; for more experienced multiskilled CSRs, it can be a hybrid; and for the senior CSR, it can be the Control Tower.

Capability of the Control Tower

- Provides a graphical user presentation of customer service information, giving the CSR an easy-to-use display of information.

CONCLUSION

Fundamentally all this innovative technology is for naught if at the end of the day it does not serve some vital business objective. In the case described here, the goal is to create value in the eyes of customers and

potential customers—particularly enough value in the "call experience" that they are "delighted," will buy your goods and services, will
buy more of them or will buy them again, and are less likely to try a
competitor's product or service. Your vision of customer care should
define how your corporation will differentiate itself on the basis of this
perceived and delivered value. Your customer care business policies
and procedures should ensure that commitments made by the customer service representative are carried out, on time, every time. Using
technology should enhance your ability to provide your customers with
a competitive difference.

About the author

JOE KULAK

Mr. Kulak is an independent consultant with over sixteen years experience
applying information technology and telephony solutions to complex business
problems. His experience includes: managing the Customer Care Consulting
Practice of Coopers & Lybrand L.L.P. in New York, and as an executive for EDS
Communications Strategic Business Unit, he was responsible for designing and
implementing world class call centres for EDS and its customers.

Computer Telephony Integration in Action

HOW SOME COMPANIES—AND CUSTOMERS— ARE BENEFITING

Fred Gallagher,
TKM Communications, Markham, ON

IF IMPROVED CUSTOMER service is your objective, and a call centre environment is a critical component of your operating practices, your organization should carefully consider obtaining computer telephony integration (CTI). Why? CTI focuses on elevating the treatment of the customer during a direct contact experience, a customer call. Typically, this is an inbound call initiated by the caller to the organization; or, as we shall see, it can also consist of a blend of inbound and outbound calls. This three- to four-minute event might be your only direct contact, or moment of truth, with your customer. Therefore, the call must achieve customer delight and the potential for positive word-of-mouth referral, otherwise the customer's propensity to use your product again will diminish because his or her expectations of your customer support will not have been met.

WHO IS THE TYPICAL CALLER?

One must make the following basic assumptions to appreciate the value of focusing on this call.

- The caller has called into call centres at least once before and has experienced the typical delay before an agent answers the call. The

majority of organizations without CTI focus on answering 80 percent of all calls within 20 seconds. Targets more aggressive than this
are usually deemed to provide diminishing levels of return.

- Most callers today expect the agent to have a computer screen and
also expect their purchases to be somewhere in your database, but
they are not surprised if you don't find it.

- If the customers are calling during what they believe are business
hours, they expect to be greeted by a live agent. They are prepared
for the possibility of an automated attendant, but hope that it would
be just for routing purposes, which they can navigate with only one
or two keystrokes. This assumption does not rule out the use of
automation for comprehensive applications such as telebanking;
however, customers should be informed ahead of time that they will
be calling into an automated service.

- In summary, the customers are expecting to be greeted by a live
agent; they expect a minimal delay in being answered; and they
would be pleasantly surprised if you knew who they were.

WHAT IS THE TYPICAL CALL?

The next step is to analyze the typical customer call and determine
where the introduction of automation will realize benefits for the caller
and the call centre.

Our analysis of the value of introducing CTI into the call centre falls
into two major areas:

1. The benefits of using CTI to connect the caller, your agent, and your
   database to the telephone call, which takes the initial 10 to 15 percent of the call. This has been the traditional focus of CTI implementations. Even though that procedure consists of only a small
   part of the call, it has the most important effect on how the rest of
   the call will turn out.

2. The benefits of using CTI to manage the telephone conversation
   between the caller and your agent, including the resultant disposi-
   tion and follow-up. This is the stage where good implementation of
   CTI will mean the difference between just satisfying the caller and
   actually delighting the caller.

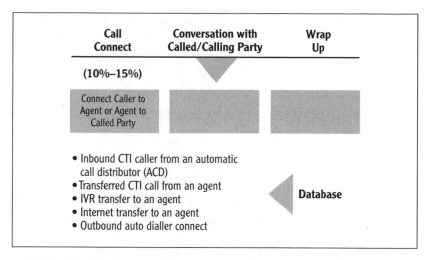

FIGURE 1: The Benefits of Using CTI to Connect the Caller, Your Agent, and Your Database to the Telephone Call

As Figure 1 depicts, the initial part of the call establishes the connection between the caller and the agent. In a typical connection process in an environment without CTI, the call is routed to a pool of agents managed by the telephone system's automatic call distributor (ACD) software. When the call arrives, the agent welcomes the caller and begins the identification process. This process will include identifying the caller, finding out whether the person has called before, and why he or she is calling today.

In a CTI-enabled environment, there is an intelligent communications software link between the telephone system and the computer. The link, often referred to as "CTI Middleware," provides the messaging and control functions that are the foundation of CTI applications. The Holy Grail of CTI applications is the "screen pop," which refers to a process consisting of three important steps—each of which takes only a fraction of a second:

- The telephone system initially passes the caller's telephone number and/or the number called to the CTI-enabled computer application.

- The next step is to determine which agent will answer the call. A CTI "Coordinated Screen and Call" application will monitor which agent receives the call via the ACD software, or a "Host-Directed Routing" CTI application will use the caller's data to route the call to a specific agent.

- The final step will be to display on the answering agent's computer terminal all the pertinent customer data. The data will vary by application and organization, but usually will include customer name, call history, and a pre-fill of this data into the initial application screen.

IS YOUR COMPANY A CANDIDATE FOR CTI?

The screen pop process can deliver true value to your organization. In fact, ask yourselves the following 10 questions and if you can answer yes to any of them, you are a likely candidate for screen pops.

1. Should we be treating some callers differently?
2. Are our regional campaigns effective?
3. Should we route some calls to specific agents?
4. Are we trying to establish a closer bond between callers and specific agents?
5. Can we verify the caller's security before we answer?
6. Should we redirect this call to the accounts receivable department?
7. Do we have customers who should never be answered by a machine?
8. Would we like to return calls to callers who hung up in the queue?
9. Would we save significant money if we reduced the length of the call by 15 to 25 percent?
10. Is there potential to up-sell—that is, sell additional products—to this customer?

HOW THE ROYAL CANADIAN MINT BENEFITED FROM INBOUND CTI

The following comments and description of the implementation of screen pops at the Royal Canadian Mint will help you gain a true appreciation of the benefits of the screen pop process.

It's really neat…it saves time…wow!…I think it's perfect…It's a beautiful thing…Everybody loves it…It's really fast.

Comments such as these are becoming a daily reality for the group of customer service agents at the Royal Canadian Mint, a Crown corporation that specializes in the marketing and sales of coin-related products and services to over 40 countries.

The Royal Canadian Mint, known fondly as "the Mint" reengineered its call centre in Ottawa by integrating its IBM AS/400 and Centrex telephone system using IBM's CTI Middleware product, CallPath/400.

The new telephony application monitors all incoming calls, captures the caller's telephone number, searches the customer database for a match, and automatically "pops and fills" the order entry screen for the answering agent. The application will also determine which 1-800 number was called and select either the Canadian or the US order entry screen to populate.

The objectives of integrating the AS/400 application and the Centrex telephone system were to improve customer service and increase agent productivity. The integration process has not only met these objectives, but also eased the Mint's efforts toward profitability and allowed the Mint to significantly expand its customer base.

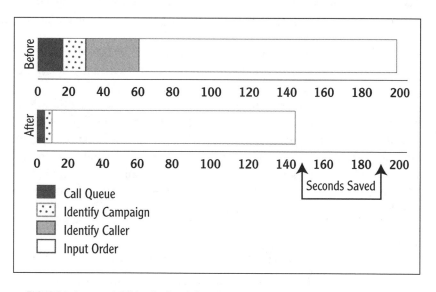

FIGURE 2: Impact of CTI for the Royal Canadian Mint

As Figure 2 shows, before CTI was installed, the agents spent the first part of the call looking after the Mint's needs because it had to know who was calling and where the person was calling from. Now with the new telephony application, that information is automatically provided, so the agents can immediately focus on the customer's needs. Clearly, everybody benefits.

The Mint reduced call duration by 15 percent. With an average call duration of three minutes, this resulted in significant productivity improvements and 1-800 cost savings. It also increased the amount of time available to service the caller's needs and therefore improved the up-sell opportunity.

The Mint is also sensitive to callers' needs for privacy and will not record a caller's telephone number without his or her permission.

The Management Information Systems department is equally enthusiastic. Callers comment that the system response time is now unbelievably fast. Even though the AS/400 is doing more for the agents, they are using fewer system resources because they now do fewer alpha searches to identify callers.

The new system has also reduced the number of host sessions per agent from two to one. Previously each agent toggled between Canadian and US host sessions while answering the call. Now CallPath does the selection for the agent prior to presenting the call; so the agent just needs a single host session.

But one of the most rewarding experiences a visitor will encounter is the overwhelming enthusiasm of the customer service agents in the Mint's call centre. "It's a beautiful thing" truly says it all.

We have just seen an example of how CTI can benefit the handling of inbound callers. Similar benefits can be achieved by using CTI to automate the placement of outbound calls to the customer. The premise here is that the more time the agent has to actually talk to the client, the better serviced the customer will be. Ault Foods, one of the pioneers in the use of CTI, has accomplished just that, while significantly improving agent productivity.

HOW AULT FOODS BENEFITED FROM OUTBOUND CTI

Any milk today? Every day Ault Foods' telesales personnel ask this question in thousands of calls to convenience stores across the country. Ault is best known for its Sealtest dairy products. Ault knows that the key to success is regular contact with the retailer and it is always in search of solutions to make that easier.

Ault used IBM's Callpath/400 CTI Middleware in its order entry and customer service departments. Its objective was to have the AS/400, which processes the orders, to dial and monitor the progress of outbound telephone calls to the retailer. This would reduce the average call duration, with an objective of achieving a minimum productivity improvement of 20 percent. The actual result was an increase of average orders per agent from 150 to 250 per day. A 66 percent increase!

How It Works

- The agent uses the AS/400 terminal to flag the calls he or she needs to make.

- Callpath/400 selects the first customer to call and issues a command to the Northern Telecom Meridian/1 PBX to dial the customer via Bell's Megalink ISDN (Integrated Services Digital Network) service.

- If the call is successful, the AS/400 displays the customer details on the agent's screen, and the agent can now take the order.

- When the agent finishes entering the order, the AS/400 submits it for processing while simultaneously placing the next call.

Why It Works

The agents were very involved with the implementation process and contributed many ideas to the final design. The result therefore reflected the true needs of telesales personnel. The agents also liked the autodial process because it removed many of the mundane aspects of the order process, especially now with multiple area codes within large cities such as Toronto.

Customer service managers were involved early in helping to justify the new installation, and they contributed enthusiastically to the overall design. The significant productivity benefits achieved would never have been realized without their commitment, teamwork, and adaptability to change. In addition to increasing the order rate, CTI now provides them with an immediate update on which agents are active, which customers they are talking to, and how they are progressing through their call list.

Executive management from the chairman down knew that a complex project such as this could only come in on budget if they formed a winning team.

The message of Ault Foods' experience? Technology can be used to bring you and your customer closer together. The key is *effective teamwork*.

How can you argue with a 66 percent productivity increase in today's economy?

WHAT TO DO ABOUT ABANDONED CALLS

For one reason or another customers sometimes hang up while in the queue waiting for an agent to answer. Callers usually "abandon the call" because the wait time they are experiencing is longer than they anticipated when they initially placed the call. Expectations are therefore not being met on this call. Such a call is a major customer service concern of most call centre managers. Keeping the percentage of abandoned calls to a minimum has become a prime measurement of call centre quality, but accomplishing this can be difficult.

The use of CTI functions such as the screen pop will reduce the number of abandoned calls because the length of calls will be shortened, therefore reducing the number of callers in the queue and the subsequent wait for an agent. Unforecasted peaks of calls will, however, still continue to occur and result in a surge of abandoned calls. But, CTI to the rescue! The following case study illustrates how Ault Foods used CTI to turn abandoned calls into customer satisfaction.

Like the Mint, Ault Foods implemented screen pops, which capture the caller's telephone number and display on the agent's terminal the customer's typical shopping list when he or she calls in to place an order. The CTI application also automatically adds new telephone numbers to the customer information database. This latter feature has allowed the caller identification rate to increase from the initial 65 percent of all calls to an envious 95 percent plus rate. The automated screen pops save about 20 to 30 seconds on each call.

While implementing screen pops, Ault Foods realized it could also be immediately notified by a CTI application when a caller abandoned the call while waiting for an agent. To leverage this capability, Ault implemented a CTI Abandoned Call Return application. This application tracks callers who abandon while they are in the queue and uses their telephone number to search the database and identify them. The CTI application then places a call-back request in the outbound queue of the agent responsible for that territory. The customer then receives a personal call within minutes of hanging up. Ault's customers, which include retail stores, food service providers, corner stores, and hospitals have been universally delighted with their call-backs. Their perception is that Ault Foods really cares about them and will go to any measure to assure complete satisfaction.

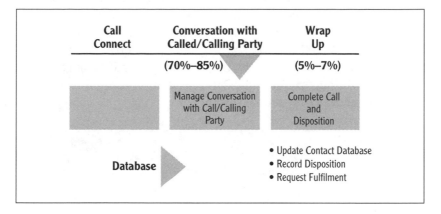

FIGURE 3: The Benefits of Using CTI to Manage the Telephone Conversation Between the Caller and Your Agent

If CTI has done its stuff right, the caller is now connected to the agent, both parties know each other, and they are both in a good frame of mind. The next few minutes will determine whether they stay that way. Advanced implementations of CTI will leverage the use of the Customer Contact Database to significantly improve the level of customer service. Figure 3 illustrates some of the key functions that should be focused on. Mutual Life of Canada is a prime example of an organization that implemented this strategy and went beyond just satisfying the caller to actually delighting the caller.

HOW MUTUAL LIFE GUARANTEES CUSTOMER SATISFACTION WITH ITS CALL CENTRE

Mutual Life of Canada, lead company of the Mutual Group, is located in Waterloo, Ontario. The Mutual Group, with more than $30 billion in assets under administration, offers a wide range of financial products and services to individuals and businesses.

Mutual Life of Canada is one of Canada's leading providers of employee benefit plans. The company annually processes more than three million cheques for health and dental claims. To support this high level of customer interaction, Mutual provides customer service over the telephone through an "Infocentre" staffed with customer service specialists (CSS).

The Infocentre was the first of many steps taken by Mutual to advance beyond the concept of what we all know today as "customer service." The financial services world is becoming more complex, the choices are more difficult and product differentiation can very often be confusing for the client. Every company, from the small business on the Internet to the big one with branches across the country, is trumpeting customer service as the differentiator.

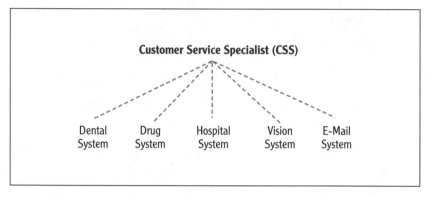

FIGURE 4: Mutual Life of Canada—Before CTI

Just saying it was interested in customer service was not enough. One of Mutual's first objectives was to establish the Infocentre to offload the task of administering the group benefit plan from the human resources department of each of their clients. This initiative would increase the number of calls to Mutual's Infocentre by 300 percent; however, it was enthusiastically received by both the administrators and the individual employees of Mutual's clients. The CSSs began directly receiving calls from members inquiring about claims eligibility, claim reimbursement, benefit coverage, deductibles, etc.

By directly supporting the individual employees, Mutual was able to make them happier participants of the plan their employer or sponsor had implemented. Happier employees means happier employers. Very fundamental, but also very smart!

If you build it, they will come. Mutual guarantees service levels to its clients. Guaranteed service levels definitely set you apart from your competitors; however, they can place significant demands on the management of your call centre.

As a result of the Infocentre's new and guaranteed service levels, Mutual saw call volumes tripling almost overnight. This could be a wonderful trend, but it could also strain call centre staffing and training facilities.

Now every agent could be a star! To cope with the drastically increased workload at the Infocentre, Mutual used a flexible client-server solution, using IMA's EDGE CTI Middleware to consolidate and simplify the view of its suite of host applications and present a single image of the customer to the CSS. A unique characteristic of the new system was that the design and development of the CSS workflows could be performed by a business analyst using EDGE's point-and-click GUI (graphical user interface).

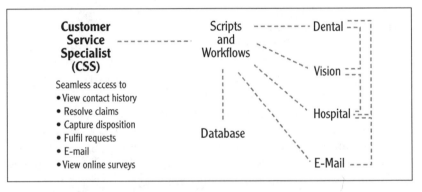

FIGURE 5: Mutual Life of Canada—After CTI

By applying the specialized, expert skills of the analyst during development time of the call flows, Mutual ensures that each CSS is using the most efficient method of handling the call. Complex transactions are simplified into a series of steps, and callers are treated consistently on every call. In effect, each CSS now has the opportunity to benefit from the pooled expertise of many years of claims processing.

As well, rather than having to remember which screen to switch to, the agent is now moved through the call by the caller's responses to prompted questions. Therefore, training time has been significantly reduced, and the CSS now has the opportunity to focus on the customer's unique needs and become a star!

Call consistency is a two-way street. It's not unusual in this business to have callers work the system—that is, they might call in to inquire about the eligibility of a new claim and in a typical ACD environment, their call will be taken by the first available agent. If that first agent doesn't perceive the claim as eligible, the caller might be tempted to call in again, be connected to the next available agent, and get a second opinion.

When a Mutual CSS makes a commitment, he or she is committing the organization. With the new system, the CSSs have an edge on their callers to ensure that the second opinion is consistent. Every call is now tracked, so if a client does call back, even if it's only a few seconds later, notes on the previous dialogue appear on the CSS's screen. The caller still has the opportunity to discuss or escalate the claim; however, all discussions and commitments are tracked by the system until the case is closed. Therefore, all clients are treated fairly and consistently, and abuse of the process is minimized.

"While I have you on the line, may I ask you a few questions?" How can you refuse? The CSS has just solved your problem and now he or she is prompting you for your opinion on some changes Mutual or your employer is thinking about implementing. You have just been empowered! This is one of the best examples of the use of up-sell scripting.

Using its new system, Mutual can develop and implement a new survey script in less than 30 minutes. The survey script can then be activated globally or just appear when an employee from a particular client or group of clients is on the phone. The survey appears automatically while the CSS is stepping through the workflow.

At the end of the survey period, Mutual consolidates the results into an executive report and presents it to the client. It has proved to be an absolute customer delight.

Results

The customer's reaction to all these initiatives has been outstanding. Mutual Life of Canada is in an industry that sells promises. The ability of an organization in the insurance industry to succeed is directly related to how well it keeps its promises. Mutual has received letters from its customers confirming that they feel Mutual has done an excellent job of delivering on its promises. Here is what one wrote: *A major reason for our decision to market our insurance plan was our desire for a true partnership with the carrier, and we heard and saw substantial evidence that the staff of Mutual shares this philosophy.*

And another: *Your infocentre system of tracking calls and documenting conversations is terrific. . . . Even when the infocentre person advises on a particular expense that turns out to be ineligible, the method of delivering the news was direct, honest, accurate, and personable.*

IS THE EXPENSE AND EFFORT OF OBTAINING CTI WORTHWHILE?

In summary, you have just read the stories of companies that use CTI to improve the treatment of the customer during that three- to four-minute event—the telephone call. Was the installation worthwhile? Well, if you ask their customers, you'll hear the answer loud and clear: Yes!

About the author

FRED GALLAGHER

Fred Gallagher is president and founder of TKM Communications, located in Markham, Ontario. Growing very rapidly, TKM Communications has established a reputation as being one of Canada's leading call centre solution providers, consistently delivering high quality and comprehensive applications.

TKM Communications' focus has been the development and integration of "customer interactive solutions." These include automated services such as Interactive Voice Response systems, Fax-on-Demand systems, and Paging servers. In addition, TKM Communications has been a pioneer in implementing advanced computer telephony integration (CTI), customer-agent solutions such as screen pops, expert agent routing, power dialling, agent workflow, and Internet-to-call-centre integration. TKM Communications' Web site is <WWW.TKM.COM>.

CHAPTER TWENTY-ONE

Leveraging Technology to Create Strategic Advantage

AN EATON CREDIT CASE STUDY

Susan Miller and Jacqui Thomson,
Nortel (Northern Telecom) Canada,
Brampton, ON

Eaton Credit Corporation proves there's no limit to superior service when state-of-the-art technologies can be merged into a powerful customer-contact application.

In the credit industry, trust is a two-way street. A consumer seeking credit must provide evidence of his or her worthiness and then live up to that assurance in all future dealings. The credit provider, for its part, must commit to providing timely, personalized service or risk losing customers to a more responsive competitor.

This commitment to delivering the best possible customer service is one of the founding principles of Eaton Credit Corporation, the company that manages credit card operations for the Eaton's department-store chain, as well as for private-label credit cards for several other Canadian companies.

Eaton Credit has long recognized the vital role of communications technology in making business practices more responsive to customers' needs. It was this vision that drove the company's Toronto-based National Call Centre to implement an advanced computer telephony integration (CTI) application, meshing and leveraging Nortel and IBM technologies to create a highly responsive, customer-conscious service environment.

FIRST CONTACT

Eaton Credit is a substantial corporation in its own right, consistently ranking among the top 250 Canadian companies. Like all service-based businesses, Eaton Credit must be acutely sensitive to customers' changing expectations and the nuances of building and maintaining fruitful, long-term relationships. Accustomed to a world where vast amounts of data are available in an instant, consumers naturally expect to access their credit card accounts and resolve transaction issues quickly and efficiently.

To tackle this challenge, Eaton Credit's National Call Centre launched the "First Contact Resolution Project." Its mission is to achieve world-class levels of customer service by bringing together the best people, processes, and technologies—both internally and among Eaton Credit's strategic partners. The ultimate goal is to further differentiate Eaton Credit from competing credit card operations by giving service agents the tools they need to resolve customer inquiries and ensure total satisfaction, as the project name suggests, on first contact.

Crucial building blocks for this project were the selection of appropriate technology and, just as important, the choice of partners with the right balance of quality and expertise to carry Eaton Credit's ambitious goals forward into the next century. Of the many technical issues on the table, the most fundamental was the need to link the customer database on Eaton Credit's IBM mainframe to Nortel's Interactive Voice Response (IVR) technology and integrate this into the Nortel Call Centre.

BUILDING ON PARTNERSHIPS

The main priority for the First Contact team was to look beyond the specifics of systems and platforms to find workable solutions. That meant enlisting support from all its strategic partners—all within an extremely tight time frame.

"The particular applications we were trying to develop didn't have many forbearers in Canada," explains Bruce Clark, director of Quality Assurance at Eaton Credit and the project's principal champion. "This was an all-encompassing, 'big-bang' project that required fundamental change on our data side, corresponding change on our voice side, and an effective integration of the two."

When the project got under way at the beginning of 1996, a further challenge was added to its mandate. Because of the cyclical nature of the retail business, the team had only nine months before the busy, year-end holiday period—when call volumes typically double—to accomplish its goals.

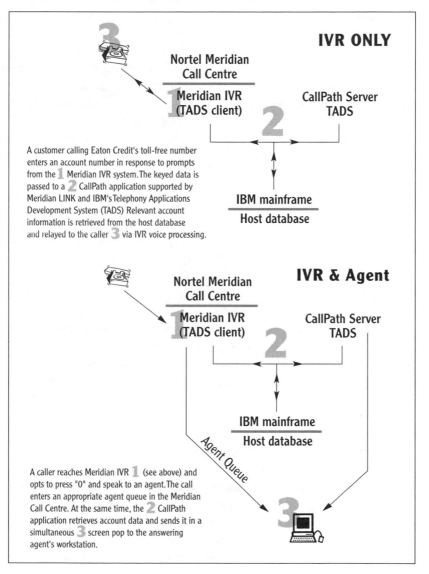

FIGURE 1: Credit Card Inquiry System

WHERE TWO WORLDS MEET

In broad strokes, technical execution of the First Contact project was quite straightforward: to take Eaton Credit's computing applications, in which the company had made a significant investment, and mesh these with the versatile features and proven reliability of its existing call centre platform.

Eaton Credit implemented a three-tier client-server environment in front of its mainframe, and redesigned the call centre agents' computer screens to use a Windows-based graphical user interface. The new interface enables agents to access multiple host applications at the same time; it also accommodates "screen pops" of customer-related data from the host (a screen pop is a process whereby the customer's identification and data are automatically displayed on the agent's screen when the call is received).

How Does It Work?

From a technical standpoint, this pioneering integration of its CTI application was a complete success. But has it met the project's ultimate goal of setting new standards in customer satisfaction?

Eaton Credit's primary CTI application is the Credit Card Inquiry System. Incoming calls to a 1-800 number are identified and routed to its IVR (see Figure 1). Each caller is greeted by the system and prompted to key in his or her account number using the telephone keypad. Further touch-tone commands can be used to perform routine account inquiries—for example, requesting a balance, tracing a transaction history, activating a new card—in real time, without assistance from an agent.

If a caller is reporting a lost or stolen card, or if at any time he or she opts to hit "0" and speak with an agent, the CTI application delivers a simultaneous screen pop of appropriate account information to the answering agent's desktop. The result is a time saving of 20 to 40 seconds per call. Customer service is not only quicker, but also more personalized. Agents have all the relevant facts before them, including any data entered in the IVR, and are better informed to meet customers' needs. Callers, meanwhile, are spared the annoyance of having to repeat information or start the inquiry process over from square one.

RESULTS MADE TO MEASURE

The First Contact project has yielded benefits across the board for Eaton Credit. The primary goal of the initiative—to make customers happier and reinforce long-term loyalties—has been met. In the first few months that the CTI application was up and running, survey responses showed an 8 percent increase in customer satisfaction. Anecdotal feedback from agents and cardholders indicates that this positive trend is continuing.

At the same time, the new system has increased productivity at the National Call Centre. Shaving 20 to 40 seconds off each call handled by a live agent yields a productivity gain approaching 50,000 hours annually. Freed from the necessity of retrieving database files or keying in basic information themselves, agents are able to focus their energies on resolving customer problems, which in turn boosts staff morale.

Eaton Credit has also realized significant savings in technology costs. In the past, the call centre used a third party, 72-port IVR system. The new, improved configuration requires only a 24-port IVR, resulting in a dramatic reduction in associated telephone trunking costs.

As welcome as these productivity and hard-dollar gains have been, however, they cannot eclipse the ultimate measure of Eaton Credit's success: cardholders are being better served and are clearly expressing their satisfaction with the improvement.

SUCCESS IS ITS OWN REWARD

In the past, Eaton Credit's dependence on proprietary, non-open technology platforms severely limited management's ability to develop strategic call centre solutions. Today the vision that drove the First Contact project, supported by the cooperative partnerships between Nortel, IBM, Bell Canada, and Synamics, is not only bearing fruit in the form of a vastly improved call centre, but has also prepared the ground for future service enhancements as the company moves forward.

While the marked improvement in cardholder satisfaction may seem to be reward enough, Eaton Credit has received further, unexpected confirmation of a job well done. For an unprecedented fourth consecutive year, in 1996 the company was awarded the prestigious Canadian Information Productivity Award (CIPA). Sponsored by several

of Canada's most respected information technology and business organizations, the CIPA honours industry leaders who have made innovative and highly effective uses of information and communications
technology.

The technological breakthroughs that linked the best of the best—
IBM computing and Nortel call centre solutions—have enabled Eaton
Credit to protect its investment in both technologies while ensuring
continued forward momentum. As customer expectations grow
increasingly refined, the National Call Centre is well positioned to keep
pace by introducing ever more sophisticated CTI applications.

The technology is impressive, but at the end of the day, the real
credit goes to a company that has stayed true to its roots, doing whatever is needed to keep customers coming back.

About the authors

SUSAN MILLER and JACQUI THOMSON

Susan Miller is Nortel's national director, Solutions. Since joining Nortel in
1986, she has focused on network design and consulting. In her current role,
Miller has been responsible for the development of the Canadian Nortel Call
Centre Business Plan and has worked with Bell to deliver call centre solutions
to the Canadian financial industry.

Jacqui Thomson is market manager, Symposium Marketing, at Nortel's global
headquarters in Brampton, Ontario.

CHAPTER TWENTY-TWO

Top Eight Keys to Creating a Customer-Focused Database

Pat Finerty, Coopers & Lybrand, Toronto, ON

Your organization has been using databases to effectively transact business with customers for a long time. These operational databases usually support transaction processing related to the administration of your general ledger, billing, and a wide range of high-volume activities. These databases are often referred to as "legacy systems" and were designed to optimize the efficiency of processing a large number of relatively simple, well-defined tasks as inexpensively as possible. Typically they are mainframe-based systems, requiring a technical support team to administer. Without them, not only would your organization be uncompetitive, but it could not function.

Tomorrow's organization will be equally reliant on another type of database to compete and thrive in our increasingly competitive business environment. A customer database specifically designed to handle an entirely different set of tasks is rapidly becoming a necessity for companies to capture and hold their customers' loyalty. For the purposes of this chapter, database marketing is any fact-based marketing activity that is driven by information from a database and that relates to customers, prospects, or markets.

Organizations today are discovering that information on customers and their purchasing habits, which is trapped in their legacy systems, is an extremely valuable untapped asset. It is untapped because few organizations have successfully made the transition to providing their marketers with easy access to this information. By taking note of the eight keys to successfully developing a customer-focused database your company can dramatically increase the chances of realizing the benefits of database marketing.

THE EIGHT KEYS

1. Focus on a finite set of applications.

By its very definition, database marketing can support a wide range of activities—for example, developing customer segmentation strategies, implementing rapid-response marketing initiatives such as win-back programs, and applying sophisticated analytical tools to the contents of the database to cull previously unsuspected relationships between different customer groups and behaviours (a form of data mining).

The applications available to marketers who can leverage the whole range of information available on their customers and markets are limitless—for example, marketing costs can be slashed or redirected through developing more targeted offers, revenue can be enhanced through the development of timely cross-sell and up-sell programs, and new products and services can be developed through recognizing the unique needs of high-value customers.

However, attempting to realize all these benefits at once virtually ensures the failure of database marketing efforts. Projects that attempt too much too soon will quickly become unmanageable. While you are developing a case to support the initial investment, identify the entire range of opportunities, but set priorities and specific outcomes associated with one or two applications that have been agreed upon.

These applications should be realizable in no more than 12 months. If initial implementation extends beyond that, your scope is overly ambitious.

2. Ensure that the database contains a link to one or more strategic imperatives for the organization.

The types of data contained in your database will be driven by the specific application that has been given highest priority by your organization. If you simply want to develop cross-sell and up-sell strategies, you may not need customer information at all. A detailed analysis of transactional data may allow you to develop an understanding of various purchase affinities (groupings of purchases that occur frequently) and this may, in turn, allow you to develop effective up-sell triggers at your point of sale. Gas retailers have easy access to this transactional data, but a simple analysis of sales is not enough. To be effective, many gas retailers focus their efforts on driving incremental gross margin, not just sales. Therefore, their transactional database must be able to effectively derive gross margin, the strategic imperative, from the transactional data pertaining to price, brand, and cost of goods sold. This link can greatly increase the complexity of the structure of the database because price can fluctuate daily or even hourly while the cost of goods sold is fixed for more extended periods of time. But the link is essential for success. Without that critical component, the value of the database is questionable and continued investment should be curtailed.

Gross margin is not the only strategic variable an organization may require the database to contain. Other organizations are driven to maximize return on equity or minimize customer defection, often referred to as "churn." To facilitate the link to critical components, a number of organizations in the financial services and telecommunications business have felt the need to restructure operations. These companies have reorganized by replacing product managers and line of business managers with customer segment managers. This change is in direct response to the need to either reduce churn in particular high-value customer segments or capture a greater share of customer spending within the organization's sphere of operations. The development of the appropriate methods and measures to capture and track these strategic imperatives must be accomplished within the context of a marketing database effort.

3. Answer simple questions first.

Sophisticated data mining techniques such as rule induction, neural networks, and fuzzy logic can represent real opportunities for marketers. However, attempting to leapfrog to these techniques before establishing some fundamental building blocks will prove disastrous.

If your marketing database does not support simple ad hoc querying of a useful set of customer and/or transactional information, supported by some simple visualization of results, you are not yet prepared to take the next step. The importance of the querying capability cannot be overstated. Without the ability to interact with the data and validate results, your marketers will never internalize, or take ownership of, the information extracted from analysis. And without very strong validation of results, the rest of the organization will often question the strategic direction suggested by the information coming out of the database. Only when the marketers successfully internalize the results analysis, and clearly and convincingly present this analysis to the organization will breakthrough results follow.

Building even simple query capabilities can be very challenging in a high-volume transaction-processing environment. A large coalition marketing program was unable to produce more than a dozen queries per week after only one year of transactions had accumulated in the database.

It is far more productive for an organization to implement a relatively simple marketing database that facilitates queries and drill down on results, than to attempt to implement neural networks or other less intuitive technologies in the early stages of an implementation.

Database Marketing Questions	Data Mining Applications
Who are my most profitable (highest ROE (return on equity) or highest ROI (return on investment)) customers?	Neural networks are modelled on the neural pathways of the brain and use combinations of on/off pathways to "learn" which combinations of variables are related to desired results of your application.
What is the most effective way to communicate with my most profitable customers?	Induction develops "if-then" rules based upon the statistical significance of data items to a desired result (e.g., response to offers).
Which marketing activities work well? How well do they work?	Visualization supports the interactive display (often animated and abstract) of many-dimensioned data.
What is my most effective channel (store, branch, region)?	Nearest neighbour can be used for classification of database records based upon the historical records most similar to the current record.
What is the difference between the most and least effective channels?	Ranks results based upon closeness to desired results.
What is the nature of the opportunity for performance improvement?	Decision Trees and Rule Induction—CHAID and other techniques that assist in developing relationships between data variables and the desired result in a hierarchical structure.

4. Dedicate a team of information systems and marketing professionals to deliver the solution.

Without a team that understands your data, the underlying technology, *and* the marketing application requirements, the sought-after benefits will be elusive. This holds true whether you are in a build or buy situation.

Senior IT (information technology) executives are beginning to see the problems associated with marketing databases as unique in that they require a great deal of effective collaboration to build or implement a purchased system that is flexible and effective. At a large Canadian financial institution, past difficulties in completing collaborative technology development between IT and marketing led the marketing department to attempt to build a marketing database without IT's support. As a result, the vendor and end users could never effectively differentiate between system requirements that dealt with decision support and operational implementation.

Remember, most technology vendors are technologists first. They may attempt to supplement their project teams with industry experts, but you cannot assume they understand the subtleties of your business from both the technical and business standpoints. Technology vendors tend to assume that your organization functions in a similar fashion to your competitor's. While this may be true in many respects, it is the effective treatment of your unique business and technical issues that will have an impact on your project's success or failure. Building a high-performance team of marketers and technology professionals is essential to achieving your objectives.

It is important to clearly differentiate decision support and knowledge creation from program implementation. Decision-support and knowledge-creation activities support the organization's ability to understand where opportunities exist to further its strategic objectives. For growth strategies, decision-support systems may lend new insight into untapped markets or uncaptured share of an individual customer's regular spending. A typical decision-support database therefore needs highly developed, iterative ad hoc query capability. This supports the discovery process of immediate feedback to questions. A second typical component of a decision-support system is market data. Market data helps the end-user put context around opportunities for improvement through insights into the total size of the market or competitive positioning.

While the pursuit of knowledge must ultimately lead to marketing activity to be of true value, attempting to simultaneously implement operational marketing capability (such as narrow cast capability, campaign management, or rapid response marketing initiatives) while developing completely new insights into customer behaviour can jeopardize your database implementation.

5. Ensure that a consistent vision exists among the following key project team members:

- Executive sponsor authorizing the resources.
- Marketing champion ensuring that the application meets expectations.
- Any other business units benefiting from the implementation.

To ensure this consistency exists, you will find it helpful to include within the project specifications not only details of the original deliverables, but also what the initial implementation will not do. These deliverables must be defined in terms of the activities supported first, and the system functional requirements second.

Ensure that all team members are using the same language. At both a large Canadian telecommunications company and a large Canadian bank, marketing database projects were more than six months into implementation, yet executives directly responsible for the deliverable had no clear idea of core concept definitions such as updating versus refreshing or householding versus customer consolidation.

6. Do not be afraid to develop internal expertise.

While outside expertise is often essential to correctly define your requirements and select the most appropriate technology, an organization committed to leveraging customer and transactional information will, at a minimum, need to develop internal expertise in

- Online analytical processing.
- Structured query language (SQL) and other relational database technologies.
- Statistical analysis.

While many vendors claim that software has now become intuitive enough for non-technical marketers to undertake any and all analysis required without having any in-house technical expertise, the reality is that there continues to be a need for expertise in defining models for multidimensional analysis, leveraging relational databases, and validating results.

A side effect of this need to develop internal expertise is the necessity to operationalize the learning and knowledge discovery that evolves from your customer-relationship management processes. A tremendous amount of effort is expended during the early stages of a company's exploration of database marketing. Often this learning occurs in the hands of a small number of technical experts and marketing champions. While this core group of technical experts is very necessary, the key to generating continuing benefits from their efforts is to capture the learning within the processes themselves. When new insights into customer behaviour are developed, processes should be created that are triggered by specific spending patterns or customer service activity. Only once these processes are in place can the marketers move on to continuously build upon the learning gained from the marketing database.

7. Insist on quality data.

Be prepared to compromise on all parts of your marketing database wish list, except the quality, consistency, and timeliness of your information.

When you define the contents of your marketing database, there will be customer or sales attributes that will be unavailable, historical data lost, or details on transactional information deemed too expensive to maintain. These shortcomings can be addressed through new data-gathering processes, improved quality assurance in your legacy systems, and any number of other measures, once the value of the data has been demonstrated.

However, no compromise can be permitted in the quality, consistency, and timeliness of data key to the deliverables of the database marketing project. These factors are all relative to the application being developed. In the area of knowledge discovery, tolerance for data completeness (quality and consistency) may be much greater than an operational implementation. Timeliness is also a function of intended application. Overnight feeds may be necessary for win-back programs or attempts to pre-empt defection from customers quickly reducing their usage of a particular product (American Express characterizes these customers as "precipitous decliners"). For loyalty schemes such as the Airmiles™ Reward Program, many of the database applications drive selective communication via coupons and individualized messages on statements and in the quarterly newsletter. For these applications, the timeliness of data is driven by cut-off dates for data extracts and print runs four or five times per year.

8. Leverage vendor strength.

When you purchase an existing marketing database from a vendor, focus on realizing the benefits of the vendor's strengths before customizing to compensate for perceived vendor weaknesses.

Due to the complex nature of many marketing database applications, firms often choose to purchase existing solutions. However, every organization perceives its needs to be unique (especially for marketing applications) and thus requests customization. The temptation to "get it right the first time" is great, and many organizations take many weeks, months, or even years attempting to incorporate all special requirements in the first implementation. This is a mistake.

A better approach is to leverage a vendor's strengths first. Only by gauging your ability to successfully realize benefits in this area can your organization assess the risks and rewards of a high volume of custom development. If no benefits can be realized from your vendor's system without a great deal of customization, the vendor selection process may be flawed and should be revisited.

CONCLUSION

Investment in a marketing database is critical to an organization's survival. Open markets have intensified competition, and differentiating products and services is more difficult than ever before. Companies that ignore the need to manage and nurture their customer relationships do so at their peril. Without a concerted effort to capture and act upon the information hidden in your customer and transactional data, your marketers will be forced to compete with promotions and price, or reduce operating costs.

Price reductions, promotional activity, and investments in new technology to increase efficiency will be quickly replicated by your competition. The only true source of long-term competitive advantage is an investment in capturing and leveraging the one asset that cannot be replicated by the competition—your organization's relationship with existing customers. Follow the advice given and provide your team with an opportunity to successfully establish customer-focused database.

About the author

PATRICK FINERTY

Patrick Finerty is a manager with Coopers & Lybrand's International Centre of Excellence in Customer Satisfaction. Patrick works with clients to develop programs and technology that assist them in making more effective use of strategic organizational knowledge. His areas of expertise include data warehousing, database marketing, loyalty marketing, customer-relationship management, call centre operations, and direct marketing.

CHAPTER TWENTY-THREE

Are You Ready for Electronic Commerce?

Stanley A. Brown, Coopers & Lybrand, Toronto, ON
and Doug MacCallum, Ironside Technologies,
Toronto, ON

Does your company need to improve sales, enhance customer relations, and increase operating efficiency? Many organizations faced with those challenges have responded by investing in technology —in many cases, not wisely. Some companies seem intent on playing follow-the-leader—investing in the latest technology rather than the right technology for the company. This is particularly true when it comes to the Internet and electronic commerce.

Rather than making a costly mistake, your company must determine its priorities and the appropriate technology required to achieve them. Then you'll need to put a schedule in place to ensure that the company stays on track. As a guide, here are some of the questions to ask and some of the answers that best-practice organizations have found in their quest to achieve competitive advantage through electronic commerce.

WHAT IS ELECTRONIC COMMERCE?

Simply defined, electronic commerce is a means of transacting business electronically—in many cases over the Internet. As quoted in a Gartner Group Inc. summary report (February 10, 1997), "The migration to electronic access will be so pervasive that by the year 2000, two-thirds of all enterprises using call centres will expand their systems' capabilities to accommodate robust electronic access, and will conduct one-third of their transactions electronically."

Until recently, most Internet applications were used for either academic purposes or information, including research, private publishing, broadcast publishing, correspondence, e-mail, and document delivery (page retrieval).

Commercial applications on the Internet have been primarily e-mail (which requires human response and has a significant time delay) and form completion, including limited forms of order entry, quotations, price or inventory inquiries, online catalogues, and other static applications. But they have not received widespread acceptance as business-to-business applications, possibly because they have not been truly customer-friendly or interactive.

STATE OF ACCEPTANCE TODAY

A survey conducted in the fall of 1996 by the International Customer Service Association (ICSA) asked respondents how often their organizations used the Internet for various activities. As shown in Table 1, almost half use e-mail frequently and browse other home pages occasionally. More than one-fifth occasionally connect for videoconferencing.

TABLE 1: Business Use of the Internet

Purpose	Never	Occasionally	Frequently
Send/receive electronic mail	18%	35%	47%
Browse other home pages	22%	48%	28%
Connect for videoconferencing	75%	22%	2%

Source: ICSA (*Customer Service Benchmarking Report*, 1996)

Sixty-five percent of respondents published their own home page, and of those, 69 percent indicated that it services both businesses and consumers. Two-thirds of these respondents reported that their company's home page information is updated by batch—that is, a fixed number of changes are made at one time. More than a quarter (28 percent) indicated that their home page information is updated in real time—that is, information is constantly updated with each transaction.

Services Provided Electronically

All responding companies offered a number of different services either through their home page or through e-mail. As Table 2 shows, product or service information for viewing on a home page and correspondence with customers through e-mail were the two services mentioned most frequently.

TABLE 2: Services Provided Electronically

Service	Home Page	E-Mail
Product or service information (for viewing only)	82%	22%
Product or service information (available to download)	46%	13%
Product or service availability/inventory information	18%	10%
Correspondence with customers	21%	57%
Order-taking	18%	27%
Order status information	5%	20%
Complaint submission	13%	33%
Billing statements/reminders	0%	3%
After-sale support	13%	20%
Mailing list registration	13%	15%
Intranet support	13%	7%
Other	3%	5%

Source: ICSA (*Customer Service Benchmarking Report*, 1996)

Forty percent of respondents answered the question "If you accept orders through your home page, what percentage of your total orders are received through the Internet?" The median answer was 1 percent. Eighty-three percent of those orders required further processing.

Those companies taking orders over the Internet, through either their home page or e-mail, reported taking customer payments in the ways shown in Table 3.

TABLE 3: Payment Method Percentages for Orders Taken over the Internet

Charging to a customer account	25%
Credit card number by phone/fax/postal service	18%
Credit card number by e-mail	17%
Credit card number via home page	10%
Electronic funds transfer	8%

Source: ICSA (*Customer Service Benchmarking Report*, 1996)

Advertising and Marketing

In addition to providing services over the Internet, some customer service units are using the Internet to advertise and promote their products or services. About one-fifth use e-mail to promote new products or services, and just under one-fifth advertise on other Web sites.

Of those companies using e-mail to promote new products or services, 42 percent customize communications on the basis of a customer's purchasing history.

Research

Several questions on the survey dealt with using the Internet to conduct research. When asked what research methods were used, respondents indicated that they most often get reports of "hits" at their site. See Table 4.

TABLE 4: Research Method Percentages

Reports of hits at your site	38%
Reports of visitors movements at your site	17%
Surveys available to download from Web site and return by fax or mail	15%
Electronic mail surveys	10%
Interactive online dialogue	7%
Other	3%

Source: ICSA (*Customer Service Benchmarking Report*, 1996)

About a quarter (23 percent) indicated that they use the Internet to find new customers. Reported methods of finding new customers include advertising, having a home page, and getting involved in chat rooms. Many reported that simply offering information online helped them find new customers. And when asked if they use the Internet to *develop relationships* with individual customers, almost a third (32 percent) indicated that they do. Most indicated that they communicate with their customers through e-mail, either handling inquiries or initiating contact with a potential customer.

In addition, more than half (52 percent) reported that their organization uses the Internet to conduct research on competitors.

When asked what they would like to do with the Internet but can't do yet,

- 17 percent indicated they would like to take orders over the Internet.

- 8 percent indicated they would like to process orders online.

Other common responses included providing customers with information regarding their individual accounts and offering status and payment information.

When asked about problems using the Internet, respondents indicated that common concerns included available resources and security. Despite these problems, three-quarters of those answering the question "Do you feel your organization has benefited from Internet access?" responded positively, noting it has given their organization access to global markets, allowed an exchange of information between themselves and their customers, and provided them with new and efficient research tools. These companies reported positive customer comments and inquiries about additional access and service over the Internet.

A study conducted by Coopers & Lybrand in May 1997 found similar revealing results. Its IDEAS study, representing in excess of 800 respondents, produced the following key findings about electronic commerce:

- **Importance.** When asked how important having a Web site was to their organization today, 72 percent of respondents indicated that it was either critical or important.

- **Current Adoption.** When asked which of the following interactive online services were provided online or via the Internet, and which were the most important, the respondents provided interesting answers. See Table 5.

TABLE 5: Services Provided Electronically

	% Provided Online	% Provided by Internet	% Most Important
Technical support	15	11	13
Order processing	30	12	19
Fax on demand	24	4	2
Order status	15	2	13
Account inquiries	21	5	12
Bill payment	17	3	2
Product or price inquiries	20	24	10
Inventory inquiries	8	3	3

Source: Coopers & Lybrand, *IDEAS '97* (Toronto, May 1997)

The Internet is seen to have important applications, in particular, for order processing, technical support, and order status. And the ability of organizations to embrace it, based on perceived limitations, is quite high.

WHAT CAN ELECTRONIC COMMERCE DO?

The new generation of Internet software applications, has created single, integrated applications that provide for real-time business-to-business transactions, including

- Interactive, real-time online order entry
- Order status reporting (directly accessible by customers)
- Identification of possible substitutions (in the event that a back order is required)
- Quotations/quotation status
- Connectivity to EDI (electronic data interchange) back-end
- Advertising

- E-mail

- Announcements

- Product introductions

Business-to-business electronic commerce will be the fastest growing business transaction alternative before the end of the century. The only limitation is management's mind-set concerning the possibilities and the degree of control that will be given to customers.

CAN ELECTRONIC COMMERCE REALLY OFFER A STRATEGIC ADVANTAGE?

A research study by the Yankee Group (Boston, January 1997) suggests that companies in North America will be conducting US$134 billion in business on the Internet within the next four years, compared to the US$120 million currently being conducted. Customers are demanding new, more convenient, more informative access to your organization. Offering that access electronically will soon become the standard, not a strategic advantage.

HOW MUCH INVESTMENT IS REQUIRED?

The costs of establishing an online presence vary greatly depending on the complexity and extent of the services you plan to offer customers. Your primary costs will include

- An Internet Web server

- A robust software application package

- Applications that allow real-time online communication

- An integrated firewall

- System integration/consulting fees

WHAT ARE THE BENEFITS OF ELECTRONIC COMMERCE?

Organizations that are active in electronic commerce have found that, on the revenue side, they have been able to

- Reach new markets.

- Increase loyalty among existing customers.
- Increase order size by at least 10 percent.
- Offer direct marketing opportunities.

But enhanced revenue is not the only benefit. Reduced operating costs have also been achieved. They include

- Reduced cost per order (in the range of $5 to $8 per order).
- Reduced routine enquiries to the customer service representative.
- Improved order accuracy (order confirmations and invoices can be downloaded by customers).
- Reduced back orders (customers can immediately choose substitutions, if necessary).
- Reduced returns.
- Reduced cost of document production and distribution (documents/catalogues and specifications sheets can be downloaded at the customer's site).

HOW DO YOU CHOOSE THE RIGHT INTERNET SOFTWARE PRODUCT?

Decisions about Internet software products are some of the most difficult to make; however, to help you, here are a few things to consider:

1. Your Internet software application must be secure. This means that additional firewall protection may be required.
2. Your application must be capable of being integrated with your existing order entry and inventory management system.
3. Your Internet application should allow for some degree of flexibility.
4. Your software should be fast and easy to use, to ensure prompt customer service. (Java software is mandatory.)
5. You must have the ability to monitor usage of the site, so that you can identify what features customers are using or having difficulty with.
6. Of course, your Internet application must be cost-effective.

WHAT ARE THE STEPS TO ESTABLISHING AN ONLINE PRESENCE?

At a recent executive briefing conducted by Coopers & Lybrand, and Ironside Technologies, the following approach to going online was suggested:

1. Decide what applications and services you will provide to customers electronically and the phases required to implement those services.

2. Identify the Internet software application that meets those needs.

3. Decide where your site will run. Will it be part of a production system or reside on an isolated server?

4. Meet with the people in your organization who will provide the content for your Web site—your marketing team, programmers, and graphic designers.

5. Integrate your Internet software application with your existing legacy systems.

6. Research Internet Service Providers (ISPs) who can get your company on the Internet. Most will handle TCP/IP (Transmission Control Protocol/Internet Protocol) as well as address and domain name registration.

7. Begin planning for security and firewalls by determining the level of customer access required and the usage monitoring needed.

8. Test your site internally, check every link, and locate your site through more than one Web browser.

9. Register your site with all popular search engines and publicize it to your customers and vendors.

10. GO LIVE!

11. Measure activity. Check for pages that no one ever looks at and check links to ensure there are no "orphans" that are unreachable.

12. Keep your site interesting and up to date so that people will come back to it. Assign a Webmaster to monitor content and keep it current.

WHAT IMPACT WILL ELECTRONIC COMMERCE HAVE ON CUSTOMER RETENTION OR LOYALTY?

The ability to conduct business transactions online is a service requirement for today's customers.

Today, it is a point of differentiation in a sea of "me to" organizations. To earn loyalty and repeat business, organizations must become what customers value most, a business that is easy to do business with. They must be flexible, and provide service in a manner that allows the customer to contact and do business with an organization, at their convenience, not at the convenience of the supplier organization. As stated in the Overview of Part Four, companies with "superior" service quality enjoy twice the return on sales, twice the return on investment on an additional 13 points at market share over companies with service quality rated as "inferior." In addition, the study reveals that companies with superior service quality gain market share year to year, while companies with inferior service quality lose market share.

When all is said and done, the Internet may be the key for those that are bold enough. And the rewards can be significant.

About the authors

STANLEY A. BROWN and DOUG MACCALLUM

Stanley A. Brown is the partner responsible for Coopers & Lybrand Consulting's International Centre of Excellence in Customer Satisfaction, located in Toronto. He is also the author of *What Customers Value Most: How to Achieve Business Transformation by Focusing on Processes That Touch the Customer* (Toronto: John Wiley & Sons Canada, 1995).

Doug MacCallum is regional vice-president of sales for Ironside Technologies, which provides leading business-to-business software and solutions to the marketplace. MacCallum spent 10 years in sales and marketing with IBM and was director of channels for AT&T Paradyne Canada.

Part Five

Best Practices in Workforce Management: The Importance of the People Factor

Technology and people must go hand in hand. Faster, smarter technologies must be seen as tools to equip an organization with faster, smarter customer representatives. But that cannot happen without the right training. Earlier we discussed two of the three leading trends in customer support centre environments as found in the Coopers & Lybrand 1997 *IDEAS* study. Here we discuss the third trend, workforce management.

The most common workforce challenges reported by *IDEAS* respondents include

- The need for continuous skills upgrading.

- The need to improve utilization.

- The need to better facilitate teamwork.

- The need to increase productivity.

- The need for cross-functional training.

There's more. However important external customers are for the success of your business, the real key to success may in fact be your internal customers—your customer service representatives (CSRs). CSRs are the new front line. To be successful, they require excellent client-service skills, strong product knowledge, and an understanding of the operating equipment in use.

Numerous tools are being used by best-practices organizations to help their employees become effective CSRs. These tools include the following:

- The use of standard benchmark models across the organization to assist in evaluating the strengths and weaknesses of each call centre.

- Silent monitoring and incentive programs to provide additional assurance of high customer service levels.

- Performance support systems, which combine several technologies, including expert systems that provide advice.

- Computer-aided instruction.

Nintendo provides an excellent example of workforce management in action. By focusing on employee training, the company was able to increase flexibility in staff utilization, which resulted in increased profitability. Today, 80 percent of Nintendo's staff are now cross-functionally trained. In fact, service personnel working across established departmental boundaries is the norm in the company. This has resulted in a staff cut—going from 600 to 400—with faster and more qualified responses to customer queries. Not only has Nintendo dramatically improved customer service ratings, but it has also cut costs by $1 million.

Best-practice organizations also take a strategic approach to workforce management, as you will note in the chapters that follow. Part Five starts with John Kressaty's perspective on empowering customer service representatives. He contends that high-performance work teams, which should be organized around natural work groups, should not have the standard department manager but rather a coach or facilitator who keeps them on track and advises them when necessary. Another perspective is provided by Susan O'Dell and Joan Pajunen, who believe that service-empowered people are those who understand the big picture; have insight into the expectations of the key stakeholders in the business—the customer, the employee, the shareholder; are knowledgeable about the company, its products, and their jobs; and are sufficiently skilled to ensure they can perform successfully in a variety of situations.

The next article, by Bob Parks and Alexandra Lang, deals with another dynamic of teams—the need for cross-functionality. The authors show why this is important: every time a customer does business with an organization, a large number of visible and not-so-visible employees are responsible for managing that experience. Why have so many people involved? Why not limit the potential for inconsistency and error through multiple hand-offs? Cross-functional training is the answer. In the next chapter, Professor John Daly discusses the issue of leadership and his belief that highly effective leadership in a customer-driven firm has some core characteristics that are consistent across types of organizations and business sectors. He highlights some of the main characteristics that set apart great leaders from others.

We then move from teams and leadership to the process of measurement and performance enhancement. Jack Green's article is based on his belief that quantitative measures of performance don't offer the staff member enough information to take ownership of their work outcomes; however, effective qualitative measures, along with procedures for continuous assessment, do. Green describes how to incorporate qualitative performance standards in the mix of performance-assessment tools and how these can compensate for the inefficiencies of assessing performance solely using quantitative tools. The last chapter in Part Five, by Sandip Patel, introduces a new, but far-reaching concept—"the knowledge worker." Sandip shows how technology and people should work together to achieve improved customer satisfaction. He points out that as organizations transform their customer care operations, utilizing intellectual and experiential capital on a continuous basis is critical to creating and sustaining a customer focus and superior service standards. To succeed in this, work flows and technology must facilitate the capture and dissemination of knowledge, as well as the collaboration and sharing of learning among employees. This connotes a new role for employees of the organization in leveraging context-specific knowledge to deliver value to their customers. The role shifts from that of a processor (of widgets or information) to that of a knowledge worker.

How an organization achieves best practices in workforce management is not a quick-fix formula that can be picked off the shelf and installed; nor is technology the solution. There are many pieces to this puzzle, and our contributors offer some best-practices considerations.

S.A.B.

CHAPTER TWENTY-FOUR

Empowering Customer Service Representatives

HIGH-PERFORMANCE WORK TEAMS IN A CUSTOMER SERVICE ENVIRONMENT

John E. Kressaty, S.C. Johnson Wax, Racine, WI

IN THE EARLY nineties, high-performance work teams (sometimes called self-directed work teams) started to surface in the customer service environment. These teams consist of customer service representatives who are empowered to work with customers to improve the efficiencies of the supply chain. Since the customer service representatives spend more time talking to customers than anyone else in the organization, it makes sense that they be empowered to handle any situation. High-performance work teams can enhance the functions normally performed by the customer service representative because they can manage any situation.

High-performance work teams, which should be organized around natural work groups, do not have the standard department manager but rather a coach or facilitator who keeps them on track and advises them when necessary. One way to form these teams is according to the geographic regions being served. The members of these teams also each participate in "Resource Teams," which specialize in specific areas of importance such as productivity, quality, recognition, and communications. The Productivity Team monitors workload balance and general practices that can increase productivity when they are adjusted or improved. The Quality Team monitors the practices and training of the high-performance work team members to ensure the training is effective. The Recognition Team helps develop incentive programs and determines the different award programs offered during the year. The Communications Team strives to use all tools available to create effective communications that can be executed with the least amount of effort.

The team members meet regularly with personnel from other departments—including sales, marketing, manufacturing, distribution, communications, and information services—to ensure a smooth supply-chain process. The teams control the working conditions and atmosphere in the department, which enhances their performance and allows decision-making to delight the customer and benefit the company.

EMPOWERED REPRESENTATIVES IN ACTION

The customer service professional must be empowered to fulfil the corporation's strategic plan. The necessary skills for such empowerment should be given by coaches and upper management during the initial training of these front-line people, and constantly reinforced through incentives and team-building activities. The training for the teams would include problem-solving, decision-making, conflict management, peer appraisals, negotiation, and team-building. This group training encourages the team to make effective decisions and fosters continuous improvement.

Customers notice the increased effectiveness of the empowered customer service representative in the high-performance work team. Customer survey results evidence this by the high rating customers give to the front-line customer service people. Top managers making customer visits hear that their customer service department is an asset to their business. Company employee opinion surveys, too, show that employees realize they are empowered. The ratings for "feeling empowered" by employees have shown improvement since the surveys of the eighties and early nineties in companies that conduct such surveys. Departments that are not empowered reflect this in their low employee-empowerment ratings; and employees in those departments indicate a desire to become empowered.

An example of empowerment in action is the following story of a burn victim. The customer service department of a major skin care company received a call from a hospital in Hawaii. The hospital explained that its local supplier was out of stock of some critical skin cream that it was using to relieve the discomfort of a nine-year-old burn victim. The hospital had tried everywhere in the islands to get the product, but to no avail. The customer service representative told the hospital that it would have the product the next day, even though it was Saturday. The customer service representative was aware that the minimum quantity shipment was 50 cases. She was also aware that the hospital was not set up as a direct customer. Nevertheless, she requested four cases of the product from inventory, took them to an overnight delivery service, and arranged for them to arrive at the hospital on Saturday.

Two weeks later the manager of the customer service department received a letter from the hospital's administrator. The administrator explained that the patient's parents were very impressed with the way in which the company had responded to the hospital's need for the product, and said that the hospital would now purchase the company's products regularly. The hospital administrator also noted that the company had a number of divisions, one of which provided hospital solutions for cleaning, disinfecting, and other maintenance needs. The hospital administrator indicated that he would be recommending to his director of environmental services that the company's products be used in the hospital's maintenance program.

There is no way to calculate the revenue earned by this company for the acts of the empowered customer service representative who sent four cases of product to the hospital at no charge. This story is an excellent example of empowerment at work and what it can mean to any business.

Here is another one. A customer was breakfasting at a restaurant, but was not feeling well. She had a cold and her throat was sore. The waitress heard her talking about her condition and brought her a throat lozenge from someone in the kitchen. The customer's breakfast arrived, but since she was not feeling any better, she hardly ate the meal. The waitress came back, noticed her customer had not eaten, and cleared the table. The waitress told the customer that she would not have to pay for the breakfast she had hardly eaten. She wished the customer better health and invited her to return when she could enjoy a meal.

This empowered employee made it possible for her customer to have a heart-warming experience. The customer has told other people of the great service, and she will come back to eat at that restaurant.

Here is an example of how team empowerment can deliver fast results. A major manufacturer of packaged goods received a call from its largest customer late on a Friday afternoon, requesting that 1,200 cases of product be shipped overnight to some 28 stores. Complying with that request required cross-functional support. Although not all team members were available, the empowered employees pulled together a high-performance response and made sure all processes were in place to meet the customer's needs. High-performance work teams can take that type of action when they are empowered to meet the objectives of their companies, whatever the circumstances. All employees must know what the objectives are and possess the skills necessary to perform the processes required to reach the corporation's goals.

HOW TO ESTABLISH HIGH-PERFORMANCE WORK TEAMS

These are the steps you can take to establish high-performance work teams in a customer service environment.

1. Create a "customer-driven" philosophy that can be clearly communicated and accepted by team members.

2. Identify a natural work group (for example, according to geographic regions being served) to form the different teams.

3. Establish the resource teams discussed earlier (productivity team, quality team, etc.) to support the various natural work groups. The actions of the work teams must be reinforced with appropriate and timely incentives.

4. Design and conduct training programs that teach the varying skills needed by the individual team members, as well as improving individual job skills as required to bring all members to the same skill proficiency.

5. Develop and implement the appropriate measures for success, and monitor results regularly according to a scheduled timetable. It is important to constantly observe the team's performance. The 360 degree feedback tool is acceptable to use as part of the performance appraisal process. Feedback from customers, peers, and other cross-functional areas helps to identify the customer service representative's

strengths as well as areas that need improvement. Customer, team, and employee opinion surveys can also be used.

Once teams are established, continuous training and skill development for all team members are a necessity. High-performance work teams are dynamic organizations that must be constantly nourished and revitalized.

Establishing high-performance work teams empowers customer service representatives to work with customers to improve supply-chain efficiencies. The result is improved response to customer needs, which enhances the revenue and profit generated by the customer service transaction.

About the author

JOHN KRESSATY

John Kressaty received his MBA from California Western University and has worked for S.C. Johnson Wax for 26 years. He started as an area sales representative in the New Jersey region and is currently director of customer service, North American Consumer Products. Kressaty is a past president of the International Customer Service Association.

CHAPTER TWENTY-FIVE

Developing Employees Who Can Deliver Best Practices in Customer Service

Susan M. O'Dell and Joan A. Pajunen,
Service Dimensions Inc., Toronto, ON

W HEN IT COMES to developing employees who can deliver a best-practices level of customer service, not just any old people will do. You need people who can make decisions close to the action, create a personal service experience for each customer, and contribute good ideas to the corporate plan. And you need them to do this regardless of their distance from head office or length of service with the company. You must be prepared to empower your people.

WHAT IS EMPLOYEE EMPOWERMENT?

Employee empowerment may be one of the most misunderstood and therefore abused concepts in customer service today. Somehow management developed the notion that one could simply hand over responsibility for customer satisfaction to front-line individuals and everything would turn out fine.

What happened in reality is that after transferring into the hands of the staff the power to please the customer, executives and owners watched in horror as employees made inappropriate decisions that adversely affected shareholders, other employees and, ultimately, customers. It's no wonder we are beginning to see service company leaders grab back the reins in order to protect their business. But hanging on for dear life is no answer either. The best practice is to devise a training and developing system that creates service-empowered people.

WHAT ARE SERVICE-EMPOWERED PEOPLE?

Service-empowered people are those who understand the big picture; have insight into the expectations of the key stakeholders in the business—the customer, the employee, the shareholder; are knowledgeable about the company, its products, and their jobs; and are sufficiently skilled to ensure they can perform successfully in a variety of situations.

While there is no single set of human-resource practices common to companies that have a high proportion of loyal customers, there are some approaches that most share. Here are some examples.

Job Descriptions. Every job description of every employee, from the newly hired part-timer to chairman of the board, indicates how each position relates to the rest of the organization and states the requirement to satisfy all three stakeholders.

Selection. These companies have, through a controlled selection process, acquired a significant percentage of employees who share the traits that distinguish those who thrive in an operating environment designed to deliver an excellent customer experience.

Education. Beyond training and development, these employees are invited to understand the business of the business. They know the real profit numbers and what to do to change them. They are educated in the moods of the customer and can impress you with their knowledge of the competition.

Rewards and Consequences. Employees at all levels can cite examples of behaviours that would have a positive or negative effect on any or all of the three stakeholders and the resultant reward or consequence. It is clear to all concerned when each is deserved.

Best practices are built on a strong set of basic principles. We will highlight these and explain how they can be extended to create a service-empowered team.

Job Descriptions for Every Employee

Job Description Basics

Whether formal or informal, job or position descriptions should be based on accountability. And they should focus on outcomes rather than tasks. It doesn't seem to matter whether the description is written formally in management-by-objective style or more informally. The key is that it focuses on "what is to be achieved" rather than on "how to achieve it." Believe it or not, a job description can even be communicated orally, but if set down in writing, it forms an easier reference point and can be referred to in discussions about performance.

Accountability-based job descriptions help ensure that staff know why they have been hired and therefore how to measure their own success on the job. To assess whether you have accountability-based job descriptions, think of the job of someone who reports to you. Then write down one outcome you expect from that person's performance. Okay, now ask: "Does the employee know this outcome is expected of her and why it is important to the customers? Can she identify the indicators that tell her when it is well done?" If the answers are no, you may be encouraging your employees to focus more on the "how" than the "what." Or worse, giving them no focus at all.

Service-Empowering Job Descriptions

Everyone in an organization is accountable for protecting the best interests of the customer. That means everyone has an obligation to all three stakeholders—to make this a good place for customers to do business; a good place for all employees to do productive, satisfying work; and an attractive place for shareholders or owners to invest their capital in.

In an organization that really understands the concept, we find the same accountabilities in all the job descriptions. But how can the chief operating officer have the same accountability as the part-time front-line person just hired? Easy. They are each accountable for looking after the needs of all three stakeholders. It is just the scope of command that changes.

While the executive looks far into the future and the front-line employees deal with the current reality, all focus on delivering an integrated experience for the customer and meeting the needs of all three stakeholders. They all understand their interdependence on one another, where to go with or for information, and the importance of timing. When the customer help-desk clerk who hears two callers in a week say that the competitor's telephone system is much better, he knows the value of that information, whom to get it to, and how. From another perspective, an executive who hears, at an industry workshop, about a consumer trend can often have this confirmed in minutes by front-line staff.

Best-practices companies ensure that everyone in the business focuses on his or her accountability to each stakeholder and thinks about how every action and decision affects all three. Staff know that if something is good for the customer and good for the employee, then it's likely to be good for the shareholder as well.

People Selected Because They Will Thrive

Selection Criteria Basics

This increasingly sophisticated aspect of human-resource management is still all about matching the right person to the right job. Since the best predictor of future behaviour is past behaviour, the best selection process gets at evidence of past performance. Make sure those who hire others in your company can tell you exactly what they look for in a candidate and how they know they have found it. Ensure that they are looking for evidence that the candidate delivered the output, rather than concentrating on "how" the candidate did it. If you are selecting on the basis of gut feel or an outmoded system, you aren't getting the best talent.

Seek out others in the industry who have the reputation for hiring successfully and ask them to share their process and selection criteria with you. If you are in a seasonal business where you have to hire scads of people in a short period of time, study a service organization such as the Walt Disney Company, with its thousands of seasonal hires every year.

Service-Empowering Selection Criteria

What are the innate characteristics of employees who thrive in organizations that deliver consistent quality service? Two traits are found in a high percentage of employees in these companies. While the specific tasks required at the fast-paced front line may be different from those required in the future-thinking executive suite, the same traits can in fact be shared by all. The first trait is curiosity.

Curiosity Keeps This Cat Alive

Why is curiosity such a valued trait? The reason is that without it, the ever-changing customer will be viewed through yesterday's glasses. Little glitches that appear in systems and procedures will be ignored until they turn into full-blown problems. The customer who says "I used to come here all the time" won't be asked what made her stop coming or what brought her back. Employees without curiosity can unpack a carton of merchandise without really seeing its contents. And without curiosity, employees accept instructions at face value instead of asking why.

Although often more difficult to manage, curious employees are worth their weight in gold. Send them out to learn about your competition and they will come back with information you never dreamed it was possible to acquire. Turn them loose on customer research, and they will come back with information as valuable as that from an expensive study.

To find evidence of this curiosity trait, you can ask questions that require the respondent to tell you of a time when they were curious about something, what steps they took to satisfy their curiosity, and the results of their actions. Use questions that begin with "Tell me about a time when." Ask why things are done a certain way in the applicant's existing job. Or create a situation that requires curiosity, and ask: "How would you handle this situation?" There are also inexpensive surveys and tests that can be administered to test the curiosity level of an individual.

When You Win, I Win

The second valued trait is more difficult to describe, but equally powerful in action: the desire to be of service to others. It is the genuine joy of participating in problem-solving, meeting a need, or offering a kindness to a stranger—and finding the act its own reward.

In organizations with a team dedicated to serving, we find an accounting clerk excited about developing a new payroll system that saves supervisory time, buyers who thrive on the moments they interact with the customer, or an executive who sneaks in time to work on an industry task force. These are individuals who think that serving someone else is a neat thing to do and can't help but find ways to do it.

Like curiosity, this trait can be uncovered with good interviewing techniques and aptitude tests. Look for situations in which the person had the opportunity to be of service. Things you want to hear are

- Great listening skills and credit given to others.

- An indication of self-fulfilment in problem-solving.

- A genuine pleasure in performing the service act.

Things you don't want to hear are indicators that the person has an opinion of customers that places them in an unfavourable light. It's amazing how many service providers really dislike serving their customers.

While knowledge and skill are the basics of a selection program, service-empowered people also bring some innate traits that can only help your organization and your customers.

Education Beyond Training and Development

Training and Development Basics

All too often, decisions are made to build new stores, to buy new technology, or to start a new promotion without any consideration as to what that same money would do if spent on training and development of employees in the company. — Michael J. O'Connor[1]

It is much easier to spend money on bricks and mortar than on a human asset, for the following reasons:

- The delivery is immediate; you see it in weeks instead of years.

- The result is visible; you can see and feel where the money went.

- The outcome is predictable; you know what you will get for your money and can even predict the maintenance cycle.

But it isn't so when it comes to people. They don't all respond the same way to the same initiatives. An attempt at a human "renovation," or training investment, may actually benefit the competition if your staff turnover is high. Perhaps that is why one retailer we interviewed said he wouldn't put the staff in training until they had proved their staying

---

[1] *International Trends in Retailing* newsletter (Arthur Anderson & Co.)

power by lasting three months. Imagine! Three months of customers in the hands of an untrained person. It's like assigning a pilot-in-training to the flight that is expecting a stormy turbulent ride.

Why is this so prevalent in the service sector when it is so obviously wrong? Maybe because a great deal of money has been spent on training in the past only to deliver insignificant results. But the training may have been poorly designed or, more likely, the wrong training was delivered.

Another reason we find a deficiency in training is that it is treated like an inoculation—once is enough. "Oh, our employees already had that training" is a common response when we suggest that there is a lack of communication skills or knowledge of a goal-setting process. Yes, but they aren't using it. Did you know that up to 80 percent of all training dollars are wasted if the lessons aren't consistently followed-up or coached? This fact may be the reason why business is so reluctant to invest in any more training. The last round didn't stick.

The basics of a training system are the following:

- Ensure that responsibility for training and protecting the training investment is in the job descriptions of every manager, supervisor, and executive.
- Train employees before letting them loose on customers.
- Separate knowledge training from skills training.
- Prioritize the training.
- Follow up.

Service-Empowering Training

Beyond those basics, what kinds of education and development do we find in an organization of service-empowered people? There are three.

1. Orientation to the Vision and Culture

All staff need to understand the vision, the strategy, and their role in the plan. And they need to know it within the first few hours of starting work. Those first few hours of orientation are your chance both to demonstrate that your culture is committed to people and to behave as if they were your most important resource.

2. Education about Business

Educate every employee in the aspects of margins, profit, and return on investment. Is it worth sharing such sensitive information? Just ask New Brunswick Tourism, whose summer employees quickly figured out how their behaviour could help meet the provincial objective of "getting customers to stay a little longer and spend a little more," when they were asked to create a business plan for a fictional Tourist Information Centre.

Employees can plan their own actions better when they understand the implications for the business. Although you may at first feel uncomfortable sharing gross margin, expenses, and profit numbers with employees, this practice is often later credited as being a primary contributor to a company's increased service levels and profit.

3. Understanding of Customers

Employees who think the way customers do provide valuable information and make better decisions. Every one of your employees is a customer to somebody, and you need to find a way to help them see your business through those same critical eyes. One way to increase that ability is to send them out to experience a "foreign" environment in the shoes of the customer.

For example, when you are a gas retailer you can't go to an environment much more foreign than a lingerie boutique. What could those who sell gasoline and convenience products learn from a visit to a specialty women's store? A great deal, actually, as the employees of one gas retailer discovered. They learned about customer discomfort and as a result were able to look at their own sites and find ways to make new or infrequent users feel more at home. They saw some applications of technology that they could use to speed up the transaction and that made them realize customers would arrive at their sites with higher expectations. And they saw first-hand how customers wander all over the retail map in unexpected ways. Next, a visit to their own competition helped uncover opportunity areas where they could improve their service at little or no additional cost and move ahead of the competition.

Beyond the basics of good training and development, a company that wants service-empowered people makes education and learning a way of life, from the first orientation session through to sharing facts about the business, then to providing continuous activities to learn about customers. This creates a team that is ready to be held account- able, take the consequences for service glitches, and share in the rewards that quality customer service brings.

Rewards and Consequences

Reward Basics

Employees thrive on recognition and reward—not pay, but recognition. Of course you must be competitive in your compensation package, but the big difference between companies with great internal morale and those with poor morale often seems to be related to the reward system. In high-morale companies, there is great pleasure in achievements, with lots of public recognition, and swift, predictable consequences for non-performance.

While designing effective reward and consequence systems takes time and effort, the important thing is that employees and manage- ment alike understand why a reward is earned or a consequence deserved. Both must be consistently applied.

Service-Empowering Rewards and Consequences

An advanced system puts the information about performance into the hands of the empowered employees. They are the first to know whether they are about to be rewarded or suffer a consequence. And they know what each will be.

When a bonus cheque is received or a reprimand given, the empowered employee is not surprised; the person knows what he or she did to get this feedback and is already planning future actions.

Rewards and consequences should be tied to outcomes that please as many different stakeholders as possible. Making sales, for instance, pleases only one stakeholder—the shareholder. Instead, ensure rewards are related to measures that matter to others—for example, an employee suggestion that benefits the customer, improves job perfor- mance, and saves the company money.

But most important of all is that service-empowered staff under- stand how the rewards and consequences are tied into the overall strategy and what can be done to affect results. This system not only is fair, but is also perceived to be fair.

IS IT SAFE TO LET GO?

When customers arrive at your business filled with anticipation that their expectations will be met, who will they find in charge of your business? Will they find employees who are in touch with customer expectations and who have the knowledge and skill to deliver an appropriate experience? When the answer is yes, it is safe to let go. With the right training and development practices, employee empowerment is the best way to ensure customer satisfaction.

About the authors

SUSAN M. O'DELL and JOAN A. PAJUNEN

Susan M. O'Dell and Joan A. Pajunen are founding partners of Service Dimensions Inc., Toronto, an international consulting firm specializing in the retail and service sectors. This article is adapted from a chapter contained in O'Dell and Pajunen's book *The Butterfly Customer: Capturing the Loyalty of Today's Elusive Consumer* (John Wiley & Sons Canada, 1997). Along with their work with major domestic and international companies, the pair are accomplished speakers and have written numerous industry articles and papers, including a best-practices study of training and development for an Ontario government report on the retail sector.

CHAPTER TWENTY-SIX

How Cross-Functional Teams Are Making Their Mark on Customer Support Centres... and the Bottom Line

Bob Parks and Alexandra Lang,
Kaset International, Tampa, FL

THE POWER OF combining several perspectives into a common focus on customer experiences almost always provides the cutting edge—even though the cross-functional teams thus created can seem at first like a double-edged blade. Because team members usually work in different "silos," their views of the world can dramatically affect their opinions of "what should be." At first, they may not even agree on who the customer is.

The experience of one insurance company clearly illustrates the dilemma—and its ultimate solution.

THE PROBLEM

Large numbers of the insurance company's customers were defecting early—often during the first year or two of coverage. The primary root cause soon became clear: poor management of customer expectations and resulting experiences.

During the underwriting cycle, underwriters collected risk information, often through the agents. Compensation for agents and underwriters was based primarily on revenue rather than profit, and their focus was often short-term.

Depending on the size of the risk, premium audits typically took place six months to a year from the time that the customer's coverage began. At that point the company would discover that the size of the risk had been underestimated. Within a few days, the unsuspecting customer would receive a rather curt notification letter from the company. The letter said not only that the insurance premiums were doubling or tripling, but also that the customer was expected to pay additional premiums for back coverage. No explanation or sympathy was offered. Needless to say, these customers often left without paying another red cent. Their expectations had been completely mismanaged.

THE STRATEGY

The insurance company pulled together a team to identify the causes of, and solutions to, customer defections in its workers' compensation business. The team began to go through the usual "forming, storming, and performing" process. The underwriter saw the independent agent as the customer, whereas the premium auditor and loss control analyst saw the insured (the end-user) as the customer. After all, underwriters dealt only with agents, whereas auditors and loss control analysts talked only with insureds.

After significant brainstorming, the team decided to focus on the insured since this customer held the purse-strings and ultimately made the decisions. The team members also decided, however, that they needed *agent participation on the team*, since the agent was a critical link in the service delivery process, and his or her service affected the ultimate customer's perspective.

THE SOLUTION

This particular team came up with recommendations that changed the way the company did business. It revised agent and underwriter incentives, and often did the premium audit at the front end. Additionally, it re-examined and redesigned communications ("moments of truth") with customers. Jargon and curt language were removed from correspondence. Letters were rewritten in customer-friendly and clearer language. Most important, the company managed customer expectations at the front end.

THE RESULT

Four years after the process started, revenues and profitability, instead of dropping each year, were restored to levels achieved before the defections started occurring. Customer defections in the first two years had been reduced by 80 percent. This is just one example of what a cross-functional team, focusing on customer experiences, can accomplish.

THE RATIONALE

Every time a customer does business with an organization, a large number of visible and not-so-visible employees are responsible for managing that experience. Picture the series of events that take place when a customer pays a bill, gets electricity turned on, buys a car, jets across the country, or buys some groceries. How many employees are involved, directly or behind the scenes, in making that a pleasant or even a value-added experience for the customer? Each one has an opportunity to enhance retention and loyalty. When all those employees are in sync, driven by a common purpose and participating in a process they have helped design, they can make a tremendous difference in customer perceptions. Customer perceptions drive customer behaviours. Customer behaviours are barometers of customer loyalty—and ultimately determine bottom-line success.

Even the slightest malfunction anywhere along the line can leave the customer with, at best, a forgettable experience and, at worst, reason to defect to a competitor. Cross-functional teams with a common focus—namely, customer satisfaction—can turn the tide. They will then have successfully broken out of their organizational silos.

A CUSTOMER-FOCUSED PROCESS FOR CROSS-FUNCTIONAL TEAMS

Many organizations have discovered a proven process that aligns divergent viewpoints, creates extraordinary customer relations, motivates employees, and boosts the bottom line. Simply put, the process is based on listening to customers, determining which improvements will make the most difference to them, and then assigning cross-functional action teams to analyze the customer concern and come up with a solution.

Identify Cycles of Service

To improve customer loyalty beyond what can be accomplished through skill training and department or unit initiatives, you need to identify processes that affect large numbers of important customers. One way to do this is to use the concept called the "cycle of service." Strategically important, high-leverage cycles can be selected by senior management as the focal point for proactively designing and managing customer experiences.

A cycle of service begins with identifying a customer need and it ends when the need is met. For example, a customer wants to obtain health coverage; a customer wants information about her policy; a customer wants to file a claim; or a customer wants to clarify a bill. In each case the customer goes through a predictable sequence of interactions or experiences (moments of truth) until that need is met.

Each moment of truth has the potential to be neutral (unmemorable), negative, or positively memorable!

Sine Qua Non: Listen to Customers

The customer's need is best identified through qualitative, transaction-based, customer feedback. This information gives teams a common focus and goal.

Once a cycle of service has been identified, transaction-based customer feedback is useful for determining the positive and negative aspects of the cycle. Asking customers to rate a recent experience numerically, then asking what went well, what didn't, and how the organization could improve the experience can yield priceless information. Simply put, that process collects customer feedback that is quantitative enough to track change, yet qualitative enough to diagnose and drive change. When they examine the data, even people who don't have direct customer contact often see the customer's influence on their area of responsibility.

Using the information from customer feedback, you can then direct and track efforts toward improvements that will make a real difference to customers, and increase their loyalty. That information also makes clear that loyalty-building customer experiences result from a cross-functional effort because those experiences are affected by *horizontal workflows*. A cursory examination of the process that supports any customer interaction makes that perfectly evident. Cross-functional process flows are, however, often ignored in strategic service-improvement planning. This happens when organizations look at processes within departments only, instead of cross-functionally across departments, and thus miss opportunities to eliminate redundancies.

Consider the following example. The customer service centre for a telephone equipment supplier wanted to improve service, so it began by collecting transaction-based customer feedback. This call centre was the primary point of contact for customers who were obtaining bids and ordering equipment.

When the customers were called and asked about recent transactions they had had with the call centre, they had plenty to say. A variety of problems emerged—problems that could not be solved in the service centre alone. For example, wrong orders were being shipped or, when they were correct, were being shipped to the wrong locations.

The root causes of some problems that customers were experiencing were not immediately apparent. Miscommunication between customer service representatives in the call centre and the pickers and packers in the warehouse seemed to occur too often. Also, some problems appeared to relate to information technology systems, but nobody knew for sure.

Get the Support of Upper Management

Let's continue with the telephone equipment supplier story. The manager of the service centre attempted to involve his peers (the warehouse manager, marketing manager, logistics manager, and IS [information systems] manager) in solving the problems. His attempts were unsuccessful because other priorities got in the way of their involvement. He was in charge of customer service, and they were not (or so they thought). And he was frustrated because he was being held accountable for the customer feedback he was collecting, yet he was unable to solve their concerns.

It wasn't until the president of the company became involved that significant cross-functional problem-solving began. Only when the operational management team realized that the problems were important to the president did they begin to act as a cross-functional management team. They began to take ownership of customer experiences —not just their organizational silos.

Efficient cross-functional problem-solving requires leadership from top management for continued organizational alignment.

Involve People Closest to the Customer and the Process

Here is an example of cross-functional problem-solving by involving the right people. A retail bank called customers who had recently visited a branch to make a deposit. The bank discovered that the most frequent complaint involved having to wait in a long line of cars at the drive-thru window. Customers would became even more frustrated when they discovered that only one of the three drive-thrus was open. Management knew this was potentially a problem of great importance, since market research had revealed that high-value customers were more than twice as likely to use the drive-thru as low-value customers.

First, a cross-functional *management* team was assigned to the problem. Team members thought the solution was obvious—open more windows. Then they decided to involve some people *at the branch level*, since these were ultimately the people who would be affected by any decision to do things differently. Now the cross-functional *action team* included several head tellers from various branches, a branch manager, an operations analyst, and a back-office branch analyst.

What they discovered was revealing. And they came up with a key solution within an hour of their first meeting. Everyone agreed that the biggest cause of the problem was that the bank had an unwritten policy of putting its least experienced tellers at the drive-thru windows. Within a week, the cross-functional management team drafted a new, written policy according to which only the most experienced tellers would work the drive-thrus. The next time they asked for customer feedback, responses indicated that the problem had been eliminated.

People who do the work, who are closest to the process, know what's going on. They could come up with great solutions, but often they aren't encouraged to come together to solve problems.

Develop a Common Language, Common Skills, and a Common Goal

A common language and set of customer-focused concepts create a common-ground foundation on which various cross-functional players can work together to make value-added improvements.

Moments of Truth

Typically, an interaction (or transaction) between your organization and a customer is a "moment of truth"—a moment in time when the customer comes into contact with your organization, either directly or indirectly. It is the moment in which customers have an opportunity to compare their actual experiences of your service with their expectations for the experience or service. Consciously or unconsciously, customers give you a report card grade on how you measured up. If you satisfied them by meeting their expectations, you get a C. If you disappointed them, you get a D or F for your effort. If you delighted or dazzled them, you get a B or maybe even an A.

These moments of truth will likely occur thousands of times each day. The outcomes of each contribute to whether your customers continue to do business with your organization or go to a competitor. Customers who have had a bad experience are reported to tell 10 to 15 people about it; those who have had a positive memorable experience tell 4 to 5 people about it. Those whose expectations were simply met don't usually tell anyone. So to maintain and build customer loyalty, you must make sure that your customers are having positive memorable experiences. This requires you to proactively manage your customers' moments of truth.

Two Kinds of Service

There are two opportunities for customers to experience moments of truth when they interact with your organization. These correspond to the following:

1. **Core Service.** Core service is what the customer is paying for—for example, an accurate policy statement; an accurate, on-time, claims settlement and payment; or an accurate bill. If the core service is perfect, you typically get the C grade; if not, you get a D or an F. It is difficult and expensive to consistently and positively surprise your customers with the core service you provide. Just keeping them satisfied is usually challenging enough. But satisfaction won't necessarily make them loyal, especially if a competitor lowers its price or creates a better mousetrap.

2. **Customer Service.** Customer service typically involves how the customer gets treated by your service providers. Poor customer service

stories abound. The "bureaucrat" is well known as the rude person who is too busy meeting his or her own needs to meet the customer's needs. In addition to the treatment received from service providers, policies and procedures also influence customer service. Being put on hold for what may seem like an eternity, having to explain the same story three times to three different people in three different functions, or being transferred around several times to get a question answered—just to fall into a black hole—are common examples of poor service. Terrific treatment by service providers can temporarily keep customers from defecting, despite occasional breakdowns in core service and policies/procedures. If those breakdowns or detractors persist, however, even the most empathetic and caring service providers will not be able to keep customers from finding other options.

Interestingly enough, about 80 percent of the *negative* things people remember about a moment of truth concern core service or policies and procedures. On the other hand, 80 percent of the *positive* things people remember relate to they way they are treated by the organization's people.

Training programs that are designed to develop individual service provider's skills and motivation to deliver dazzling customer service contribute significantly to a cross-functional team's cohesion and add value to the organization's business. Team members can be taught how to improve the quality of core service and customer service. Executives can learn concepts that increase their understanding of the strategic value of customer loyalty.

Create Strategic as Well as Action Teams

Many organizations operate in vertical silos, so ongoing cross-functional management teams can make a big difference for the customers. Cross-functional teams also change the way managers view their positions; they discover that they have responsibilities beyond their immediate silos. They realize how their decisions affect customer experiences and how these decisions are tied to overall profitability.

Often, cross-functional action teams are needed to solve a specific problem. These teams, made up of people closest to the problem all along the customer's cycle of service, may be disbanded when the problem is solved. Members can go back to their regular responsibilities or contribute their knowledge and experience to another action team.

The key is to provide all employees, at all levels, with portable skills—team and communication skills that are valuable no matter which team they are contributing to. Cross-functional team members sometimes spend considerable time learning other roles and getting to know how the other team members work. When everyone has the same skill set, much time can be saved. This leaves time to spend working on the problem at hand.

Build a Strategy for Enhancing Customer Loyalty

A Health Maintenance Organization (HMO) wanted to improve the experiences for patients who telephoned for medical advice. Frequently, those calls required follow-up and call-backs. Patients complained that the call-backs could take days. Management initially thought that the "advice nurses" could solve the problem on their own. Understandably, the advice nurses were frustrated.

Fortunately, the organization had set up a cross-functional management structure that focused on solving patient problems and improving overall patient experiences. A cross-functional action team convened for several meetings and took on the task of identifying the causes of the delays in following up with patients who had telephoned for advice. The team included an advice nurse, a physician, a member of the chart room, and an analyst from Information Services.

Several root causes were identified. The primary cause was that patient charts were often missing. And the chart was needed for follow-up, either by the nurse or by the physician. The cause of the missing charts was that they were cumbersome to sign out and physicians often neglected to do this. The solution was to convert the charts to the same scanning system that was used in the lab. In fact, the IS team member pointed out that the HMO already owned the software licence for the scanner. As a result of the cross-functional effort, no more charts were lost and overall patient follow-up improved.

CONCLUSION

The right solutions for customers and the organization frequently require cross-functional problem solving.

Customer loyalty can be the unifying focus encouraging cross-functional teams to find new ways to manage customer experiences. Customers whose service expectations are consistently exceeded are significantly more likely to remain loyal to a business. Customer loyalty results in major financial payoffs, including customer retention, customer referrals or advocacy, and add-on sales of other products and services offered by the business. In short, customer loyalty is a profit strategy, whereas customer churn (defection) is a costly way to do business.

Great things can happen for the customer when decisions that were once made by only one of the functional or departmental heads involved in the total customer experience process are now made through consensus by multifunction teams. While this change can present a significant paradigm shift for some management styles, a careful strategy can ensure that turf protection issues do not become barriers to progress.

The cross-functional ownership of each decision that affects the customer leads to choices that benefit the customer and the organization. Experience has shown that there are other benefits to this approach as well. It has the potential for enhancing interpersonal relationships, reducing bureaucracy, eliminating rework, and subsequently reducing operating costs.

About the authors

BOB PARKS and ALEXANDRA LANG

> Bob Parks is a senior consultant at Kaset International, a company that provides consulting services and training products to assist service organizations in their quest to deliver unsurpassed service quality resulting in customer loyalty. Since joining Kaset International in 1992, Bob Parks has worked in a variety of service industries, helping organizations implement transaction-driven, customer-feedback processes. He also assists organizations in using customer feedback to drive their improvement efforts.

> In addition to his work at Kaset International, Bob Parks has 10 years of experience in the insurance and financial services industry. His formal education includes an MBA in finance and marketing from the University of Chicago.

> Alexandra Lang is corporate communications manager at Kaset International, where she has been for 17 years. She has managed Kaset's quarterly customer publication *in-touch!* since 1984. She has written or contributed to articles for several external publications, and has interviewed and written about customer-focused executives in many countries. She also edits Kaset's front-line/supervisor subscription newsletter, *The Customer Service Professional.* In addition, she is responsible for public relations and management of the corporate library.

CHAPTER TWENTY-SEVEN

Leading a Customer-Focused Organization

John A. Daly, University of Texas, Austin, TX

O<small>VER THE LAST</small> 20 years, the notion that successful organizations must be customer-focused has become well accepted. Reflecting this is a plethora of books, magazine articles, and training materials outlining just what it takes to be customer-focused. A consistent strand through all this literature is the belief that customer-driven organizations need highly effective leaders. But how do great leaders create and manage successful customer-centred firms? Are there particular things the best leaders do that others might learn from?

In this chapter, we show that highly effective leadership in a customer-driven firm has some core characteristics that are consistent across types of organizations and business sectors. Obviously, a complete exposition of the characteristics of effective leaders is far beyond the confines of this chapter. But we highlight some of the main characteristics that set apart great leaders from others. As we move through these characteristics, it becomes apparent that many of the factors that define an outstanding, customer-focused leader are identical to the factors that mark a successful customer-oriented firm.

BELIEVING IN THE VALUE OF A STRONG CUSTOMER FOCUS

Strong and effective leaders deeply believe that focusing on customers is critical to the success of their organizations. This is partly because of the obvious financial returns that accrue as a function of a vibrant emphasis on customers. Numerous studies demonstrate the fiscal returns associated with long-term retention of customers.[1] Many projects also show a strong relationship between positive customer service and employee motivation: better service is associated with higher employee satisfaction and commitment. There is also considerable work demonstrating the marketing advantage of a strong customer focus: companies prefer doing business with organizations they see as customer-centred.

Leaders display this belief in the centrality of customer focus in many ways. Obviously, the leader's commitment to a mission that emphasizes the value of retaining customers is important. But effective leaders do more—they make a focus on customers part of their core personal values. They believe in it so much that it becomes part of their essence. They use a customer focus as a primary judgmental criterion for every move they make within the organization:

- They hire people who share their value for customers.
- They endorse investment strategies reflecting a customer orientation.
- They demand a strong and positive customer focus in their personal interactions.

Having a customer focus as a primary value aids the company in maintaining alignment—everyone is going in the same direction: toward maintaining outstanding customer service.

In demonstrating their focus on customers, leaders constantly remind people in the company of the centrality of their clients to the success of their organization. Executives make choices each day about what to highlight in what they say and do. Some choose to emphasize

---

[1] See J. Heskett, W.E. Sasser, and L. Schlesinger, *The Service Profit Chain: Linking Profit and Growth to Loyalty, Satisfaction, and Value* (New York: Free Press, 1997); and F. Reichheld and T. Teal, *The Loyalty Effect: The Hidden Force Behind Growth, Profits, and Lasting Value* (Cambridge, MA: Harvard Business School Press, 1996).

internal issues of budgeting, management, and planning. Others emphasize sales. But customer-focused leaders accentuate their organization's attention to customers. The importance of customers is often communicated in subtle ways. For instance, in one faltering manufacturing business, a new executive charged with turning the company around quickly changed all the artwork that filled corporate headquarters. In place of the beautiful pictures of woodlands, mountains, and beaches that used to decorate executive offices, and the large and sometimes garish travel posters that dotted employee work areas, today one finds nothing but photos of customers using the organization's products. When asked why he made this change, the executive said that there was an implicit message in the artwork. Before he got there, the message the art communicated was something akin to "I want to be somewhere else." Today the message is "Customers use our products every day—remember that what you make affects other people in meaningful ways."

DELIVERING MORE THAN OTHERS EXPECT

A traditional notion in the literature on customer focus suggests that to achieve outstanding service, organizations must exceed the expectations of clients by delivering more than is expected. The same goes for leaders—effective leaders deliver more than their various constituencies anticipate.

In delivering more, leaders have three choices: They can deliver (1) more *products,* (2) better *processes,* or (3) greater *people skills.*

1. *Product deliverables* are items such as new computers, cellular phones, and up-to-date software that help employees get their jobs done. While critical to success, solely offering product deliverables doesn't give leaders a distinctive, long-term, competitive advantage. Why? Because whatever products one person provides today, other leaders in the organization can offer tomorrow.

2. *Process deliverables* refer to activities that make the work of people easier and more efficient. Reengineering business processes, creating procedures akin to supply-chain management, and reducing bureaucratic hassles are typical examples of process deliverables. Again, though, while critical to business success, a process deliverable can be imitated by others.

3. The one class of deliverables that cannot be cloned is *people deliverables*—those distinctive personal and interpersonal skills that leaders offer and that are difficult, if not impossible, to match. Leaders offer themselves! Indeed, every characteristic of leadership described in this chapter is an example of people deliverables.

In most companies, leaders emphasize deliverables whether they are products, processes, or themselves. Some innovative leaders, however, not only try to bolster deliverables but also try to better manage expectations. When it comes to expectation management, there are three principles to consider.

First, leaders *choose* colleagues, employees, and even customers on the basis of expectations. Too often, people end up working with others who do not share common expectations. And when there is a mismatch in expectations, problems quickly emerge. Take the case of a New York-based entrepreneur. His company has grown from one employee (himself) to more than sixty in the last five years. During the growth process, he learned the value of actively choosing employees and clients. For example, in his third year he acquired a small competitor along with the competitor's five employees. He quickly discovered that three of those employees didn't share his drive, his imagination, or his work ethic. After many battles he finally found positions for the three employees outside his company. Why? Because as long as those three were around, nothing was easy. They simply had different expectations about work than he and the other employees had. He'll tell you there is nothing more torturous than having an employee who expects to work seven hours a day in an organization where everyone else expects to put in a good ten hours.

And the same principle of choosing is just as important with customers. While the maxim that the customer is always right is obviously silly, the principle that the customers you choose to do business with are always right is absolutely correct.

Second, effective leaders manage expectations by underpromising and then overdelivering. While this maxim is problematic if taken to extremes, it is valuable to remember that leaders maintain their personal and organizational credibility by seldom, if ever, overpromising. They don't make commitments to customers or colleagues that they cannot keep.

Third, rather than just being responsive to the expectations of customers and employees, great leaders often create expectations. Business leadership is about creating expectations others never imagined. CNN, the Sony Walkman, and *USA Today* are all products that were cast as failures in virtually every preliminary marketing survey. Nonetheless, leaders of those companies defied the research and created expectations for consumers that have changed the way people live. Parenthetically, when a business creates an expectation, it also has greater control over it, thus making it easier to continually deliver more.

BEING ATTENTIVE AND RESPONSIVE

Leaders pay close attention to those they work with and to their customers. The skills taught to call centre employees for use when interacting on the phone (for example, smile, be responsive, use names of customers) are just as important for leaders. Great leaders make others the palpable focus of all their attention. But attentiveness is only the first step. Leaders also need to be responsive—which doesn't mean always agreeing with people. Rather, it means working at understanding them. A critical fact is that most people want understanding far more than they want agreement. If you agree with me but don't "get it," then the agreement is cheap. On the other hand, if I know you understand me, then even your disagreement may not bother me that much. Leaders of customer-focused organizations are not in the business of agreeing; they are in the business of working toward understanding.

Two aspects of responsiveness merit special attention when it comes to customer focus. The first is how savvy leaders decide to attend to some issues and not to others. In most situations there are far too many issues to address at one time. So how does one decide which issues to attend to first? Research on customer focus shows that some leaders make use of something akin to an importance-performance matrix (see Figure 1).

On this matrix, leaders plot all the issues they think they might wish to consider along two dimensions: (1) how important that issue is, and (2) how well the organization is performing on that issue. Imagine then a line across the centre of the graph and a line drawn down the middle of the graph (the dashed lines in Figure 1). In the figure, the leader's attention ought to centre on box 1—issues that are vitally important but which are currently being performed poorly. Ineffective leaders spend too much time on items falling in the other boxes—none of which include items of pressing importance. This matrix is often used by innovative businesses to identify important opportunities for solving customer concerns. In those cases, customers' perceptions are plotted, giving the organization valuable insights into consumers' opinions of both the importance of different deliverables and the quality of those deliverables.

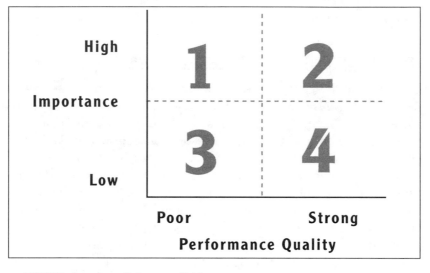

FIGURE 1: Importance-Performance Matrix

The second aspect of responsiveness on the part of leaders of successful customer-driven companies is the need to grapple with some tough challenges. Three of the most common are the following:

1. **Awareness.** How aware is the leader of people's expectations of her or him? How often does the leader seek out information from her or his various constituencies. Leaders who seldom seek information about expectations will spend enormous amounts of time, effort, and probably money offering deliverables that are unimportant to the people they are working with and for. Great leaders find numerous ways of constantly discovering expectations. One leader of a mid-size organization in the western part of the United States regularly holds sessions with employees at every level of the company, seeking their opinions and expectations. He meets with his board quarterly, but is in touch with every member of the board far more often. He constantly talks with major customers and vendors to learn of changes in their business. No wonder he is so successful!

2. **Progressiveness.** The special things you deliver today won't be special tomorrow. People never seem satisfied for a long period of time. Witness the proliferation of employee benefits, the burgeoning expectations for "free" amenities, or the constant dissatisfaction with software that is not the newest. As a consequence, savvy leaders spend a good portion of their time dreaming up something to deliver next, not resting on their laurels. An executive who can be heard uttering a refrain such as "They're never happy...They always want more" is suffering from burnout.

3. **Responsibility.** Leaders understand two key points about responsibility. First, you cannot ask others to do things they perceive you would not be willing to do if you were in their position. Too often, poor leaders are seen to expect things from their employees that the employees know the leaders would never do. In one large company, the chief executive officer went on what she called a "personal responsibility" campaign. She wanted employees to take responsibility for neatness, for timeliness and courtesy, for all the little things that make an organization work. She was smart enough to recognize that what she did herself would affect the success of her campaign. She started arriving earlier and parking in a noticeable spot. She made a special point of greeting people, wearing her name tag, and picking up trash in hallways and restrooms. Her campaign, not surprisingly, was a success; for when employees noticed she was doing the things she asked others to do, they became more willing to do those same things. Their attitudes and behaviours reflected her attitude and behaviour.

   Second, responsibility means that every employee is accountable for customer loyalty. In some businesses, the rule is simple: whoever picks up a client's call is responsible for ensuring a solution for that customer's concern. No one can pass responsibility to anyone else. This is especially true for leaders, since they assume the mantle of leadership when they assume the position.

CREATING LOYALTY AND PRIDE

Successful leaders are people others want to work for every day. They generate loyalty to themselves and their mission. In the simplest sense, leaders get others to want them to be successful—they get adopted.

Clearly, a full description of all the ways leaders generate loyalty is beyond the very limited space available in this chapter. However, we know that one thing extraordinary leaders do is build a sense of pride among their employees. Research tells us that employees' pride in their work and organization leads to better customer service, higher levels of sales, greater commitment, and generally higher morale. What creates employee pride? Some studies suggest that task pride—the pride an employee feels in working at some job—results from five variables:

1. a sense of accomplishment; a belief that what was accomplished was

2. distinctive;

3. challenging;

4. personally valued; and

5. under one's own control.

In addition, organizational pride emerges when employees feel not only proud of their tasks but also that the organization they work for has a positive public reputation. Effective leaders create work environments and public awareness that generate pride and, consequently, loyalty.

STAYING DEPENDABLE AND CONSISTENT

Research on customer focus has demonstrated the critical importance of demonstrating reliability. In some empirical work, reliability or dependability comes out as the single most important facet of outstanding service. The same goes for effective leaders of customer-focused organizations. They exemplify the reliability that they expect in their employees and in their products or services. In short, they keep their promises. One managing director of a firm in Great Britain took this notion to heart. He noted that his company offered customers ironclad guarantees for any product they purchased from the company. He noted, as well, that many internal units of his company provided "service-level" guarantees to other parts of the organization. It occurred to him that perhaps he ought to do the same—offer a personal guarantee to his employees. Devising such a guarantee took time. But in the end he emerged with a personal document that laid out those things he was committed to unconditionally. Items on the guarantee included such things as returning calls the same day, follow-up as promised, and regular meetings with his key leadership team. In discussing the process of creating this document, the managing director had some important ground rules for whatever appeared on his personal "commandments." Everything listed had to be realistic, measurable, doable, believable, and ethical.

PRACTISING GOOD COMMUNICATION

Communication is the single most important responsibility of a leader. Top executives spend upwards of 80 percent of their time talking and listening. The list of communication competencies required of a successful leader is extensive. It includes such things as listening effectively; clearly communicating messages; interviewing and asking questions in ways that generate useful information; being persuasive and influential; being good at working as a team member in meetings, as well as managing meetings; negotiating decisions; arbitrating disputes; building and maintaining relationships; selling ideas; giving speeches, briefings, and presentations; and presenting a positive impression through both verbal and nonverbal means.

One communication skill that gets less attention than perhaps it should is the ability of outstanding leaders to relate interesting, pointed, and clear stories to people within and outside their organizations. The use of narrative as a strategy for informing and influencing others has only recently begun to receive the attention it deserves. Narrative can have great impact. Stories communicate to listeners important points in ways that other forms of communication seldom do. Stories are also useful as a means of communicating personal values.

One CEO of a small, but highly successful organization proved the value of narrative by relating the experience of his first three weeks at the company. He recollected that after giving employees speech after speech about the importance of outstanding customer service, nothing much was happening. One day, he stood up at an "all-hands" meeting and starting talking, in story-like fashion, about a conversation he had recently had with a customer. He talked of the anguish the customer experienced when deliveries were late; he spoke of the embarrassment the customer faced when talking with his own customers. By turning what could have been a drab reporting of statistics into a vivid story, this executive mobilized his employees into understanding why he wanted a focus on customers.

EMPOWERING AND DELEGATING

Effective leaders are willing and able to delegate important tasks to others. Why is delegation so important? Here are three reasons. First, the workload that leaders face is immense. There simply is not enough time to get all the work done. Second, the tasks are becoming increasingly complex. Leaders cannot be competent at every aspect of their organization. Third, delegating and empowering others is the only way leaders can train others to take on roles that will allow for easy succession.

If delegation is so important, why isn't it done well in many organizations? Often it is because leaders want to maintain total control. They believe that by delegating, they are sacrificing control. In fact, just the opposite is true. You gain control by giving it up. By allowing others to perform some tasks, the leader gains the time to manage other tasks and explore new responsibilities. Spending too much time managing downwards limits the amount of time one has to manage upwards. Or in some cases, leaders don't delegate and empower others because they don't know how to do so effectively.

While this chapter is not about delegation, some critical ground rules are worth looking at here. First, delegate outcomes, not processes. There are many different ways to accomplish a task, and the effective leader tries to let the people he or she has empowered find their own way to an agreed outcome. Overmanaging the process drives people crazy if they've been given the responsibility of achieving a task. Second, good leaders delegate some things they like to do. This sounds counter-intuitive. Shouldn't they delegate tasks they hate? No! Why? Because if a person doesn't like to engage in those activities, why would he or she expect others to like them? Indeed, the effective leader often delegates tasks he or she really likes. The consequence is that the people working for the leader come to like those same things that attracted the leader to the job. Third, delegate an entire activity, not part of it. When leaders assign only portions of the task, employees are not well motivated to do them. Employees who are responsible for the entire task often have a much stronger commitment.

In the realm of customer service, it is essential to delegate responsibility to, and empower, representatives. No leader will be able to interact with every customer every time. Moreover, leaders often don't understand the issues customers raise as well as employees do, since the latter are generally much closer to the end-user. And clients want to talk to people who have authority (thus empowerment), but don't want to go through the hurdles that often arise in getting to the leader.

Clearly, this brief description of some of the major personal characteristics of leaders in customer-driven organizations is limited. Many other skills and competencies are important—business acumen, strategic thinking, marketing skills, financial and accounting competencies, to name but a few. But the goal of this chapter was to identify some of the critical personal characteristics of leaders. And even a cursory review of these features reveals that organizations reflect their leaders. All the attributes associated with leaders described here are also characteristics of customer-focused organizations. Leadership is work. And to lead a customer-centred organization requires the same sorts of skills that an organization requires to be successful.

About the author

JOHN A. DALY

John Daly is Carter Professor of Communication and Management at the University of Texas at Austin. He is president-elect of the National Communication Association and recently completed a term on the board of directors of the International Customer Service Association. Author of more than 90 scholarly articles and four books, he has consulted with over 100 major public and private organizations on topics related to bolstering customer loyalty. The companies he has worked with include 3M, IBM, Apple Computer, Marriott, Continental Airlines, Merrill Lynch, Consolidated Edison, State Farm, Dun & Bradstreet, Halliburton, and a wide variety of U.S. federal organizations, including the White House.

CHAPTER TWENTY-EIGHT

Using Qualitative Performance Measurement to Achieve Performance Improvement

Jack A. Green,
Entretel Incorporated, Oakville, ON

QUALITATIVE VS. QUANTITATIVE MEASURING

Performance measurement in call centres is often limited to the numerical data collected by the automatic call distributor (ACD), such as average call time, number of calls taken, and time in queue. Where sales is an element of the job, measurement of "conversion rate" (percentage of inbound calls that result in sales) or sales volume may become part of the performance measurement mix. The advantage of using these numbers as a performance measurement tool is the ease with which they can be collected and their apparent total objectivity— they are untouched by human hands so the "numbers can't lie."

These measures are, by themselves, an inadequate indicator of success for a call centre. (I'll call these measures "quantitative" because of the objective manner in which the numbers are tallied, as opposed to "qualitative" measures that assess the quality of the customer interaction.) They do not measure some elements that are critical for success (for example, Was the correct information given? or, Was the customer handled effectively?), and they are inexact calibrators for the dimensions they purport to assess. These numbers fail, for example, to interpret why average call time is excessive for a particular employee—and thus fail to indicate how the employee could improve call handling time or how to increase the number of sales if the conversion rate is too low.

Since the quantitative numbers also fail to measure the quality of the calls handled by individual staff members, feedback on performance quality is typically based upon "tips" (usually on what not to do) provided by a supervisor who has overheard a telephone conversation. Even when the supervisor monitors both sides of the conversation, one problem with this type of feedback is that it is subjective and therefore open to interpretation and debate. It also places ownership of the staff member's performance with the supervisor, who provides a report card on a sampling of overheard calls. True ownership requires that the person who has responsibility for his or her performance also has the wherewithal to assess where improvement is needed and take corrective action—that is, the ability to affect performance. So ownership of staff members' performances should more appropriately belong to the people who "hear" each and every call made—the staff members themselves. Quantitative measures of performance don't offer the staff member enough information to take ownership; however, effective qualitative measures, along with procedures for continuous assessment, do.

Incorporating qualitative performance standards in the mix of performance-assessment tools can compensate for the inefficiencies of assessing performance assessment solely according to quantitative tools. Objective, assessable standards can also be the basis for the following:

- Analyzing training needs, designing a training program, and assessing the success of a training initiative.

- Establishing a relationship between performance level and reward system ("pay for performance" system), and providing a road-map for employees who wish to improve performance and reap greater rewards.

- Creating a structured coaching program that can help coaches focus on behavioural areas that will result in improved results (effectively established and communicated qualitative standards can even allow for self- and peer-coaching programs, freeing up valuable supervisory time).

- Assessing staff suitability for the call centre position, identifying those who are not making the grade, and clearly communicating why they are not making it.

- Screening prospective new employees.

- Establishing internal job levels or tiers for creation of an internal career path.

TEN-STEP PROCESS FOR ESTABLISHING QUALITA-TIVE TELEPHONE PERFORMANCE STANDARDS

When you set formal qualitative performance standards, it is critical to ensure that they are relevant to effective performance of the job, can be objectively assessed, and are "bought into" by the call centre staff. Here are some of the steps to take in establishing such standards.

Step 1: Create the team.

The first step is to form a team that will have responsibility for creating the performance standards. Ideally, the team should include representatives of front-line staff. This encourages the staff to buy in and increases the likelihood that the standards selected will be valid ingredients of effective job performance.

Step 2: Determine success factors.

The team establishes the set of criteria that lead to the success of each call (and that the staff members can control). The criteria are based on the organization's mission statement, department service objectives, customer and industry surveys, and sales targets. The process may involve auditing a number of taped calls to determine what behaviours contribute to a successful call. This brainstormed list is then massaged into a workable number of key *success factors* (generally fewer than 25, although some teams initially start out ambitiously with more—until the call-assessment process is found to be too cumbersome). Typically included in this list are items such as effective listening, effective questioning, effective tone of voice (empathy, professionalism, confidence), effective greeting, effective closing, and using the caller's name.

Step 3: Break each success factor into its components.

For each success factor, the team then determines which behaviours contribute to or detract from successful performance. For example, for "effective listening" the list may include the following:

• Representative does not re-ask for information provided earlier in the call.

- Representative acknowledges receiving or understanding information provided or questions asked.

- Representative gives varied listening responses (for example, "Yes," "I understand," "okay," "I see").

- Representative gives answers that fit the question asked.

- Representative practises "active listening" techniques—that is, summarizes, paraphrases, repeats.

- Representative does not interrupt the caller or mentally drift away from the conversation.

Step 4: Establish a scoring system.

A scoring system must be created. A Yes or No assessment of whether the target behaviour did or did not happen on a particular call is often seen as the simplest way to rate performance. This may be appropriate in some cases (for example, "Did the rep confirm the caller's account number?"). A problem with this scoring system is that it doesn't acknowledge improvement in performance, only perfection. Most organizations intend the qualitative performance standards to form the basis for coaching and motivation as well, so opt for a scoring system that identifies levels of effectiveness in performing a key success factor.

For most factors, a scoring system offering four levels of performance rating is preferable. For example:

Effective use of "hold." Use the hold feature when leaving the call for any reason. Explain why the hold is necessary; provide the alternative of a call-back (as appropriate); ask permission to hold (and provide the opportunity for the caller to respond); check back after 30 seconds; thank or apologize after the hold period.

The Levels of Performance are:

1. Three or more parts of the above were missing when the call required them.

2. Two of the above parts were missing when the call required them.

3. One of the above parts was missing when the call required it.

4. All the above parts were included when the call required them.

Step 5: Determine the criteria for each score.

For each success factor, the team determines which components (Step 3) will determine each scoring level (being either included or excluded from the call). The challenge here is to make these as objective and observable as possible and to optimize reliability—that is, the consistency with which two people's assessment of the same factor on the same call will result in the same rating. Where objectivity is not attainable, "consistent subjectivity" can be accomplished by having rating staff agree upon examples that satisfy each scoring level, then working to become consistent at assessing calls against these examples. This might be appropriate if an organization chose, for example, to assess tone for the degree of empathy, friendliness, or professionalism.

Staff should periodically compare assessments of the same call to identify any drift from consistent subjectivity. Once identified, this drift can be remedied by having teams assess a number of calls and discuss their assessments, until consistency is again reached. Accept that 100 percent consensual reliability is an unreachable goal, and take care not to become bogged down at this step. In one organization, none of the 150 telephone-based staff were receiving feedback three months after implementation of the assessment process because management could not agree on what constituted a score of 2 and a score of 3 on one standard. While this debate raged on, many staff were scoring 1's or 2's on a number of standards without benefiting from feedback on how their behaviour was negatively affecting the company's customers!

Step 6: Run a test trial of the standards.

Once standards have been calibrated with observable levels and corresponding scores, and once the organization has determined the level that staff are expected to score on each, the "success factors" can be considered "performance standards." The next step is to test the system using a taped sample of calls made or received by a target group of staff. Each call is then debriefed, or discussed with the person who made it. The standards, or the criteria for establishing scores for each level within the standard, can thereby be reviewed and fine-tuned as necessary.

Step 7: Communicate the standards.

Communicating the standards to the rest of the staff must include the "what" of each standard as well as the "why" and the "how" for achieving the standard. Focused training is required at this stage and should allow the staff members to practise each standard and assess their level of performance on each. If the standards are well designed, trainees will be able to determine, on the basis of their practice (role play) and assessment ("How am I doing on this standard now?") exactly what needs to be done to improve their score and performance.

Step 8: Coach performance vis-à-vis the standards.

Once the standards have been appropriately communicated, staff members will be capable of listening to tape recordings of their own calls and identifying where their performance falls short of target. For perceived fairness, staff should be given the opportunity to align their performance with the standards before formal assessment. Therefore, as the next step in implementing a set of qualitative standards, staff members must have the opportunity to practise the standards, listen to their own taped calls, assess their performance and performance improvement needs, and receive coaching.

Step 9: Formally assess performance: the audit.

The first step in formally assessing qualitative performance is to establish a system for taping calls, ideally without the staff members knowing which calls are being taped. Then, based upon predetermined criteria for call selection (the call should be a minimum length, not just a "sorry, wrong number" call) and a system of randomized call selection, the calls for the audit are selected. Performance on the calls are then assessed using the qualitative performance standards. For perceived fairness, it may be advisable to have periodic informal audits done for coaching purposes by internal staff, and the formal audits conducted by an objective third party.

Step 10: Use the audit results.

The benefit of establishing performance quality measures is not just to collect another new set of numbers, but in how these numbers are used. Some of the uses are outlined below.

- If the standards have been established to **assess training** effectiveness, the results of this assessment will be compared with a pre-training assessment of a sample of taped calls (collected before training and the process of establishing standards were begun).

- If the purpose is to rate higher and lower performers for **reward** purposes, then the opportunity for coaching and periodic reassessment must be made available. The reward system that is established must be communicated in advance and the connection with performance should be logical and perceived as fair.

- If the purpose is to support **performance improvement** and to provide staff with a road-map for achieving the quantitative results (such as higher sales), the results must become part of a pre-established system of feedback and coaching.

- If the standards are to be used to objectively **assess suitability** of current staff for the call centre job, the organization must determine whether to allow the opportunity for coaching and then base the decision on a post-coaching reassessment.

- If the standards are to be used to **screen newly hired employees**, the levels of achievement expected for those beginning the call centre job must be set, and a telephone screening process designed. Then a telephone screening interview to assess applicant performance against those standards is conducted.

- If the qualitative standards are part of the **establishment of job levels** within the call centre, for career pathing purposes, the qualitative performance requirements for each job level must be set. The qualitative standards must then be incorporated with other job level standards such as product and technical knowledge, and written performance or coaching skills.

Whatever the purpose, it is critical that the results of the measurement process be used. If the results are not used, the value of the process is negligible, and there is no point to collecting the numbers.

SEEING THE PROCESS IN ACTION

This process has been successful in creating usable qualitative standards in a number of organizations in a range of industries. One, a charitable organization that we will call "Christian Charity Canada," implemented a set of qualitative performance standards in 1996.

The Objectives of Christian Charity Canada

Christian Charity Canada, a division of an international Christian charitable organization, began in 1996 to position its call centre technologically to track and analyze its extensive donor market. To optimize donor retention and satisfy the changing needs of this "client base," it was considered necessary to upgrade its call centre's professional staff. Christian Charity Canada recognized that as society and markets evolve, organizations that plan to enjoy continued success must move with them. And with donor and potential donor expectations and motivations changing as well, the management at Christian Charity Canada believed that its charitable mandate was too important not to keep up with the changing times.

The first phase of the change process involved determining donor expectations, defining current levels of service delivery in relation to those expectations, and determining what Christian Charity needed to do to meet and exceed donor expectations. Then, conducting a gap analysis, the organization determined what, specifically, needed to be done to reach its goal. As part of the process, the organization redesigned the Donor Service team system to increase its ability to respond to donors' focused information requirements. Christian Charity also re-established quantitative performance standards based on adjusted expectations of what could be accomplished in each donor telephone interaction (in addition to standards such as average call time, this included dollar standards for areas such as delinquency calls or renewals).

Improving the qualitative performance of staff interactions with donors was considered critical. Christian Charity planned to accomplish this by setting qualitative standards, establishing processes to assess and sustain these standards, and training staff to perform to these standards. Christian Charity also wanted to ensure that the staff on the phones (for whom the main hiring assessment criteria had been a willingness to do the job and willingness to work the shifts) were able to perform at a level compatible with the organization's objective of improved service standards. The qualitative standards were then to be used as a performance tool for assessing staff suitability in the new environment. These are the steps Christian Charity took:

1. Creating the team. The team established to set the standards included supervisory staff, call centre managers, training staff, and human resource department staff. Most of the supervisory and training staff were recently promoted "from the trenches;" all worked closely with the front-line staff, so all had a strong sense of how calls were handled and what constituted a successful call.

2. Determining success factors. The team analyzed audio tapes of the various types of calls received or made by the two target departments, Telephone Operations and Donor Services, to assess what was happening qualitatively to meet donor expectations and to find the gaps between telephone performance and donor or caller expectations. They developed a list of the success factors necessary for meeting the donor expectations. This process was facilitated by an external consultant, who, among other things, supplied a template of success factors from which the team evolved its own list. Success criteria for Christian Charity included the following:

- "warm" transfers and reception
- use of hold
- use of caller's name
- call control skills
- value-added close
- avoidance of "dead air"
- providing an appropriate Christian message
- use of empathy
- explaining service steps
- "advocacy"—highlighting the positive
- extending oneself when the opportunity arose
- "selling" Christian Charity versus simply providing information

The taped calls used in this analysis were selected according to a randomization system and kept for a later audit. These would eventually constitute a base line against which performance improvement could be measured. Because qualitative standards had yet to be established, as well as communicated, the plan was to measure the performance of the team as opposed to scoring individuals (once the standards were set and communicated, assessing and reporting individual performance were legitimized).

3. Breaking each success factor into its components. Based upon their analysis, the team members were able to assess what behaviours contributed to and detracted from expected performance on each of the success factors.

4. Establishing a scoring system. Initially, the Christian Charity team members considered that a Yes/No rating system would be easier to use as a basis for call assessment. Then they conducted Steps 5 and 6 of the standard-setting process. Step 5, determining the criteria for each score, resulted in Yes being perfect performance on the success factor, and No being anything less. When Step 6, the running of a test trial, was conducted, the team encountered problems with the Yes/No system: the strict interpretation of the standard resulted in a low range in distribution of scores (for most standards, everyone scored No), yet to set the Yes threshold at less than perfect removed the objectivity of the system and legitimized mediocre or less than ideal performance. The potential demotivating effect of a system in which everyone scored very low was also a consideration. So the team decided that for most success factors, a four-level rating scale would be used.

The team also set some mandatory standards. Others were given a weighting, so that when all the scores were added up to form an overall rating of the call, the scores on those standards were doubled. Thus a high score on one of those standards had an increased positive effect on the overall score and a low score on a weighted standard had an increased lowering effect. The areas weighted were those considered critical for call success, but which were weaker in Christian Charity's call centre than the team preferred. Examples of weighted standards were "giving relevant pertinent and accurate information" and "clear enunciation."

5. Determining the criteria for each score. With four levels for most standards, determining criteria for each level became more complex and thus demanded more time than the establishment of a Yes/No system that rated performance on a standard as "perfect" or "anything less than perfect." For some criteria, clean objectivity was not achievable and "consistent subjectivity" became the goal. To accomplish this, two staff were assigned as the designated listeners who had final say on the rating of the calls. Concurrence and consistency on the more subjective ratings (and there were only a couple of these) would be easier with only two people.

6. Running a test trial of the standards. At this step, some differences in interpretation were identified. Some raters assessed some items more leniently than others, so criteria were made a little more explicit.

7. Communicating the standards. A training program was designed to communicate the standards. It included components of the following:

- Providing opportunities for participants to practise.
- Teaching participants how to rate themselves on each standard.
- Providing opportunities for participants to listen to their taped practice calls to assess how they were performing vis-à-vis the standards.
- Supporting the participants in their action plans for improvement.
- Making taping equipment available after training so participants could manage their own skill-improvement and -maintenance process.

8. Coaching performance vis-à-vis the standards: Supervisors/coaches at Christian Charity were trained to coach staff, using tapes of actual calls. The coaches conducted internal, informal audits, and the results were used for feedback and coaching. This was in addition to providing the opportunity to staff members to tape their own calls and assess their performance (peer assessments were encouraged as well). Staff were aware that all this would culminate in an externally conducted, formal assessment of a random selection of their calls.

9. Formally assessing performance—the audit. Three months after the performance standards had been communicated and the coaching had begun, calls for each employee were randomly selected and an audit was conducted. Overall scores on each standard were compared with the results of an analysis of the calls done before the standards had been set, and individual scores achieved on the post-training audit were reported. Detailed scoring sheets with the auditor's comments were provided as were the tapes of the calls upon which the audit was based. These were used for feedback to the staff and for coaching purposes.

10. Using the audit results. The results of the audit had multiple purposes.

- Supervisory staff used the results for coaching purposes and to confirm that performance had improved substantially.

- The effectiveness of the training program was assessed, and areas for remedial training were ascertained. Christian Charity training staff were trained to deliver the qualitative skills training program and were able to select and deliver those parts of the program that needed to be reviewed with the staff.

- Staff who were less effective were counselled and moved into positions that involved more database management and administration, positions with significantly less telephone contact with clients. In addition, a plan to merge two departments (a telephone-based group and a data-entry group) and have them do one another's jobs was aborted, partly as a result of the data-entry group's consistently low performance on the standards.

- As new call centre staff are hired, they are interviewed over the telephone and the standards are used as part of the assessment process.

The Christian Charity's setting of qualitative standards resulted in a process to communicate to staff very specifically what the organization's performance expectations were, to show staff how to achieve the quantitative results the organization had set as targets, and to provide support and assistance in assessing and coaching staff to create a world-class call centre.

These results can be attained by any organization willing to commit to the process of developing a set of qualitative performance standards. The call centre job is unique in that every aspect of it can be measured, so performance can be optimized. It is a shame to waste the opportunity by not measuring and coaching for improved call quality.

About the author

JACK A. GREEN

Jack A. Green is the director of Entretel Incorporated, a call centre performance management consulting organization based in Oakville, Ontario. Jack Green has an MBA from York University, BA Honours from the University of Guelph, and various teaching and counselling certifications. He has written and co-written articles for a number of periodicals, such as *TeleMarketing Magazine, Sales and Marketing Magazine, Canadian Banker,* and *HR Reporter.* He is sought after as a speaker at call centre conferences across North America.

CHAPTER TWENTY-NINE

The Role of the Knowledge Worker in Customer Care

Sandip Patel, Coopers & Lybrand, Boston, MA

WHAT IS "KNOWLEDGE" AND WHY SHOULD YOU CARE?

In today's information economy, a knowledge era is fast emerging, and as organizations transform themselves to become more competitive, the challenges required to achieve success have also changed. The focus of these challenges has shifted from cost reduction alone to growth and globalization. The knowledge economy requires the recognition and leverage of an organization's intellectual capital to gain competitive advantage. Broadly speaking, intellectual capital is not limited to patents and other R&D assets; it includes the collective experience, competence, and customer relationships of an organization's employees that are used to move the organization toward its strategic goals.

In other words, this intellectual capital, or knowledge, is not just information. It is the context-specific awareness of what is possible, how to do it, and when it is appropriate to do so. It pertains to the tacit knowledge in the minds of the workers and is based on experience and expertise. Having this knowledge is often what distinguishes superior from mediocre performers. Such knowledge, when used in the right context, creates value for the enterprise, value which is shared and used to exceed performance targets. The Gottlieb Duttweiler Foundation, a Swiss think tank, has estimated that organizations use only 20 percent of available intellectual capital on a day-to-day basis.

In service-oriented companies, customer service is an important element of growth, much talked about and considered very important, but not used to exploit the intellectual capital, or knowledge about the customer, that can be captured and leveraged from employees' experiences and interactions with the customer. For example, the marshalling of knowledge into actionable information has helped Skandia thrive in newly deregulated insurance and financial markets around the globe. In fact, the company has leveraged its knowledge of effective processes and best practices to develop structural assets—manuals, software, and other resources—that can be customized to meet the needs of brokers in all markets. Specifically, Skandia believes that its market value is driven by both its intellectual capital and its financial capital. Intellectual capital, in this context, is derived from the organization's processes and infrastructure: employees' capabilities, relationships, reputations with customers, and their power to innovate. In order to measure and grow intellectual capital, Skandia focuses on four areas that help to balance investments and contribute to sustainable growth:

1. **Customers:** the perspective of the business from the point of view of customers and markets.

2. **Processes:** the profile of the internal excellence of operations (for example, productivity, efficiency, effectiveness).

3. **Employees:** the individual and combined competence and capabilities of employees.

4. **Renewal and development:** the capability to recycle concepts in new markets or create a new concept in a mature market to capture a valued position.

Skandia uses this strategic model to identify the driving forces in its operating environment and create new opportunities while still managing to refine existing operations. This model ensures that every "knowledge worker" in the organization focuses on priorities that are of strategic importance to the organization.

As organizations transform their customer care operations today, leveraging intellectual and experiential capital on a continuous basis is critical to creating and sustaining a customer focus and superior service standards. To succeed in this, workflows and technology must facilitate the capture and dissemination of knowledge, as well as collaboration and learning among employees. This connotes a new role for employees of the organization in leveraging context-specific knowledge to deliver value to their customers. The role shifts from operating as a processor and communicator of information to a user of knowledge. The new role requires the employee to have the competence of identifying, collecting, and using context-specific knowledge—implicit and explicit—to add value to every customer interaction.

Depending on the organization and the nature of its business, different categories of knowledge may exist that are germane to the effectiveness and quality of service delivery. For example, Figure 1 illustrates a high-level knowledge architecture for an insurance company. It is not enough to identify the specific knowledge needs to establish a customer-focused organization—the infrastructure (process, measures, culture, and technology) required to effectively leverage such knowledge is critical to add value to customer interactions.

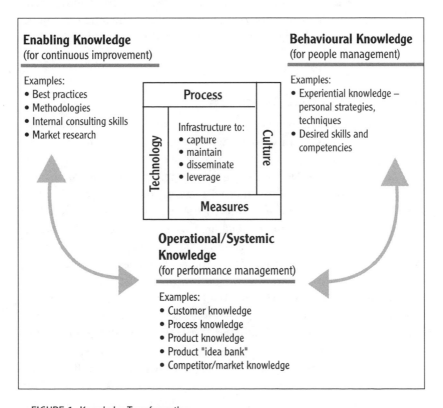

FIGURE 1: Knowledge Transformation

The U.S. Department of Labor estimates that by the year 2000 at least 44 percent of all workers will be employed in data services, for example, in gathering, processing, retrieving, or analyzing information. This will mean a fundamental change for many organizations. The ability of an organization to transform, share, and leverage information and intellectual/experiential assets into enduring value for an organization's customers and its people is what we term "knowledge management." Coopers & Lybrand Consulting (C&L) studied 10 companies that were known for best practices in knowledge management. The study showed that the purpose behind the knowledge management efforts of the companies could be broken down as follows: customer intimacy, 40 percent; operational excellence, 40 percent; and innovation, the remaining 20 percent. One of the key challenges these organizations faced was determining how and where to get started. The basis of determining the focus and starting point for knowledge management was looking at how their business made money, what knowledge was needed to do that better, and which things they could do first for immediate business benefit.

THE KNOWLEDGE WORKER

We have developed and successfully applied the concept of knowledge-based process design in working with organizations to redesign their customer care operations. The basic premise of this concept is that in any customer care environment, there are service representatives who are distinctly superior performers, who win accolades for excellent customer service, and who are "loved" by the customers they assist. These representatives are the true knowledge workers in the organization and stand out as model service providers, in spite of similar training, manuals, and information available to their colleagues. We have determined that each of these individuals is a better performer through a combination of experiential knowledge, personal strategy, mind-set, personality, and behavioural competencies. Our work has focused on making these knowledge dimensions explicit and applying them to the design of workflow, training, and support systems for customer care. These knowledge dimensions vary across industries, as well as across businesses within the same industry, depending on the business strategy of the company. Technology must be effectively applied to assist in the execution of business strategy and create value for the enterprise.

Understanding the role of knowledge in process and competency design and using technology to execute such designs have enhanced customer care functions.

In our work with service organizations, we have found that tacit knowledge in the mind of a customer service representative is an important driver of the quality of service. This knowledge dimension is often not considered in designing customer care processes and is very difficult to codify and incorporate in the service delivery process. Such tacit knowledge includes

- A solid understanding of the service dimensions and the service value chain.

- Recognition of the moments of truth and how customer perceptions are moulded.

- Knowing the individual customer—the drivers of loyalty, the points of intimidation, what that customer really cares about, where the customer fits in the needs cycle, and what drives that customer's questions.

- The ability to stay with the customer's agenda, to elicit the appropriate information, and to make a lasting impression in the mind of the customer.

Customer Call Centre in a Financial Services Company

Coopers & Lybrand Consulting recently assisted a life insurance company with the consolidation of all its customer service centres into a centralized service organization at the head office to establish consistent service quality, facilitate cross-selling at each point of customer interaction, and gain cost efficiencies. The consolidation has been very successful, with significant operational efficiencies and a workflow that supports a "one stop" service for customer calls. The project team consisted of a cross-functional team of service representatives, facilitated by C&L consultants. This process of participative work design resulted in the service representatives internalizing the process of continuous learning and improvement to create, assimilate, and proliferate their work processes. An important outcome of the process redesign project was the definition of the information requirements for the design of a customer service workstation as a performance support tool for the service professionals.

At the end of the project, the review and feedback indicated that there was a lot of knowledge in people's heads that never made it into the workstation. It was clear that notwithstanding the availability of performance support tools and tenure of employment, some service professionals had an inherent competency that made them better than others. This competency also enabled some service professionals to adapt to and internalize the new service paradigm quicker than others. In a customer service organization, routine processing is ideal, but changes in products and customer needs are frequent, if not strategic; therefore, continuous learning becomes essential. The leadership was quick to recognize that it was the ability to continuously learn and internalize that made exemplary service professionals. An effort was launched to understand this knowledge dimension and establish performance profiles and knowledge-sharing practices that were critical for delivering sustainable quality customer service. The results led to a better understanding of the desired competency profile for the service professional of the redesigned service organization, the development of a training and hiring strategy, and recommendations for enhancements to the customer service workstation. The results can be summarized as follows:

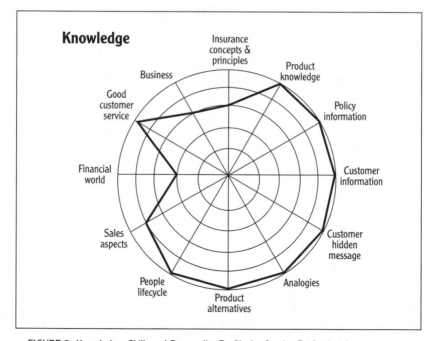

FIGURE 2: Knowledge, Skill, and Personality Profile for Service Professionals.

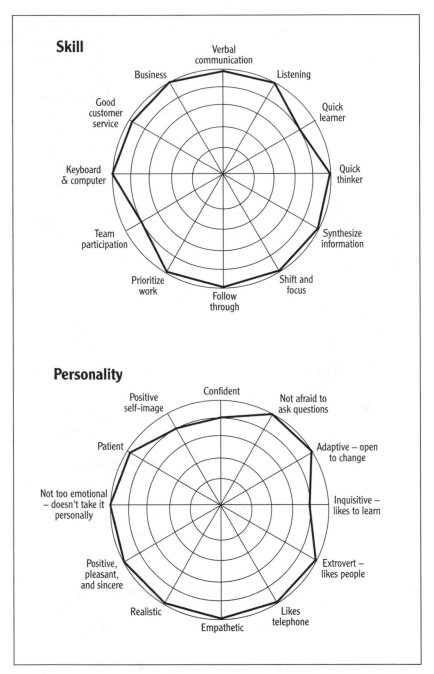

FIGURE 2: Knowledge, Skill, and Personality Profiles for Service Professionals, continued

- There were specific skills, knowledge, and behavioural competencies that differentiated the superior service professionals. A set of composite profiles for knowledge, skill, and personality are illustrated in Figure 2.

- In the daily conduct of work, service professionals improvised and internalized personal strategies to deliver quality service. For example, the more experienced service professionals performed a mental task of "identifying the customer's hidden message" soon after starting to

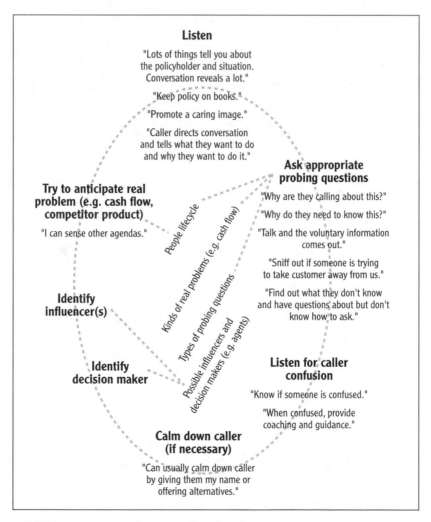

FIGURE 3: Identifying the Customer's Hidden Message

speak with the customer. This task involved little or no formal or documented information, but relied heavily on experiential knowledge. Figure 3 illustrates the activities and forms of information/knowledge used by more experienced service professionals to gain a better understanding of the customer's need before attempting to respond to a query. It is interesting to note that the representative does not rely on formal reference material or manuals for this critical activity in responding to a customer call.

- No formal mechanism existed to share, across the service organization, the experiences, knowledge, and informal practices that had proved to be effective in leaving a positive impression on the customer—for example, in some instances resulting in the service representative persuading or educating the customer to invest in a product better aligned to his or her investment goals, rather than surrendering the insurance policy. This is a particularly important quality for a service representative in a financial services company to have and is a combination of his or her skill at understanding the customer's situation, gaining the customer's trust, and providing advice that the customer can act on.

    Sharing occurred inconsistently through informal networks. Employees were being rewarded for hoarding knowledge and information. As a result of these findings, a regular knowledge-sharing process among the customer service professionals was introduced. Every two weeks, service professionals met as a team, facilitated by a moderator, to share their specific experiences with customers and determine which of these merited an entry into the "CSR Playbook." The playbook was a repository of shared experiences and personal approaches to undocumented customer situations that were germane to customer service delivery.

- Although the training was predominantly product-based, the service professionals did not need thorough product knowledge to respond to customer queries.

    The company then merged all its asset-accumulation businesses into a single retirement planning financial services business. It formed an entirely new service organization for this business, encompassing all its products. And the basic knowledge profiles and principles of knowledge-sharing developed earlier were applied to implement a consolidated customer service design delivered by multiproduct, cross-functional service teams. This case example highlights the importance of understanding and leveraging the informal practices and experiential knowledge to improve customer service organizations. And as customer care becomes the predominant competitive differentiator for companies, knowledge workers will make the difference in developing successful customer-focused organizations.

Technical Sales and Service Support in a Brokerage Firm

Knowledge is not static; it grows. Knowledge must be managed to serve as organizational memory. Although the expertise of the knowledge worker plays an important role in the quality of delivering knowledge-intensive services, it involves a period over which this knowledge matures and becomes institutionalized in the organization. According to E. Jeffrey Conklin, Ph.D,[1] knowledge workers are the scarce resource in the knowledge economy, moving freely within and between organizations. This fluidity presents the challenge of developing and sustaining an organizational memory that extends and amplifies the knowledge asset by capturing, organizing, disseminating, and reusing the knowledge created by its employees.

This concept is illustrated in a knowledge-based work design effort at a brokerage firm that operated an internal "hotlines" group—a group of representatives located in their central head office who served as the sales and service support for their 150+ sales offices. The entire field office network relied heavily on this group and called in with questions ranging from clarification about forms and policies to complicated product issues. The group perceived itself to be the lifeblood of the field sales organization and worked hard to avoid turning away even one unanswered question. The hotlines service professionals had established among themselves a knowledge-sharing culture that relied on an informal, ad hoc communications network to answer the stream of questions flowing through the unit. In addition, these service professionals had assumed the responsibility for answering technical product questions, which, in some cases, they were not certified or qualified to answer. This exposed the company to compliance risk.

---

[1] *Designing Organizational Memory: Preserving Intellectual Assets in a Knowledge Economy.* Austin, Texas: Corporate Memory Systems Inc., 1996.

An assessment of the representatives in this group identified the dimensions of their work that made them successful:

- They had developed an effective way of understanding and categorizing the caller's need.

- They had developed ways to work around system inefficiencies and organizational constraints to provide answers to incoming queries. By analyzing the workflow, "workarounds," and informal practices, the company was able to enhance systems to incorporate compliance controls and provide performance support tools to the hotlines service professionals.

- The learning curve to become an "expert" was three years. Discovering this fact was a major benefit resulting from this project. It was used to develop a content-rich training and mentoring program for service professionals in this area.

Underwriting Service Support in an Insurance Company

A company decided to reengineer its core underwriting process in order to substantially improve the process and underlying IT systems. Its goal was to achieve efficiencies in the core underwriting processes through introducing a team-based design supported by collaborative work processes and groupware technology. The company also launched the development of new information systems for underwriting, billing, and issue operations. The workflow design for both initiatives incorporated control points, information needs and flow, and role definitions.

The effective and timely sharing of knowledge between the underwriters, or the knowledge workers, was taken into account in the design of an efficient workflow. Another major constraint included the perceptions and behaviours of the people involved in the process, particularly the support staff who were called on to perform simple underwriting or diligent screening of applications prior to underwriting. These staff members had been hired predominantly as data processors and had little or no understanding of the service value chain and their role in creating value for the customer. But the company realized that having a new process and system was not enough; the employees required the right mind-set—seeing themselves merely as "processors" would never work. Their roles were transformed from untrained, reactive positions to highly trained, proactive positions.

And the people filling these positions now felt much more satisfied and happy in their work. As one observer commented on one person in that situation: "She's learning and she wants to learn…and the people in our office will take the time to teach us, which is really good."

THE ROLE OF INFORMATION TECHNOLOGY

What seems to be fairly clear in concept poses challenges in practice. The ability to capture and effectively spread an organization's intellectual capital among its employees can create significant value for the enterprise—especially if such knowledge is made available as context-relevant information to a knowledge worker. The value of leveraging knowledge lies in the potential to codify and share successful mental models, expertise, and experiences for delivering superior service to customers and gaining competitive advantage.

IT strategists play an important role in identifying the domains of relevant knowledge, establishing mechanisms to capture the knowledge during the daily conduct of work, and designing an architecture (technology and process) to efficiently share such knowledge for creating value.

SUMMARY

Knowledge is a valuable organizational asset and is the daily currency of a company's knowledge workers, in whose minds that knowledge is primarily resident. The challenge of companies is to understand the role of knowledge in delivering exemplary service and leverage it in the design of customer service delivery processes. The examples in this chapter have demonstrated that there is a real and immediate benefit to doing so.

The notion of leveraging knowledge workers to become more customer-focused, with the ultimate goal of increasing shareholder value, underscores the demise of the old paradigm of "processing" jobs in the service value chain. Every service professional in the organization must understand the knowledge, skills, and competency that he or she possesses and how it can contribute to delivering quality service to customers. Conklin, in the book referred to earlier, summarizes the challenge for the knowledge worker: "The basis of the new economy is knowledge work, and the workhorse of this economy is the knowledge worker. He or she has a strong formal education, has learned how to learn, and has the habit of continuing to learn throughout his or her lifetime. The knowledge worker, unlike the blue collar and traditional white collar worker, is an expert or specialist, because to be effectively applied, knowledge must be specialized. As a consequence, knowledge workers (unlike their clerk forebears) must routinely come together to solve complex problems—they work in teams."[2] In the world of customer service, where the perception of the customer—the measure of customer satisfaction—is moulded by an invisible voice or action at the other end of the phone line, the knowledge worker becomes the differentiator between superlative and mediocre service.

About the author

SANDIP PATEL

Sandip Patel is a partner in the Strategy Consulting practice of Coopers & Lybrand Consulting. He has extensive experience in business strategy implementation and the strategic use of technology for effective decision-making. He specializes in leading organizations through strategic transformation and in applying business modelling and simulation to redesign diverse business operations in the financial services, insurance, health care, and telecommunications industries. He is particularly interested in the leverage of intellectual capital in organizations and the deployment of performance measurement systems. Sandip Patel has an MS in Management Information Systems and an MBA from Boston University. He is an Associate Member of the Institute of Chartered Accountants of India.

---

[2] Austin, Texas: Corporate Memory Systems Inc., 1996.

Part Six

Bringing It All Together: Best Practices of Industry Leaders

It seems the key to staying one step ahead of the competition is *creating new steps* to take, rather than walking in worn paths and implementing improvements within traditional boundaries. "If it ain't broke...break it" is the operating philosophy of today's best-practices companies.

As the previous chapters have related, organizations are focusing on three key areas:

1. Consolidating and, in some cases, outsourcing certain operations.

2. Integrating customer care functions to minimize points of customer contact and maximize customer care resources.

3. Managing the workforce to equip customer service representatives (CSRs) with superior customer service and technology skills.

For those companies that have made the commitment to lead the competition in customer service, success largely depends on how they view the relationship between people and technology. Technology must be seen as an enabler of people, a tool to better equip CSRs to serve customers, not as a replacement for human contact. New technologies must be implemented carefully, with a focus on thorough training and constant measurement.

It seems that the key to achieving breakthrough customer service, however, is more than creating the perfect mix of people and technology. It also requires fundamentally changing the processes and culture of the organization to ensure that change is not just accepted, but encouraged. Improving technology or the skills of your workforce will produce only incremental change. Improving both aspects will probably produce substantial results. But achieving breakthrough customer service will happen only if you also change the rules by which your company traditionally competes and create an environment that is powerful yet invisible to the competition. And that can mean changing your organizational culture as well as your systems and processes. Ritz-Carlton did it; so did Federal Express, Home Depot, Wal-Mart, and Southwest Airlines, to name a few. It's not magic, but it does require creativity, expertise, and a complete understanding of your organization and the industry in which it operates.

The highly adaptable nature of today's best-practice companies demonstrates that being successful means more than being open to change. It means creating change.

Robert Frost in "The Road Not Taken" speaks of the bold steps taken by those who create change: "Two roads diverged in a wood, and / I took the one less traveled by, / And that has made all the difference." The examples of best practices in Part Six tell us about organizations that have taken the road less travelled and created breakthrough customer service. They demonstrate how these organizations have implemented changes that involve not just people or technology separately, but rather the entire mix of competencies—bringing to fruition Frost's conclusion, "that has made all the difference."

In the first chapter of this final part, Bill Bound and Rupert Taylor describe the breakthrough approaches being used by financial service institutions in North America and Europe. The authors provide both results of proprietary research and best-practice examples that confirm that traditional financial service providers are becoming less distribution-led and more customer-driven in order to respond to changing customer needs. In the next chapter, Ian Littman shows how the public sector in today's "change" environment is remarkably similar to the private sector. "Call them clients, stakeholders, users, beneficiaries, or the public—the government has customers just as private companies do...Many public organizations do not have this view," says Littman. He then backs this up with best-practices examples of those enlightened few that have recognized this and done something about it.

The hospitality segment, represented by the Ritz-Carlton Hotel chain is the topic of Chapter 32. The authors describe how the Ritz-Carlton's legendary service—and success—are the result of meaningful standards, effective support tools, structured and focused training, and continuous support. The success of British Airways (BA) over the past decade is also well-known. And in Chapter 33, we are told that that success has resulted from the company's unwavering focus on differentiating its service from that of its competitors. BA is continually working toward converting all those it services into "ever-elusive boastful customers."

The next chapter, about Travelers Insurance, looks at how technology and the company's focus on the internal customer have transformed

Travelers. The last two chapters in this part continue demonstrating the unique mix of competencies that are required to achieve a breakthrough. Roberts Express, a 50-year-old leader in expedited deliveries dares to offer a money-back guarantee for on-time deliveries. This is not a marketing gimmick, but an outstanding level of service that has become the company's way of life—enabled by people and technology.

The final chapter in the book is a case study of a leading-edge financial institution, which truly "broke through." mbanx, a division of Bank of Montreal, knew it had to redesign its business processes and tools to achieve its goals. Jeff Chisholm, mbanx president, explains how it did this.

The successes of the companies described in these chapters clearly demonstrate that these companies did not achieve their success through magic, but rather through dedication and commitment to being better than the competition.

S.A.B.

Best Practices of Leaders in Financial Services

TOMORROW'S LEADING RETAIL BANKS

Bill Bound and Rupert Taylor,
Coopers & Lybrand, London, UK

FOR A LONG time, the financial services industry was a place of relative stability, with well-established organizations offering quite narrow product ranges. Customers had little influence and suffered the vagaries of bank opening hours. Moreover, the true nature of life assurance and pension products remained a mystery to most.

Through the eighties and nineties, however, the industry experienced unprecedented change. Taking the United Kingdom as an example, deregulation and increasing competition have led to new entrants; Marks & Spencer, Virgin, Tesco, General Motors, Cellnet, Volkswagen, and British Gas have all moved into the financial marketplace. Traditional operators have responded with mergers and rationalizations, while the Building Societies (mutual organizations established to help people obtain mortgages) have been converting themselves into public limited companies. The range of products offered by each competitor has widened enormously, but at the same time, the extent of product differentiation has diminished. As competition has increased, aggressive sales techniques have emerged, and many customers are deluged with a plethora of junk mail.

The financial services industry continues to have an image that the media have dubbed "a failure to care about the customer." Whether or not this is actually the case, as far as customer loyalty is concerned, perceptions *are* reality. Financial service providers are increasingly seeking to improve and be *seen* to improve the standards of their service in order to retain market share and create competitive advantage. But what will this new dawn of customer service in the financial services sector look like?

CUSTOMER SERVICE IN FINANCIAL SERVICES

Coopers & Lybrand UK (C&L) sponsored and conducted research into what the retail financial institutions may look like in the new millennium. Entitled "Tomorrow's Leading Retail Bank"[1] (TLRB), this research looked first at customers of the future and identified significant and often contradictory changes in both their demographic profile and financial requirements.

Some key trends noted in the research include the fact that the population overall is aging, yet there are increasing numbers of both single parents and dual wage-earning families. The proportion of individuals in full-time permanent employment will diminish, making life-cycle cash flows much less predictable. At the same time the social safety nets will largely disappear as state provision declines, forcing individuals from all socio-economic groups to rely more on their own financial provision. Perhaps more positively, many people will become increasingly confident in handling their financial affairs and will expect the sort of standards they find in other retail sectors. Many customers will have access to, and confidence in, technology, and will seek much greater flexibility from their financial service providers.

TLRB research revealed that traditional financial service providers are becoming less distribution-led and more customer-driven in order to respond to changing customer needs and disprove perceptions of poor service levels. These changes can be grouped into four broad areas:

- Accessibility to financial services products is becoming more customer-focused through increasing choice of access points, ranging from traditional branches to the Internet.

---

[1] The word "bank" has been used to encompass all full-service retail financial organizations.

- The quality of the products and services offered is being improved to ensure that they are "right first time," reducing confusion and frustration.

- Products are being tailored to individual customer requirements.

- Customer-relationship development is taking place to create trust and build personal relationships that bind the customers into long-term, mutually satisfactory relationships.

In some respects these changes do not complement each other— for example, maintaining customer loyalty requires building relationships with clients through strong branding and marketing, but an ever-expanding array of access channels enables customers to be flexible and look across the whole marketplace for products.

In the following sections we explore in more detail the breakthroughs in customer service that financial service organizations are making to meet or exceed customer expectations.

Access

As we move into the 21st century, customers' time will be increasingly at a premium and conveniently delivered services will be compulsory for high levels of service. To this end, financial service providers are continually assessing and developing technology to offer customers access "Anytime, Anywhere, Anyhow."

The rate of development is rapid as each new opportunity is exploited. Ten years ago, the concept of telephone banking was virtually non-existent. Today, in the United States in particular, offering a telephone banking service that is available 24 hours a day, 7 days a week, 365 days a year is no longer a competitive advantage; everybody offers that service.

In banking terms, new delivery channels are developing, from branches, ATMs (automated teller machines), and telephony to a plethora of new channels, including Express Banking Shops, PC- and TV-based Internet services, kiosks, "21st century" branches (the virtual electronic bank, electronic/Internet banking) and mobile, or visiting, banks.

Already, Barclays Bank in the UK is making use of Microsoft's latest personal finance software package, Microsoft Money 97, as part of the bank's strategy to become a major player in the PC banking market.

Citibank has given an international perspective to the use of personal computing technology in the form of the Psion Organiser. The Psion, an enormously successful handheld computer, can be linked up to an ordinary telephone using a modem. It allows customers to check their balances, transfer funds, set up standing orders, and direct debits from anywhere in the world.

The use of technological innovations offers the dual benefit of enhancing customer service through increased accessibility and improving profitability by replacing higher cost channels such as branch networks. However, for established financial service operators, technology also presents a risk because it reduces the barriers to entry for potential new competitors. For example, developing a call centre requires a fraction of the time and cost associated with developing a comprehensive branch network. Many new entrants are also proving to be particularly adept at using information technology to get close to their customers.

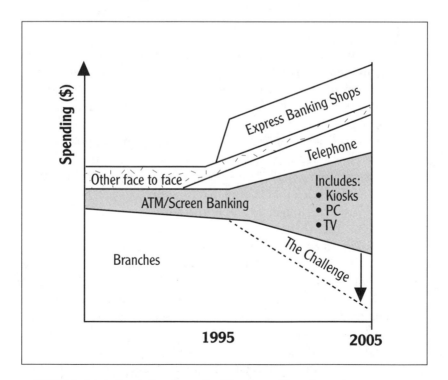

FIGURE 1: Cuts in Branch Spending to Fund New Access Channels

All these developments are placing increased pressure on the viability of branch networks. As Figure 1 shows, a cut in spending on branches is often necessary to fund alternative access channels. Despite this, for traditional banks and insurance providers, branches still remain a vital part of their service strategy. They are, however, being adapted to meet changing customer needs. For example, NatWest Bank in the UK is piloting a number of "lounge style" branches, which receive customers in a relaxed atmosphere, providing refreshments, a play area, and creche. In the U.S., Datacard has developed an instant card issuance solution, which allows customers to walk into a branch and have a credit card printed instantly.

All customer service costs money, and the development of multiple-access channels increasingly presents financial service organizations with the opportunity to segment their customer base. This enables them to focus on the most profitable clientele, while encouraging use of the most cost-effective channel for each category of customer. Of course, a bank's view of the appropriate medium may not be the customer's, but a proper understanding of customer preferences for different channels can pay dividends. Citibank in the U.S., for example, offers $50 to all customers who open a PC bank account. And Bank One in the U.S. developed a customer-segmented strategy from a different perspective. The case studies that follow provide you with the varied efforts that we, at C&L, have participated in with some of our clients as they strive to achieve breakthough customer service.

BANK ONE CASE STUDY
Encouraging Customer Migrations

Bank One was eager to align delivery channels and customer needs. The first step in this process was to understand the existing distribution environment in more detail and to develop a vision of a new retail distribution strategy, focusing on behaviour within customer segments.

To understand the existing environment, Bank One analyzed usage characteristics (transactions, products, and channels) and determined customer profitability by segment and channel. A delivery strategy was then designed with the aim of transforming the traditional delivery network into a customer-focused capability that could serve each customer segment's definition of convenience, without adding an additional layer of costs. Specific customer segments were seen to be using particular delivery channels—for example, those in retirement were still very reliant on traditional branch banking.

In determining customer profitability, the bank found that some 60 to 80 percent of customers were in marginal or loss-making relationships with the bank and that, true to Pareto's law, a mere 20 percent of customers made over 80 percent of variable contribution. In the light of these findings, the next step was to determine the changes that were required to meet the key challenge of designing a customer and transaction migration plan. The aim of such a plan was to maximize relationships with high-value customers while simultaneously migrating lower-value customers to lower-cost delivery channels. A number of methods were used to attain this. To maximize relationships with higher-value customers, various promotions, customer perks, specialized services, and personal-relationship banking were all offered. Other customers who consistently used the more costly branch channel were given personal demonstrations showing how to use an ATM. The bank thus created differential service, products, and pricing.

Quality

Along with providing varied access methods, financial service providers must provide high-quality products if they are to retain customer loyalty. Quality in the financial service context includes technically accurate advice, reliable investment promises, and "right first time" transaction processing.

In an industry where the selling of products is regulated by legislation, clear procedures and guidelines to support the trained sales force are critical. The importance of good processes is illustrated by the case study below.

DIRECT LINE CASE STUDY
Ensuring Quality Call Centre Processes and Standards

In late 1995, the PEP[2] industry remained quite inaccessible to the majority of the population in the UK. Over 100 providers fought over a small group of high earners, with purchasing decisions apparently based primarily on trust.

Direct Line operates its business mainly by telephone via a call centre and considers itself a particularly customer-focused organization. When it decided to launch a PEP product, it wanted to ensure complete customer satisfaction with the sale and processing of the product. Direct Line asked C&L to assist in the venture.

A large part of the task consisted of designing the sales and administration processes in the call centre. Processes may include, for example, "change customer details," "transfer in existing PEP from elsewhere" and "action direct debit." These and other customer-facing activities were then arranged in a logical process, each focusing on a particular customer need. Appropriate systems were designed, and standards and performance measures then set for all key processes, against which the sales staff could be measured. For example, the time taken to inform banks of direct debit instructions and despatch correspondence to customers was specified.

Because financial service providers are subject to a vast array of regulatory requirements, detailed scripts were developed so that calls would be dealt with fully and consistently every time. Thoroughly trained operators could take each customer through a short interview, explaining at every stage the regulations applicable to both Direct Line and the customer.

---

[2] PEP, Personal Equity Plan, is a particularly tax-friendly form of investment that only came about after changes in the tax laws. There was a huge rush by financial service organizations to launch these products because they were attracting high levels of investment.

Tailored Service

Even when customers know that they are receiving high-quality services, they are increasingly demanding service that is tailored to their particular needs. Broad segmentation (for example, on lifestyle needs) generally used today will not be sufficient to define customer's expectations in the future, and our research has shown that customers are likely to become increasingly intolerant of ill-targeted promotions. Leading financial service organizations will have to gather very specific information about their customers' needs and behaviours, and how they translate into buying requirements. Each organization will need to understand both the current and potential value of each of its customers and how to develop profitable customer relationships on an individual basis.

Many companies are already pursuing these concepts. The aim of Chase Manhattan Corporation in the U.S. is to treat all 25 million customers as a "market of one." For example, a mortgage borrower receives a personalized application that acknowledges his or her existing relationship with the bank. Intelligence culled from a credit bureau might indicate that a customer carries another issuer's card. This customer's next statement would then include an incentive to replace that card with one from Chase. Looking to the future, if Chase found out that a customer vacations regularly in Florida, then it would offer loyalty rewards that take the form of discounts for that area.

BNP in France is launching a new scheme called "Panorama," which is targeted at customers with at least Fr120,000 in disposable assets. The program is designed to simplify and condense information and communications received by each client, with the aim of personalizing and tailoring them to the needs of the individual customer.

Contact with customers who use call centres can also be tailored. For example, KeyCorp's call centres in the U.S. are designed to identify the caller before the call is answered (see Chapter 18 for detailed information about KeyCorp's call centres). The client can then be directed to the agent who is best suited to handle this type of customer or the particular query. At Virgin Direct, the call centre that deals with PEPs can offer "illustrations"of how the PEP could perform for the customer. If the customer requires a certain amount of income within a given period or has a certain amount to invest, the system can produce discounting or compounding rates to help the customer to decide how to make the most of his or her investment.

Customer Relationships

Varied access channels, quality products, and a tailored service may guarantee that customers feel in control of their finances; however, full customer satisfaction will not be achieved unless customers value and trust the relationships that they have with their financial service providers.

In the financial service environment described at the start of this chapter, customer loyalty, perhaps more accurately described as "apathy," was quite common. People tended to have their bank accounts with the same bank, often the same branch, for several generations. Considering switching the mortgage on a regular basis between different competitors was, if ever, *contemplated* only when moving house, and then actually *done* rarely.

Aggressive marketing, increased channel accessibility, and increasingly better informed customers have unravelled this old style loyalty. But it is commonly recognized in all areas of marketing that the cost of acquiring a new customer is much greater than retaining those you already have. Financial service organizations therefore have to strike a careful balance between, on the one hand, meeting the needs of empowered customers who can readily switch providers and, on the other hand, building a loyal client base. Figure 2 illustrates this balance.

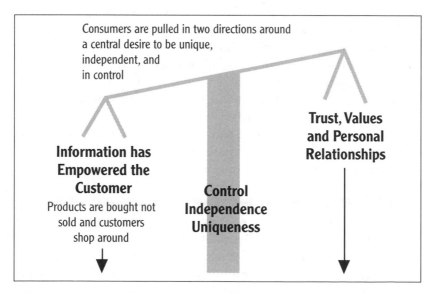

FIGURE 2: Consumer Buying Behaviour Reacting to Conflicting Pulls

If financial service organizations can no longer rely on apathy to retain their customer base, they need to develop a new approach. The TLRB research identified branding as the new tool that will create loyalty in the future and be central to success. Branding is about more than simply product and name recognition. It is part of a company's overall strategy and permeates not only the organization's processes, culture, and people, but all its dealings with external customers.

The key players in the financial services industry who have already established high levels of loyalty tend to be newcomers to the sector. They bring loyalty established in other retail arenas into financial services. Examples from the UK include Marks & Spencer (dependability), the Co-operative Bank (an ethical investor), and Virgin (value for money and fun). Other brands that have evolved within financial services include Direct Line, which has a reputation for efficiency and low-cost insurance; AMEX, which maintains its branding as the "biggest credit card provider;" and Citibank, which is ensuring that its ATM machines throughout the world all work the same way and that its branches all have similar layouts.

The objective behind branding is that customers are attracted to these organizations because they identify with their values and like dealing with their people—so much so that they regard the organization as a trusted friend. Increasing their knowledge of their customers and their potential profitability to the bank, allows financial service providers to cultivate that "friendship" so that customers progress from being one-time buyers to loyal customers who generate customer referrals.

Financial service companies still encounter many pitfalls when they try to improve branding—for instance, a lack of consistency in brand application, the failure to link each product to the overall company brand, consumer skepticism, and a tradition of media hostility. But like many other industries, the "tell and sell" era of marketing is increasingly making way for customer-focused relationships. Chase Manhattan Bank believes that customers, not products, hold the key and have begun to focus on customer preferences and individual profitability. This approach gives the bank more flexibility in relationship pricing, a technique it is now refining to incorporate into two or three pricing packages. Mindful of the ability of the lowest-cost producers to tempt customers into "cherry-picking" individual services, the bank can, for selected customers, price its packages on the basis of buying some of these services from outside. At NatWest in the UK, staff are being trained to move beyond being mere brand ambassadors to becoming mini-marketing managers. The company's mystery shopping campaign is no longer anonymous so that staff who have made significant improvements in greeting customers and offering them privacy can be rewarded.

The more traditional financial service providers have realized that it is no longer enough to tell all customers to "buy this product because it is cheap," and this has led to an increase in relationship marketing. In recent years, C&L has been working with a client, Allied Dunbar, to assess the value for money that customers obtain from its life insurance products. In an increasingly crowded and discerning marketplace, our client company has been educating its customers about the quality of its business and warning them that to concentrate on price and low front-end charges is oversimplifying their purchasing decisions. Allied Dunbar then annually rates itself against a representative sample of its financial services competitors and publishes its results. The rating is based on a wide variety of publicly available data, especially commissioned research and internal measures (for example, customer satisfaction surveys). C&L then reviews the approach, analysis, and data used to accredit the ratings. The results of this work then form a key part of the company's marketing material, and represent a real attempt by Allied Dunbar to shift customer focus from price to an appreciation of the overall service that the customer receives.

CONCLUSIONS

In order to confront increasing competition, perceived poor customer service, and changing customer demographic and economic needs, traditional financial service providers are not only having to provide innovative, high-quality, tailored products through a wide range of channels, but are also needing to build (or perhaps rebuild) relationships and loyalty with their customers.

Most new entrants to the financial services marketplace are already adept at building relationships. In addition, new distribution channels that have largely developed as a result of information technology and telecommunications make entry into the marketplace easier and cost effective. Without any past baggage to carry, new entrants are able to market themselves very aggressively and challenge the cosy network of traditional financial service providers.

Delivering high-quality customer service will be a critical part of corporate survival in financial services, but with many customers still viewing banking and insurance services as a means to an end, the challenge to develop deep and lasting customer relationships will prove particularly demanding.

About the authors

BILL BOUND and RUPERT TAYLOR

Bill Bound is senior partner in Coopers & Lybrand's Financial Services consulting practice in London, England and was one of the Board members of Coopers & Lybrand's TLRB (Tomorrow's Leading Retail Bank).

Rupert Taylor joined Coopers & Lybrand in 1993 following five years with Lloyds Bank. He specializes in distribution effectiveness, credit management, and process reengineering with a strong banking focus. He has special responsibility for developing the research into TLRB and has spoken at many conferences on the subject.

The authors have been helped in the preparation of this article by Anna Martin, a research associate working in the Financial Management Business Effectiveness Group of the UK practice.

CHAPTER THIRTY-ONE

Best Practices of Leaders in the Public Sector

Ian D. Littman,
Coopers & Lybrand, Arlington, VA

Is the public sector dramatically different from private sector companies in its need to satisfy customers? To those of us who have been heavily involved in both the public and the private sectors, the answer is overwhelmingly and emphatically "No." Those that have risen to the challenge and have achieved breakthrough customer service have done so by taking a close look at two basic concepts—customers and processes. How they treat them provides some important insight.

WHO ARE GOVERNMENT'S CUSTOMERS?

Call them clients, stakeholders, users, beneficiaries, or the public—the government has customers just as private companies do. If this surprises you, you are not alone. Many public organizations do not have this view when they start to use process management.

Your customer is anyone who receives or uses what you produce—or whose success or satisfaction depends on your actions. For most people, that user will be an *internal customer*—that is, another unit or person in your agency, whose part in a work process comes after yours or who uses your output to do his or her job.

At the Crane, Indiana, Naval Weapons Support Center, the internal customers of the procurement office are all the line units that work on weapons systems. These units depend on the procurement office to order parts and materials so that they can get their jobs done right and within deadlines. If buying problems put them behind schedule or over budget, they are the ones who hear from angry external customers and managers.

In most public agencies, middle managers who develop policies or budgets for their units are the customers of administrative officials and upper managers who develop and communicate agency-wide policies and objectives. Department heads need clear direction and feedback from the top to create effective policy directives for their staff.

In justice and law enforcement systems, litigators are the customers of investigators. Litigators need sound investigative directions to develop legal strategies and adjudicate cases successfully.

"On a day-to-day basis, cooperation among internal customers is what management is all about," noted the chief of statistical methods at Watervliet Army Arsenal in New York State. "The more we understand the needs of our downstream internal customers, the better the whole process works."

At the ultimate level, the user of the final product or service is an *external customer*. External customers can be direct, such as the retirees who receive benefits from the U.S. Army Accounting and Finance Center in Indianapolis and the naval commanders that send ships for overhaul to naval shipyards. They also can be indirect. For example, the Federal Deposit Insurance Corporation works directly with financial institutions, but the ultimate customer is the individual bank account holder. See Table 1 for further examples.

Stakeholders include those individuals or organizations who have an interest in or who are affected by a program or organization, but are not the direct recipients of its services. They do, however, have a major impact on program effectiveness, and consequently, their opinions and recommendations matter. For example, the U.S. Coast Guard's Office of Marine Safety, Security, and Environmental Protection includes the following organizations in its list of stakeholders:

- Environmental response groups
- Federal, state, and local governments
- Maritime unions
- Maritime training interests
- Classification societies

TABLE 1: Government's Varied External Customers

Government Program	External Customers
IRS Service Center Ogden, Utah	Tax attorneys Tax preparers Tax payers
Norfolk Naval Shipyard Norfolk, Virginia	Fleet commanders Type commanders Ship commanders
Johnson Space Center Houston, Texas	Congress & the administration NASA headquarters Other government agencies Scientific community Private businesses Foreign governments
U.S. Patent & Trademark Office	Engineers, scientists, and inventors Patent and trademark attorneys Private businesses Industrial information specialists Students
Defense Commercial Communications Office	Whole Department of Defense

Government Program	External Customers
Office of Physical Security & Law Enforcement, General Services Administration	All federal agencies that lease space from GSA (6,800 buildings) Building managers Federal employees Visitors to federal offices
Social Security Administration	Beneficiaries Congress

- Key congressional representatives
- Advisory committees
- Trade associations
- Foreign flag operators
- U.S. Department of Transportation representatives
- U.S. Environmental Protection Agency

The Coast Guard's Office surveys and interviews these stakeholders for their advice and opinions on its policies, programs, and effectiveness.

EVERYONE IS BOTH A SUPPLIER AND A CUSTOMER

It is important to note that for internal and external customers and stakeholders, supplier-customer relationships are reciprocal, as shown in Figure 1. For example,

- Taxpayers are customers of the Internal Revenue Service, but the IRS is a customer for the information that taxpayers give in tax return forms.

- Managers are customers for employees' reports, but employees are customers for manager's instructions on how and when to prepare those reports.

   In short, you are both a customer and a supplier for everyone you deal with. Treat your suppliers like customers, and you will have better suppliers. Make sure your customers give you the right information, and you will be a better supplier.

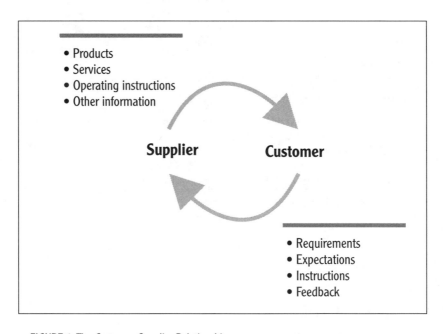

FIGURE 1: The Customer-Supplier Relationship

WHAT DO YOU STAND FOR?

The box shows mission statements from three government organizations. You might assume that your leaders know the mission already, that it is actually written down somewhere, and that it reflects what you are supposed to be doing. Usually, none of these assumptions is correct.

Mission Statements

Department of Veterans Affairs, Philadelphia, Pennsylvania
Our mission is to accurately and efficiently provide benefits and services to veterans and their families in a manner recognized as fair and responsive.

U.S. Department of Labor, Wage and Hour Division, San Francisco Region
To enforce the nation's employment standards to serve and protect the present and future workers of America.

U.S. Tank-Automotive Research, Development, and Engineering Center, Warren, Michigan
To conduct research, development, and engineering to achieve global superiority in military ground vehicles and to stimulate the transition to a growing, integrated, national industrial capability that provides the most advanced, affordable military systems and the most competitive commercial products.

VISION

Your leaders need to develop a "vision of excellence" to give your organization direction. This vision should be a description of the desired outcome of the strategic plan, the future state of your organization at some point in the future. Creating the vision for change—and then empowering your staff to achieve it—is management's most important contribution. Visions are broad, but they provide a direction. Developing a vision includes writing specific statements about desired results, which leads to identifying internal and external barriers to success and framing general strategies for overcoming the barriers. All actions in the strategic plan should contribute to making the vision a reality. Some of the essential elements of vision statements and samples from government are shown in the box.

Vision Statements

Department of Veterans Affairs, Philadelphia, Pennsylvania
Our vision is to be the finest provider of services in the DVA and to be recognized as such; to have a culture which respects both our customers and our staff and which earns the trust of veterans and their families.

City of Wilmington, North Carolina
We want Wilmington to be recognized as a great place to live, where our customers receive high-quality services, our employees work in an environment of respect and support, our leadership stimulates cooperation and innovation in our community, and our gift to future generations is an even better city than was given to us.

WHY DOES AN IMPROVEMENT-DRIVEN ORGANIZATION EMPHASIZE CUSTOMERS?

In business, understanding customer requirements has obvious importance: if customers are not satisfied with products or services, they won't buy them—and profits will reflect their disaffection. Although government doesn't usually sell its products or services, a customer-driven process is equally critical in the public sector.

In quality management, reengineering, and other process management approaches, customer needs and expectations, not agency-established standards, define quality. Take a moment to read the example in the box. No matter how fast VAROIC processes loan applications in its offices, the veterans measure turnaround from the time they mail an application to the time they receive a cheque in the mail. Which is the better definition of performance in turnaround time: veterans' perceptions or internal cycle time?

Customers Define Quality at VAROIC

The Philadelphia Veterans Affairs Regional Office and Insurance Center (VAROIC) handles veterans' GI life insurance loan applications. A top executive there said, "We had a standard of processing 95 percent of the applications within five work days from the time we received them until the Treasury Department issued the cheque. We were proud we averaged 3.3 work days per loan.

"But when an improvement team asked veterans about our service, they heard complaints that it took up to two weeks to get a cheque. The team realized that the veterans counted time from the calendar day they mailed an application to the day they got the cheque. So our standard did not meet our customers' expectations.

"The team added a special post office box number, which saved the time that the applications spent in the mail getting to us. We added a dedicated fax machine for emergency requests. We worked internally and with Treasury to streamline the application approval and cheque-mailing processes down to a 1.7 work day average.

"The immediate payoff was more satisfied customers. We also saved money by eliminating or reducing work that added little value to the application process—including time answering complaints—since our improvements have cut them by more than half.

"This taught us to tie what we do into customer expectations. We have to ask, have we aligned what we consider good service with what our customers really want?"

The commanding officer at the Cherry Point Naval Air Depot in North Carolina recalled, "For years, some of our operators made a component for a larger part. One of the operators asked the workers who used the component about its quality. 'Quality's fine,' said these internal customers. But could it be any better? 'Well, we have to open it up, drill an alignment hole, and then reassemble it. Takes us about an hour to do that.' Checking the component's plans, they found that the hole had been left out of the drawings. Now, the operators who make the component put the hole in it, which takes six minutes. We make hundreds of these a year; think of the time we wasted by not finding out what the internal customers really needed."

No matter how good you think products and services are, they cannot be considered high quality unless they meet your customers' needs and expectations. You cannot "do it right the first time" unless you know the right thing to do.

DO CUSTOMERS KNOW WHAT TO ASK FOR?

No doubt, you have had the experience of customers asking for a product or service that is partly or totally wrong for their needs. You have to talk with these customers to help them better define what they need. Often you are more of an expert on the subject than they are. But ultimately the customer validates your mutual decision on what is best.

Also, customers may not realize that it is often possible to go beyond their expectations. If you include attributes they do not expect in a product, you'll be doing that special "something extra." For example,

- The fax machine that VAROIC used in its loan processing permitted veterans to get quick service in emergencies.
- The Oregon Department of Motor Vehicles found that drivers were intensely irritated by unflattering photographs on their licences. Now, the department uses a video system that allows drivers to choose from among several pictures.

When you add these types of attributes, you are *delighting* customers. The greatest challenge is to work on the opportunities for delighting, whereby you find new ways of pleasing customers. This is one of the chief goals of government organizations that want to stay competitive with customer-focused private companies.

CUSTOMER DISSATISFACTION

Most organizations measure customer satisfaction by how well they avoid customer dissatisfaction. A common mistake is to think that if few customers complain, most are happy. Let us say that only 5 percent of your customers complain to you. Does this mean that 95 percent are satisfied? How would you feel if you learned that 96 percent of your unhappy customers will not complain and that all customers with unresolved gripes will tell them to 9 or 10 other people? That was one finding of a federal consumer products study.

Multiply the number of complaints you get by 10, and you may have a more realistic picture of customer satisfaction. Multiply unresolved complaints by 100, and you have an idea of how many people out there have heard bad things about your organization. Think about that the next time you have problems getting your budget approved or when voters fail to support your bond issue.

HOW TO GET FEEDBACK ON WHAT CUSTOMERS VALUE MOST

A key focus in business process improvement is to use and obtain results from natural work groups, which are small groups of employees and managers who operate a single process or a small number of processes, and take care of most operations within their work unit. In most organizations, these groups or self-managed teams are the mainstays of gradual improvement.

Each group trains in improvement methods as a team, then applies its new knowledge to the group's processes. A group meets several times a month to identify problems and opportunities that fall within the boundaries of their processes. Their search for improvement is guided by strategic goals, management plans, and issues discovered during core business process improvement projects.

The "do it program" at the air force development test center (AFDTC), Eglin AFB, Florida, is a good example of the use of natural work groups to roll out improvement practices to an entire organization. After gaining experience from running several process-improvement projects, AFDTC developed a special natural work group training module that included a small set of improvement tools and methods. This training was given to groups in work units where managers had completed their own team-building and planning. Most new "do it teams" quickly identified dozens of improvement opportunities. At first, the teams restricted themselves to issues that could be addressed without going outside their processes. As they gained experience, do-it teams started working together to solve problems that crossed over into other processes.

Suggestion Program

At AFDTC, the do-it initiative became the de facto suggestion program because management wanted to stress teamwork over individualism for a few years. So it waited a while before reworking its individual suggestion programs. You may wish to do the same or get started sooner. You may, however, wish to save the suggestion program for the second year. By then, all your managers should be trained in leadership and process improvement, so that they will be able to respond quickly and appropriately to employee suggestions. Without follow-through, the programs will never get off the ground, thus making your organization more resistant to change.

Here's a best-practices example that shows the true meaning of the teamwork. In July 1995, the Defence Mapping Agency (DMA) of the U.S. federal government unrolled a new road-map to get closer to the customer and improve customer service. As reported in the *National Performance Review* newsletter (Winter 1995), the reinvented DMA is organized around core business processes and features newly formed customer support teams (CSTs). Teams form partnerships with customers to plan, prioritize, and produce products, services, and information for the operational armed forces and other customers. This customer-focused approach was established after 10 months of planning by an eight-person team that relied on suggestions from employees, customers, past and present DMA leaders, subject matter experts, and private sector firms. In addition to improving customer service, the agency also

- Pruned management layers between producer and customer from 11 to 3.

- Pared headquarters staff by almost 50 percent. Staff became members of CSTs or moved to locations where the production work is actually done.

- Empowered customer support and production teams to get the job done.

- Reduced the practice of stockpiling prodigious quantities of map-sheets just in case they might be needed. DMA is instead focusing on populating a database (accessible to customers) for just-in-time production.

A PUBLIC SECTOR BEST-PRACTICES EXAMPLE

To close we provide you with another best-practices example, this one from the California Department of Motor Vehicles. Just to survive, every state agency in California must become an improvement-driven organization because the old sources of revenue growth just aren't there anymore. Natural catastrophes and economic slumps have strained the state's Treasury, while anti-tax movements by citizens block the easy way out of the state's fiscal woes. Fortunately, those agencies have a mentor readily at hand: the California Department of Motor Vehicles (DMV). The DMV serves more drivers (20 million) who own more vehicles (25 million) than in any other state. And the numbers increase daily. With a comprehensive approach to improvement that combines entrepreneurship, advanced technology, and quality management, the DMV continually reduces the time it takes to serve citizens and business customers, while holding down costs.

A good example of this, according to the American Society for Quality Control (ASQC), is the DMV's process for registering new rental vehicles. In the old process, a car rental company handed over registration papers to DMV staff, who keyed in the data, collected the fees, and issued the necessary documents, licence plates, and stickers. The three to five days it used to take the DMV to handle this process often meant that its customers—rental companies—were deprived of hundreds of dollars in revenue for each vehicle that sat idle. One company estimated its losses at well over $1.5 million per year.

To improve this process, the DMV and car rental companies in a pilot project, formed a partnership and redefined the role of the customer. From their offices, the participating companies now handle registration fee payments through direct access to the DMV database and electronic fund transfer (EFT). Registration cycle time has dropped from days to minutes, and new cars hit the road as soon as the companies attach pre-issued licence plates and stickers, which are kept in their own garages.

Benefits to the DMV (besides *very* happy customers) include the elimination of two data entry clerk positions (a saving of nearly $50,000), plus additional interest earnings from fees deposited faster through EFT. And let's not forget the increased revenues to the state from taxes on millions of dollars in new earnings by the rental companies. All these benefits will increase as more companies enter the partnership.

Although technology enabled the improvement of this process, the more basic change was the formation of a trusting partnership between the DMV and car rental companies.

Another such partnership enables automobile clubs to provide some vehicle registration services to their members, and still another allows court-appointed vehicle vendors to update court abstracts online.

Even more fundamental is the DMV's comprehensive approach to improvement, which starts with executive leadership and strategic planning, then deploys process-improvement goals and methods throughout the department. By creating a comprehensive infrastructure to drive its pursuit of equality, the DMV assures California citizens of continuous improvement in government service.

About the author

IAN D. LITTMAN

Ian D. Littman is a partner in Coopers & Lybrand's Government Services practice in Arlington, Va. He is a former state and federal employee and has over 20 years' experience in management consulting. He is the originator of the improvement-driven organization concept and has supervised improvement engagements in over 100 government organizations.

CHAPTER THIRTY-TWO

Best Practices of a Leader in the Hospitality Industry

THE RITZ-CARLTON HOTEL COMPANY

Pat Mene, Ritz-Carlton, Atlanta, GA,
and Natasha Milijasevic,
Coopers & Lybrand, Toronto, ON

PERSONALIZED SERVICE

Ritz-Carlton has won numerous awards, including the prestigious Malcolm Baldrige National Quality Award in 1992 and *Executive Travel Magazine*'s award for the best hotel group in the world in 1996. Personalized service is a Ritz-Carlton hallmark. By focusing on the delivery of highly personalized, genuinely caring service, Ritz-Carlton has built a reliable, seamless, customer-driven service delivery system designed to provide premium service. This system anticipates a guest's needs and preferences, and at the same time, reacts instantly to correct any service error and satisfy any complaint. With enormous competitive pressures in the luxury segment of the hotel industry, Ritz-Carlton is continuously setting its sights on higher goals. With the Baldrige, among other awards, under its belt, Ritz-Carlton currently has its eye on becoming virtually defect-free and reaching 100 percent customer retention in the very near future.

Since its inception, Ritz-Carlton has been driven by a clear service credo and a mission statement. We have reproduced these below.

The credo serves as a guide for the employees of Ritz-Carlton and emphasizes that highly personalized customer satisfaction is Ritz-Carlton's highest priority and is everyone's responsibility. The credo's three steps of service are further elaborated in the activities and

THE RITZ-CARLTON®
HOTEL COMPANY, L.L.C.

MISSION STATEMENT

The Ritz-Carlton Hotel Company will be regarded as the quality and market leader of the hotel industry worldwide.

We are responsible for creating exceptional, profitable results with the investments entrusted to us by efficiently satisfying customers.

The Ritz-Carlton Hotels will be the clear choice of discriminating business and leisure travelers, meeting planners, travel industry partners and the travel agent community.

Founded on the principles of providing a high level of genuine, caring, personal service; cleanliness; beauty; and comfort, we will consistently provide all customers with their ultimate expectation, a memorable experience and exceptional value. Every employee will be empowered to provide immediate corrective action should customer problems occur.

Meeting planners will favor The Ritz-Carlton Hotels. Empowered sales staff will know their own product and will always be familiar with each customer's business. The transition of customer requirements from Sales to Conference Services will be seamless. Conference Services will be a partner to the meeting planner, with General Managers showing interest through their presence and participation. Any potential problem will be solved instantly and with ease for the planner. All billing will be clear, accurate and timely. All of this will create a memorable, positive experience for the meeting planner and the meeting participants.

Key account customers will receive individualized attention, products and services in support of their organizations' objectives.

All guests and customers will know we fully appreciate their loyalty.

The Ritz-Carlton Hotels will be the first choice for important and social business events and will be the social centers in each community. Through creativity, detailed planning, and communication, banquets and conferences will be memorable.

Our restaurants and lounges will be the first choice of the local community and will be patronized on a regular basis.

The Ritz-Carlton Hotels will be known as positive, supportive members of their community and will be sensitive to the environment.

The relationship we have with our suppliers will be one of mutual confidence and teamwork.

We will always select employees who share our values. We will strive to meet individual needs because our success depends on the satisfaction, effort and commitment of each employee. Our leaders will constantly support and energize all employees to continuously improve productivity and customer satisfaction. This will be accomplished by creating an environment of genuine care, trust, respect, fairness and teamwork through training, education, empowerment, participation, recognition, rewards and career opportunities.

THE RITZ-CARLTON®
HOTEL COMPANY, L.L.C.

CREDO

The Ritz-Carlton Hotel is a place where the genuine care and comfort of our guests is our highest mission.

We pledge to provide the finest personal service and facilities for our guests who will always enjoy a warm, relaxed yet refined ambience.

The Ritz-Carlton experience enlivens the senses, instills well-being, and fulfills even the unexpressed wishes and needs of our guests.

decisions surrounding interactions with the customer. The "Ritz-Carlton Basics" describe Ritz-Carlton's guest problem-solving process as well as grooming, housekeeping, safety, and efficiency standards. Through these basics, the value of internal customer satisfaction is reinforced in an effort to eliminate internal competition (for instance, between the sales and catering departments). Finally, the motto *Ladies and Gentlemen Serving Ladies and Gentlemen* is more than a phrase— it is a culture. Some might say it is more like a religion that the employees must believe in without question.

In *Consumer Report* ratings for luxury and high-priced hotels, Ritz-Carlton routinely scores first in the luxury class with a satisfaction score exceeding that of all its competitors. Ratings of Ritz-Carlton's value, staff, and condition of rooms and facilities are all at maximum level— the only chain to receive such a score across the board. The reason for these high accolades may be that the Ritz-Carlton hotel chain does not view itself as selling food and rooms, but rather, as selling service. Company-wide, employees are devoted to the organization's principles. Internal surveys indicate that a full 96 percent of employees say that "excellence in guest services" is a top priority.

Ritz-Carlton has achieved and retained its current enviable position within the highly competitive hospitality industry through excellent leadership, superior use of information systems, strategic quality planning, a strong focus on its employees, and a well-evolved customer service measurement system. All five factors are ingredients in Ritz-Carlton's unique recipe for total customer satisfaction.

LEADERSHIP

Of the 32 Ritz-Carlton hotels worldwide, 3 are company-owned and 29 are managed by Ritz-Carlton. This set-up gives Ritz-Carlton full control over managing the people and the brand. The management philosophy at Ritz-Carlton is based upon leading by example: keeping senior management visible and readily available to employees and customers alike. Senior management at Ritz-Carlton acts as the senior quality committee and has devised the "Gold Standards" strategy.

These Gold Standards, which senior management must personally exhibit, detail how employees are expected to behave when they come into contact with customers. These easy-to-understand definitions of service quality are continuously communicated and reinforced at all levels of the organization. Through methods that include training, daily line-up meetings, and pocket cards outlining Ritz-Carlton principles, employees acquire an exceptional understanding and devotion to the

THE RITZ-CARLTON®
HOTEL COMPANY, L.L.C.

THE 20 RITZ-CARLTON BASICS

1. The **Credo** will be known, owned and energized by all employees.

2. Our **motto** is: "We are Ladies and Gentlemen serving Ladies and Gentlemen." Practice teamwork and "lateral service" to create a positive work environment.

3. The **three steps of service** shall be practiced by all employees.

4. All employees will successfully complete **Training Certification** to ensure they understand how to perform to The Ritz-Carlton standards in their position.

5. Each employee will understand their work area and Hotel goals as established in each **strategic plan**.

6. All employees will know the needs of their internal and external customers (guests and employees) so that we may deliver the products and services they expect. Use **guest preference pads** to record specific needs.

7. Each employee will **continuously identify defects** throughout the Hotel.

8. Any employee who receives a customer complaint **"owns" the complaint**.

9. **Instant guest pacification** will be ensured by all. React quickly to correct the problem immediately. Follow-up with a telephone call within twenty minutes to verify the problem has been resolved to the customer's satisfaction. Do everything you possibly can to never lose a guest.

10. **Guest incident action forms** are used to record and communicate every incident of guest dissatisfaction Every employee is empowered to resolve the problem and to prevent a repeat occurrence.

11. Uncompromising levels of **cleanliness** are the responsibility of every employee.

12. **"Smile—We are on stage."** Always maintain positive eye contact. Use the proper vocabulary with our guests. (Use words like— "Good Morning," "Certainly," "I'll be happy to" and "My pleasure.")

13. **Be an ambassador** of your Hotel in and outside of the workplace. Always talk positively. No negative comments.

14. **Escort guests** rather than pointing out directions to another area of the Hotel.

15. **Be knowledgeable** of Hotel Information (hours of operation, etc.) to answer guest inquiries. Always recommend the Hotel's retail and food beverage outlets prior to outside facilities.

16. Use proper **telephone etiquette**. Answer within three rings and with a "smile." When necessary, ask the caller, "May I place you on hold." Do not screen calls. Eliminate call transfers when possible.

17. **Uniforms** are to be immaculate; wear proper and safe footwear (clean and polished), and your correct name tag. Take pride and care in your personal appearance (adhering to all grooming standards).

18. Ensure all employees know their roles during **emergency situations** and are aware of fire and life safety response processes.

19. Notify your supervisor immediately of **hazards**, injuries, equipment or assistance that you need. Practice energy conservation and proper maintenance and repair of Hotel property and equipment.

20. Protecting the **assets** of a Ritz-Carlton Hotel is the responsibility of every employee.

company's vision, values, quality goals, and methods.

In the hospitality business, in which customer interaction is so important, it is critical that senior leaders personally instil a strong vision and set of principles in their employees. They do so by "walking the talk" and empowering their people to do whatever is necessary to satisfy their customers.

EMPLOYEE TRAINING

People are the most important part of an organization that provides such highly personalized service. At the Ritz-Carlton, human resource practices are well scrutinized for optimal effectiveness. Organizational structure and all procedures, including recruitment, training, rewards and recognition, have been moulded to fit into Ritz-Carlton's strategic plan. All hotels have a director of human resources, a training manager, and a quality leader on their staff. Within each work area, there is a departmental trainer who is in charge of the training and certification of new employees in the area.

New employees are recruited into each of the 120 hotel-specific standard job positions available using a highly predictive instrument known as "character trait recruiting." This tool is used to determine the capability of a candidate to meet the requirements of the job he or she is applying for. It is based on the attributes of employees who have been successful in that role in the past. Ritz-Carlton believes that through this recruiting method, it has reduced service variability and turnover by nearly 50 percent in the past three years.

Training begins at orientation, where the training manager and senior hotel executives work as an orientation team to personally demonstrate the Gold Standards. The next stage of the training process is the responsibility of the work area leader and the departmental trainer, who provide comprehensive training that enables new employees to master the procedures of their respective position. Upon completing this training, the employee must pass written and practical tests to become certified.

Each day, employees in every work area go through a quality line-up meeting and briefing session where they receive quality training. Through these and other mechanisms, employees receive over 100 hours of quality education to foster premium service commitment, problem-solving abilities, and the setting of strategic quality plans.

Effective involvement and empowerment result, in part, from effective quality training. To satisfy the customer, each associate is empowered to "move heaven and earth." This includes the authorization to spend up to US$2,000 to satisfy a guest.

Both individual and team recognition opportunities abound. A large number of awards are given to employees for excellence in a wide variety of areas. Top performers receive the coveted assignment of handling new hotel start-ups. In addition, employees share their achievements through sharing gratuities. Expectations are clearly laid out during the orientation, training, and certification processes. These expectations form the basis of performance appraisals. Employees are also surveyed annually to ascertain their levels of satisfaction and understanding of the quality standards.

Ritz-Carlton workers are keenly aware that attaining excellence is a top hotel and personal priority. Organization, recruiting, training, and reinforcement are all consistent with the provision of high levels of customer service.

INFORMATION SYSTEMS AND QUALITY REPORTING

Ritz-Carlton's reliable, seamless, customer-driven service delivery system is generated by its well-designed and integrated information systems and tools for quality reporting. Systems for the collection and analysis of customer-satisfaction information are used extensively throughout the organization.

At the heart of Ritz-Carlton's provision of world-class customer service are two compatible information systems: COVIA and Encore. COVIA handles centralized worldwide guest reservations; Encore, a local system, keeps records of reservations and individual guest preferences for each hotel. Employees around the world can access this common pool of customer and quality information to obtain up-to-the-minute data, including online guest preference information, quantity of error-free products and services, and opportunities for quality improvement.

All Ritz-Carlton employees are expected to collect, input, and use these data as part of their service delivery for individual guests. Each staff member (or "associate") is provided with a "guest preference pad" for the purpose of noting the special needs or concerns of his or her guests. These comments (for example, whether a guest prefers milk to cream in coffee) are entered into the COVIA system daily. As a result, employees worldwide can customize a guest's stay at the Ritz-Carlton with information obtained from the profiles stored in the integrated COVIA/Encore systems.

Ritz-Carlton's quality production reporting system summarizes all the data. Serving as a process whereby employees identify quality opportunities for improvement, these results are standardized and entered into a textbook, which is available throughout the organization. Information about quality service is also combined with marketing and financial results from each hotel to determine what quality factors are driving financial outcome. When combined with the results of frequent benchmarking studies, this quality reporting system enables the hotel's leaders and teams to better determine goals and justify expenditures.

Although a genuine, caring, human touch is at the core of Ritz-Carlton's award-winning customer service, its hallmark personal service could not be achieved without its highly acclaimed information systems.

STRATEGIC QUALITY PLANNING

The quality plan at Ritz-Carlton is really the basis of the business plan itself. The primary objectives of this plan are to improve the quality of the services provided, reduce cycle-time, improve the price/value proposition, and increase customer retention. Through benchmarking studies conducted within the hospitality sector as well as outside the industry, Ritz-Carlton has developed a disciplined, integrated planning system to achieve these objectives.

At each level of the company, teams are charged with setting objectives and devising action plans, which are reviewed by the corporate steering committee. These teams serve a threefold purpose: (1) They enable all employees to focus on a common vision of productivity and quality; (2) They empower employees to achieve this vision; (3) They facilitate improved communication and integrated problem-solving across all levels. Finally, each hotel has a quality leader who serves as a resource and adviser to teams while they are developing and implementing their quality plans.

These quality action plans are put through a screening process to ensure that they are adequately researched and resourced. Plans that pass the process are approved as being based on quality and customer-satisfaction priorities.

CUSTOMER SERVICE MEASUREMENT

The Ritz-Carlton measures customer satisfaction through various means, including regular best-practices benchmarking studies, customer surveys, and other types of market research, but particularly through making it easy for the customer to communicate with the hotel organization.

Ritz-Carlton currently benchmarks against the best in any industry through industry experts and consultants, as well as through customer satisfaction linkage with other Baldrige winners.

Frequent customer surveys form a major component of research to measure customer satisfaction. A regular J.D. Power survey asks loyal Ritz customers which service elements were important to them and how well the Ritz was performing against these elements. Another method for assessing customer satisfaction has been through the guest and travel-planner satisfaction system. On a quarterly basis, surveys of guests and planners rate their rational and emotional reactions to various aspects of product and service delivery. Ritz-Carlton believes this process to be a crucial supplement to the more objective types of customer-satisfaction survey systems and scales used.

Customer information is also gathered through other means, including travel industry research, focus groups of different market segments, preferences detected by employees coming into contact with customers, and information gathered during new hotel development.

The Ritz-Carlton makes it easy for customers to interact with the hotel staff and voice their concerns or provide suggestions for improvement. Customer service managers are on call 24 hours a day in each hotel. Guest comment cards addressed to the president are available in every guest room. And the company is also readily accessible by phone through 1-800 numbers.

The Ritz-Carlton is actively listening to the voice of the customer and soliciting customer input. Feedback received is integrated into its business strategy system to facilitate continuous improvements.

THE RESULT: TOTAL CUSTOMER SATISFACTION

Since its inception, the Ritz-Carlton has been bringing home awards on a regular basis. Recent Gallup surveys have found the Ritz-Carlton to be the first choice of customers, with a 94 percent satisfaction rating—well above that of its closest competitor at 57 percent. A nationwide study of frequent business travellers also found the Ritz-Carlton to be the clear choice of customers—again, far outperforming the next best competitor in respect of a number of quality and customer service attributes.

The Ritz-Carlton has also moved closer to its goal of 100 percent customer retention and total customer satisfaction. Complaints have dropped by 27 percent over the past three years, bringing the hotel chain nearer to its goal of 100 percent complaint resolution prior to guest departure. In addition, a full 97 percent of travel consumers had their expectations met or exceeded. While customer satisfaction has been increasing, adverse indicators of customer dissatisfaction (for example, rebates and complaints) have declined. But perhaps the most telling measure is that key national account retention has improved 20 percent—the goal being 100 percent retention. The business centre hotels have retained 97 percent of their key local corporate accounts. Also during this three-year period, Ritz-Carlton corrected the price/value concerns voiced by its customers.

At the Ritz-Carlton, the objective of the quality effort is to *never lose a single customer*. And it means it! Far from content to accept its international renown as best-practices leader across various quality measures, and first place position within the industry, the Ritz-Carlton Hotel Company continually raises the benchmark for service provision. Through superior leadership, well-integrated information systems, strategic quality planning, employee focus, and customer service measurement systems, Ritz-Carlton has earned its reputation as the hallmark of personalized, high-quality service.

About the authors

PAT MENE and NATASHA MILIJASEVIC

Pat Mene is vice-president of quality for Ritz-Carlton.

Natasha Milijasevic is a consultant in the International Centre of Excellence in Customer Satisfaction, Coopers & Lybrand, Toronto.

CHAPTER THIRTY-THREE

Best Practices of a Leader in the Airline Industry

BRITISH AIRWAYS: THE FOUR CORNERS OF LOYALTY[1]

Charles R. Weiser, British Airways,
London, UK

THE SUCCESS OF British Airways (BA) over the past decade has been the result of the company's unwavering focus on differentiating its service from that of its competitors. BA subscribes to W. Edwards Deming's view that "customers that are...merely satisfied switch. Profit comes from repeat customers—those that boast about the product or service." As a result, BA relentlessly researches, refines, and continually redefines its service offerings in order to convert all those it serves into Deming's ever-elusive boastful customers.

Delivering any service is an imperfect business. The pursuit of perfection in the service industry demands an in-depth understanding of the key drivers of not only human behaviour but also the complex support systems that facilitate delivery. We must add to the mix, in BA's service environment, the orchestration of a highly sophisticated technical operation and the requirement to serve the needs of over 72 national cultures. These additional factors make it very difficult to distil the key drivers of loyalty. There are no simple linear causes and effects, or measurements.

---

[1] Adapted with permission from *Customer Service Management*, London, England.

There is always, however, a first step in any journey. In BA's case, the company began to explore the root cause of customer defections through its customer "listening posts." Strangely, this logical first step led to some rather illogical findings. The analysis of these findings pointed to some rather interesting aspects regarding loyalty—in particular, that there is not always a direct cause-and-effect relationship between defection rates and poor company/customer interactions.

SATISFIED VS. DISSATISFIED POTENTIAL DEFECTION RATES

BA found that about 13 percent of customers who were completely satisfied with BA's service might not repurchase from the airline again—they changed jobs or had other reasons not related to their experience with the airline. At the other end of the spectrum were customers who had experienced a problem. Fifty percent of the customers who chose *not* to tell the airline about their experience defected to other airlines.

Nevertheless, a customer group was identified that was willing to communicate with BA and that may or may not have experienced a problem or simply desired to make contact with BA for whatever reason. Only about 13 percent of the customers in this group tended not to repurchase. This rate of defection was identical to the rate of defection of customers who were completely satisfied and rarely had any communications with BA.

The conclusions were quite powerful: customers who were satisfied rarely wrote or called to say good-bye and more than likely could not be saved from defecting, whereas those who wished to contact the airline, for whatever reason, were willing communicators and were more likely to be prevented from defecting in the longer term.

The primary difference between these customer types was the customer's willingness or unwillingness to perceive BA as an approachable and flexible organization—that is, the difference depended on the degree to which the customer attributed those human qualities to BA as an organization. On the whole, BA's customers recognized the imperfect world within which the airline operates. As in any relationship, customers were willing to be very resilient and positive toward BA (no matter what the situation), so long as the organization reciprocated the values found in any long-term relationship—for example, openness, flexibility, and a mutual respect for the other's rights and feelings.

The evidence of these customer types is reinforced by the fact that BA has found that no correlation exists between customer defections/ loyalty and compensation paid to customers who have experienced service failures. Customers do not think of their relationship with the airline in monetary terms. Instead, customers place a premium on the values of the relationship and how consistently they are applied. These values, as with any relationship, are perceived to be the most meaning-ful and, therefore, the most indicative of the strength of the relation-ship.

Although service failures in any company, including BA, will and should always be the catalyst for service redesign in order to limit the potential for customer defections, minimizing defections is also dependent upon a company's ability to create an open and commu-nicative culture within the company. Customer loyalty depends heavi-ly upon this "cultural development."

THE FOUR CORNERS OF LOYALTY: "NOTHING TOO BIG, NOTHING TOO SMALL"

Unfortunately, there is no best way to organize, develop, or otherwise redesign a value-based corporate culture. We do have a few hints, how-ever. First, customer loyalty should be the domain of every section of the company. Therefore, the organization as a whole should undertake some major transformations to ensure that all parts of the organization have both a clear understanding of the customer and a vested interest in propagating the corporate value system. Further, these transforma-tions never end; they become an iterative process that moves with mar-ket requirements. There is no one "answer," although there are many change programs that proclaim to provide an answer.

BA's service ethic in this context has been based upon years of cus-tomer research, which itself changes to survey different issues as they come to the forefront. The current platform upon which BA has built its recent service formula has been based upon its customers' views of its primary strengths: its global reach and the ability to tailor services at the point of delivery. Customers' needs have been transformed into a BA ethos that insists that there is nothing too big (as a global player) and nothing too small (as a flexible service organization) that it cannot or will not do for customers. This has become the "look and feel" of the service ethic, its personality. These core service values are, in turn, the basis upon which the expectations of the customer/company relationship is built.

To deliver these values, BA has undertaken over the years a number of initiatives, some linked, others not, which I describe here as the "Four Corners of Loyalty." The ultimate purpose of each corner is to support the other in order to create "enabled teams" that practise the values of the organization. Figure 1 illustrates the four corners.

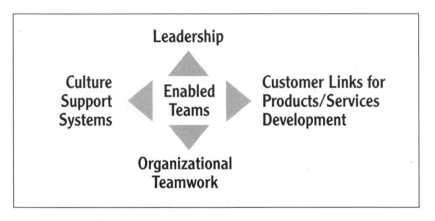

FIGURE 1: British Airways' Four Corners of Loyalty

Leadership

John Kotler, a well-known marketing strategist, said, "Management is about coping with complexity, leadership is about coping with change." Companies with "command and control" structures cannot adapt to the relentless changes of the market. Such structures stifle the creativity of staff in both coping with change and anticipating changes in the very nature of customer relationships. During BA's Leadership 2000 Programme, led by Bob Ayling and Derek Stevens (BA's CEO and CFO, respectively), "role reviews" across the company were undertaken with the objective of passing leadership responsibility from the centre to the accountable areas. Instead of fostering a paternal relationship from the centre, BA focuses on individual accountability and authority to act. Leadership in BA is not something that is "done" to people. All employees are responsible for taking the lead in areas ranging from customer relationships to operational development.

Customer Links

Proximity, or a "clear line of sight," to the customer in all operational areas is paramount so that those delivering service to the customer—directly or indirectly—gain direct access to market feedback. Over the years, BA has developed a unique brand/product management approach that is more than just product development. Rather, it is a complete feedback, service development, and delivery system designed by the marketing, customer service, sales, finance, information management, and operational teams. They design service routines, training and skills programs, management practices, and investment priorities (see Figure 2).

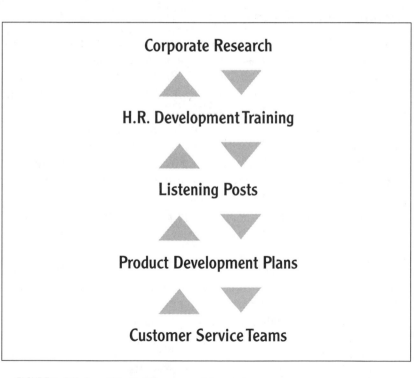

Corporate Research

H.R. Development Training

Listening Posts

Product Development Plans

Customer Service Teams

FIGURE 2: BA's Brand/Product Management Approach

The overall objective is designed to provide BA's leadership (in the decentralized form described above) with continual market stimulus regarding emergent customer views, which can then be acted upon for correction or further development. BA's Human Resources Development Training Series (originally called "Putting People First") incorporates this market stimulus into a training platform in which all BA employees (50,000) participate every three or four years. The success of these and other product development programs is monitored through the company's continuous, real-time feedback mechanisms (listening posts and daily, ongoing research), which influence future product developments and customer service initiatives. Each process is intertwined and dependent upon a flow of information from the other. In practice, the process is not always linear or sequential. It aims to offer a "window" into BA for all its customers.

Organizational Teamwork

Through the Leadership 2000 Programme, BA's entire planning and performance management systems were redesigned across the company through the leadership of Finance and Human Resources respectively—with the input and participation of their internal clients. Key Performance Indicators (KPIs) were designed that mirrored and monitored the key values outlined previously while operational targets to support these balanced the criteria. The objective was to create teams across the organization that subscribed to the company's objectives in a consistent manner and that were mutually supportive. Jack Welch, chairman of GE (US) described this type of approach as creating teams that "had the values and [made] the numbers."

Cultural Support Systems

Perhaps the most underrated aspect of creating a corporate culture that engenders the personality for which a company strives is providing a set of standards or practices that all employees can use and observe to reinforce the values that the customer is meant to experience. In BA's case, these include

- Academies
- Recruitment
- Performance management/KPIs
- Staff surveys

Academies are training centres through which all employees can develop. Employees can choose courses for personal development as well as skills upgrading so that they have the opportunity to advance to the next level in the organization or learn more cross-functional skills and enhance their leadership competencies at each level in the organization. Recruitment specifications in all areas embody both the values the company is seeking for its employees to practise and the performance measures that reward and measure those traits the company is looking for in its employees. Finally, BA undertakes employee surveys, which are used to diagnose how well the company is actually practising those traits and behaviours internally.

CREATING THE RIGHT CULTURE

In creating the right culture, your company needs to ask itself the following questions:

1. How many job categories come between the furthest employee and the customer?

   Relevance: All employees need a clear line of sight of their role in developing customer relationships.

2. What authority do employees have in asserting the company's value system?

   Relevance: Employees must have authority to turn values into practice.

3. If your company had a window into the operation from the outside, would your customers like what they saw?

   Relevance: What would you base your customer relationship on?

4. Are development opportunities available to the entire company workforce?

   Relevance: Those with authority to act need to know that top performance in addressing customer's interests can lead to advancement.

5. Do customer-research and feedback forums proactively seek out the key value-based priorities of the company?

Relevance: Don't get involved in denial or "group-think" or rationalization. A clear "fact base" needs to be established.

6. How long does it take to rectify customer issues?

Relevance: Mutual respect in a relationship demands a sense of urgency in resolving problems.

The weighting of the answers will be different for every organization. However, more important perhaps is actually their pursuit, not necessarily the answers in themselves.

About the author

CHARLES R. WEISER

Charles R. Weiser is currently responsible for BA's consumer financial services and business partnerships. His previous roles have included head of Customer Relations for BA, director of Strategic Development at Air Miles Ltd, and designing BA's Executive Club program.

Customer Service Management, from which this article has been adapted, is published quarterly for executives and managers wishing to attain quality and service excellence (see reference in Appendix I).

Best Practices of a Leader in Database Marketing[1]

TRAVELERS INDEMNITY CORPORATION

The *Cowles/Simba*
Report on Database Marketing, Stamford, CT

THE MARKET FOR property and casualty insurance has always been competitive as independent agents and those tied to specific carriers vie for a share of local markets. In recent years, however, things have become even tougher with the advent of "out-of-area" insurance writers horning in on the local markets through direct mail and telemarketing campaigns. Not surprisingly, the increased level of competition has led to higher attrition rates for insurance companies, which in turn leads to higher marketing and administration costs as the carriers seek to replace customers.

Travelers Indemnity Corporation, along with partner Aetna Casualty & Surety Company, was painfully aware of these problems—given its position of selling insurance nationwide through more than 5,000 independent agents. Its response was to revamp its strategy to concentrate on retention through target marketing.

This led to a major improvement in retention, significant returns on revenue, and the 1996 first place award for database excellence at the National Center for Database Marketing conference in Orlando.

---

[1] Adapted with permission from *Cowles/Simba Report on Database Marketing*, January 1997, p. 8–9.

Travelers' goals, among others, were to develop a strong message, build a first-class marketing database, effectively identify those customers most likely to leave, develop a customized mail program to contact them, respect the traditional role of the independent agent, and measure the results.

To achieve its targeted 1 percent increase in retention rates company-wide, Travelers believed it would need at least 15 percent (375) of its agencies to participate, provided they covered 20 to 25 percent of the company's total market.

The challenge for Travelers was getting enough agents to participate. Because they were independent, they could not be compelled to do so. Previously, the most successful marketing programs had only a 10 percent participation rate. In addition to these traditional roadblocks, this program would be even more difficult to sell because there would be no corporate subsidies to underwrite the cost. The agents would have to bear it entirely on their own.

Travelers attacked these problems and the traditional challenges across a broad front. For example, the insurance firm developed a message that focused on both the personal and the business relationships of the policyholders. It also underscored the value of the independent insurance agent, Travelers' relationship with the agent and the low-cost benefits of working with a national program.

At the same time, Travelers determined that the strength of a policyholder's relationship was based on the length of time spent working with an agency. It realized, therefore, that it had to develop different messages for different policyholders.

Travelers began by re-examining its existing database. It leveraged the one million policyholder files, which were segmented by product groups, to help develop the retention tables necessary for profiling customers and tracking the information that was crucial to sell the program to the independent agents.

Using historical data from 1990 to 1994, Travelers went beyond simply tracking retention to examining retention by the length of time a policy was held.

A company program report gave the following example: "[I]f 100 policies opened in 1990 and 10 were closed the same year, the attrition rate for 0–1-year policies was 10 percent. Tracking those same policies into 1991, if nine more of these 1990 policies lapsed in 1991, the attrition rate for 1–2-year policies was 10 percent and 81 percent overall."

This information helped Travelers coordinate its mailing program. At first the company thought it would take its tailored messages and deliver them to every policyholder in the system. But realizing that it was too costly to send everyone a full five-piece message package, the company developed a cancellation risk profile using the historical retention data it had developed.

"Not surprisingly, the longer the policyholder stayed with Travelers, the less likely he was to leave. We decided that we would optimize the retention dollars spent by focusing our 'full impact' message at the beginning of a policyholder's life cycle, then reducing the number of contracts in subsequent years," a company spokesperson explained.

Armed with this data, Travelers now had to sell the program to its agents. It was reasonably easy to prove that the agents benefited, in terms of commissions, from retaining customers for the agents—even when accounting for the cost of the programs.

But many agents noted that their particular retention rates were probably better than the averages Travelers used. Travelers agreed, but to drive home the point that additional gains could still be made, it developed similar charts for all agents holding 80 policies or more. It then used these charts to show each agent how his or her retention rates compared with Traveler's national averages.

The company then moved to develop 2,500 customized direct mail programs to fit the individual attrition profiles of each agency. To simplify the program further, the company developed a mail algorithm that put together a suggested mail program approach for each agent based on the agent's attrition rate profile. It also took into account the percentage deviation, by segment, of the agency's attrition versus the national average; the optimal creative package configuration based on the number of impressions; and the message content and cost per message.

Travelers also reinforced the role of the independent agency by making sure the communication appeared to come directly from the agency and not the carrier, which involved personalizing each letter and using each agency's name and logo.

THE PAYBACK

The results were impressive. Fifty-six percent of all agencies participated in the program in the 21 months following its launch in January 1995. The company reports: "This level of participation represents over

70 percent of all of Travelers' personal lines policies and almost four times the participation rate of any previous program in Travelers' personal lines history."

The company was even more pleased with the improvement in customer retention levels (see Tables 1 and 2) when compared to non-participating agents, attrition rates were 5 percent lower from agents involved in the program. Although many of these agents had always reported lower attrition rates, the difference had usually been somewhere around 1 to 2 percent, not 5 percent.

"If these indications hold true," says a company spokesperson, "we have reached our corporate objective in the first year of the program."

TABLE 1: Without Improved Retention (Assumption: 500-customer starting base)

	Customers	**% Lost**	**Commission**
By year 1	438	12.3	$62,875
By year 2	361	17.5	$51,822
By year 3	316	12.5	$45,362
By year 4	278	12	$39,987
By year 5	247	11	$35,457

Total commission (five years): $235,503

TABLE 2: Improved Retention 25% (Assumption: 500-customer starting base)

Customers	**% Lost**	**Commission**	**Mail Cost**
454	9.2	$65,172	$908
394	13.1	$56,559	$788
357	9.4	$51,247	$536
325	9.0	$46,654	$488
298	8.3	$42,778	$298

Total commission (5 years): $262,410
Value of retention over 5 years: $26,907
Return on marketing dollar: 8.9/1
Based on Travelers national average and an average commission of $143.55.

The attrition rates from agents involved in the program were 5 percent lower compared with non-participating agents (see Table 3).

TABLE 3: Policyholders' Attrition Rates

Year	% Attrition: Participant Agent	% Attrition: Non-Participant Agent	Difference in points
1991	16.8	20.0	3.2
1992	12.7	15.1	2.4
1993	13.1	14.2	1.1
1994	12.3	13.5	1.2
1995–March '96	12.2	17.2	5.0

About the authors

The *Cowles/Simba Report on Database Marketing* offers strategic intelligence and tactical application for database marketers. It is published monthly. For further information please refer to Appendix I.

CHAPTER THIRTY-FIVE

Best Practices of a Leader in Transportation

ROBERTS EXPRESS: FOCUSING ON THE CUSTOMER THROUGH TECHNOLOGY[1]

Vicki J. Powers,
American Productivity & Quality Center,
Houston, TX

Down IN THE windowless basement of its two-storey building lies the "heart" of Roberts Express. This freight carrier of time-sensitive shipments, which is based in Akron, Ohio, has created an information system unlike any other in the transportation industry. Customer Link™, Roberts Express's own technological development, enables the organization to combine its customer-focused environment with top-notch technology to achieve exceptional customer service.

IT'S SOMETHING IN THE WATER

The culture at Roberts Express, a half-century-old leader in expedited deliveries, breathes "focus on the customer." This organization, which offers a money-back guarantee for on-time deliveries, continually seeks new customers and new ways to serve them. Its service guarantee, which certainly doesn't leave much room for error, pays customers back 25 percent of the bill when a shipment is two hours late and 50 percent of the bill when a shipment is four hours late.

---

[1] Adapted with permission from *Customer Satisfaction in Practice*, December 1996/January 1997, published by American Productivity & Quality Center, Houston.

Regina Sacha, human resources director, believes the secret to Roberts' culture is simple. With company mission and vision statements ingrained in the organization, she said it was clear "what business we're in and how we're to be successful."

"Historically, different processes were put in place that clearly led us to successfully perform," Sacha said. "It starts with the president and his own passion and is carried throughout the organization. To absolutely have that passion that people can feel—that's what brings people here. There's an excitement for satisfying the customer."

Although Roberts Express president, Bruce Simpson, has spread his enthusiasm for the customer throughout the company, Rick Franks, director of service, believes that management as a whole has a minimal effect on the company's customer focus.

"As managers, we can only set the policies and vision to support what the front line does," he stated. "It's the individuals on the floor who have the largest impact on Roberts. They will handle the problems that come up. That's their moment of truth with the customer—how they sounded on the phone and the service they provided."

Although explosive growth can often disrupt an organization's culture, Franks believes that Roberts has done an exceptional job of keeping the culture alive in the company. In 1994, the organization hired 150 new customer service agents. Despite this large influx, the culture remains intact. One reason for this, according to Franks, is that Roberts Express promotes a large number of employees internally.

"We have a good core of people here who have worked 7 to 10 years at Roberts," Franks said. "They are the ones who pass the culture along. There's only so much an organization can do. It's the individuals who must pass the culture."

USING INFORMATION TECHNOLOGY TO SUPPORT THE CUSTOMER

Roberts Express understands how its technology drives customer satisfaction. Without innovative technology, this express delivery service could not provide dedicated transportation services in the contiguous states and Europe faster than air freight for shipments up to 1,200 kilometres. And that is exactly its mission statement: *We will delight our customers worldwide by providing fast, precise, dedicated transportation services. We will provide personal service and will be the best at doing this, guaranteed. Our primary measurement will be the customer's perception of satisfaction.*

The "guts" to this organization's success, Customer Link—a computerized information and communications system with links to computer terminals mounted on the dashboard of every truck—enables the company to plan and execute every detail of a shipment. In the environment in which it operates, where every delivery cries *emergency* for the customer, each minute is critical in the process. When a shipper calls the Roberts toll-free number, a customer assist team member will guarantee the truck pick-up in less than 90 minutes. Customers are told the exact time of pick up, time of delivery, and the exact cost.

Without Customer Link, Roberts Express could not dispatch orders, track deliveries, or inform customers of potential problems with their time-sensitive materials. By the time customers call to use Roberts' service, they are often frustrated, because it means something went awry in their process. But they feel completely confident, on the other hand, in trusting Roberts to do the job. And its current revenue of $175 million illustrates that trust.

THE MAKING OF A GENIUS

The MIS Department at Roberts Express studied many types of technology over a four-year period before deciding to create its own unique system. Two options it explored—nationwide paging beepers and meteor bounce—would offer only one-way communication. Cellular telephones would be an expensive option, according to MIS Director Joe Greulich, and would be hampered by dead spots around the country.

"Before our technology push, we had truck operators call every four hours to [tell us] where they were," Greulich said. "This was often inconvenient for the drivers and not very productive. It's annoying to have to pull over if you're on the road making emergency deliveries."

Roberts Express started using technology at a time when there were but a few pioneers. Although today many companies install satellite dishes on truck roofs, in 1989 Roberts was only the second company to go online with satellites.

"At the time, we wanted to buy a computer package, but we had to build our system from scratch," Greulich said. "It involved a total hardware and software re-configuration, as well as ground-breaking developments in database management and communications technology."

A key component to Customer Link is satellite tracking and telecommunications. The computer-like satellite terminals enable drivers to report to headquarters—without stopping their vehicles—by sending and receiving communications instantly. A receiver-transmitter mounted on the roof of each truck automatically updates the truck's progress in the computer at Roberts Express headquarters. Drivers can report unusual situations such as a traffic jam or snow storm to the agent and ask for road assistance without leaving the truck.

Greulich said that truck operators who evaluated the pilot version of this system in 1988 were a little fearful of a Big Brother mentality. With the tracking wired into the ignition system, Roberts knows the exact location of every truck in its fleet.

"We put satellites on our trucks so our customers would know that we knew where their freight was," Greulich said. "If the customer has an emergency, we need to know."

Another critical component of Customer Link is an advanced telephone system that automatically routes thousands of customer and driver calls each day to the agents who handle that geographic area. Roberts' phone system initiates customer contacts and "feeds" the entire system.

Customer Link is supported by two Sequent computers, housed in the organization's basement, serving 350 PCs located throughout the headquarters building. Agents arrange one run after another using a series of specially designed screens—all processed in real time. The system accommodates a huge amount of data, including customer information, vehicles, drivers, routes, and rates. Roberts has added significant in-house developments, such as Rand McNally mileage, online weather reports, and electronic data interchange. This technology essentially adds about 2,000 "rolling offices" to the Roberts organization, all operating as if they were located right in Akron, Ohio.

"Customer Link includes a number of special applications that have been developed in-house to fit a business niche that needs more information—faster than any other in the transportation field," Greulich said.

Customer-identification technology is one innovation that pulls up information on the computer screen before the agent greets the customer over the phone. This extra effort offers comfort for callers in an emergency situation. Greulich believes that Roberts' systems of pay, distribution, and self-directed teams are all supported—not dictated—by technology.

"My job is to enable things here," Greulich said. "What's challenging is that technology is changing very rapidly. Finding disappointments early is the key to success."

ASK AND YOU SHALL RECEIVE

Roberts Express is just as interested in getting feedback from its customers as it is in pleasing them. A third party conducts monthly telephone surveys with 150 of Roberts' most recent customers to track customer service perceptions. The survey probes service satisfaction, expectation levels, on-time delivery, likelihood to recommend the company to others, and reason for selecting Roberts.

Each month the numbers are rolled into one satisfaction score that ranges from –2 (very dissatisfied) to +2 (very satisfied). Generally, Roberts' score falls around 1.9.

"We've conducted about 15,000 surveys since we started asking for feedback in 1988," said Franks. "Even though our customer satisfaction numbers range between 1.83 and 1.96 on a 2-point scale, we will always find areas for improvement. Before we started our monthly surveys, our only avenue to measure customer satisfaction was through daily service meetings," Franks continued. "These generated comments only from unhappy customers. Our president, Bruce Simpson, a believer in Tom Peters, drove the idea to measure customer satisfaction monthly."

Roberts also conducts a driver-satisfaction survey each month with 50 of its independent truck operators. The score from this survey, which currently ranges from .9 to 1.4 on the previously mentioned scale, has just been added to the goals of its customer teams.

Customer-satisfaction numbers are rolled into a monthly research report that is distributed to every employee. The report includes summary results, month-to-month trend charts, and verbatim responses. Employees have a key interest in monitoring customer-satisfaction levels for two reasons: first, it's part of the culture; and second, employee bonuses are tied, in part, to customer-satisfaction scores.

"Each quarter, employees can receive a bonus, up to 16 percent, contingent upon reaching their objectives," Franks said. "Money is distributed to everyone in the organization. This action says two things: We must be profitable, but we can't do it at the expense of the customer."

Employees' objectives are function-specific, according to Franks, although customer satisfaction appears as a common goal for every employee. Customer Assistance Teams (CAT), for example, have seven goals they are measured against each month: customer satisfaction, driver satisfaction, delivery service system, delivery service group, pick-up service group, customer phones group, and notifications group.

"All the things we think are important at Roberts are tied to bonus goals," Greulich said. "It's not rocket science. It's a system of reinforcing metrics for how we service the customer. You must strike a balance that does the best for the company and the customer. We spend lots of time on measurement and metrics."

Roberts also implemented a gainsharing plan in 1994 to reward company performance—also tied to customer-satisfaction scores. The payout is contingent upon meeting both customer service and profitability goals. Customer satisfaction survey results determine the amount of payout employees receive.

PUTTING WORDS INTO ACTION

Roberts Express's customers never have to fear that their words are just empty sounds in the corporate building.

"The fact that we went to customer assistance teams stemmed from customer feedback," Franks said. "As we grew, the customer base grew as well. Orders were taking longer, because we asked a lot of questions. We received the same feedback from drivers who felt like just a number. We realized we needed to redesign the call centre group. Our whole goal became 'remaining small in the eyes of the customer.'"

Despite its 30-fold growth in the 1980s, generating revenue from $3 million in 1982 to $75 million in 1989, Roberts purposely made changes to appear small in the eyes of its customer. In 1989, it reorganized its customer service and dispatch employees into self-directed CATs. Teams of six to eight employees handle certain geographic regions and work with the customers in that area. Incoming calls are automatically dispatched to the appropriate CAT. Teams handle customer service and dispatch—all with more responsibility and much less management intervention.

The team approach seemed like the way to make the whole process work to everyone's advantage, explains Virginia Addicott, director, Safety and Contractor Relations. Customers would benefit from a more efficient system, and drivers would benefit from not having to interact with different dispatchers for each order. Employees would benefit from job enrichment with additional responsibilities.

MOVING TO THE NEXT STAGE WITH CATs

By August 1992, CATs had replaced the Customer Service and Operations departments entirely at Roberts Express. Today, it's a matter of adding teams as the volume of business increases.

The CATs have proved so successful that a new project was initiated in August 1995 to move to the next stage with this concept. The organization created Service Teams Empowerment Program (STEP) as a work-environment-changing program targeted at moving empowerment beyond the buzzword and living it every day.

"The Services leadership team wanted the front line to be able to make decisions that affect customers," Sacha stated. "That was the mission that was put forward. Once we defined a 'statement of empowerment,' we had to determine how to make it happen."

Sacha described the process as a refocusing of jobs. A number of different functions—such as service quality, contractor relations, and human resources—make up each team. One of Roberts' telling statistics illustrated how 50 percent of an agent's time supported the customer, while 50 percent included other responsibilities. As a result, the organization built competency models for service agents and team facilitators, because their roles and responsibilities were getting "squishy."

"This new framework allows us to look at people holistically and look at the mind-set. We have set a performance standard to measure people," Sacha said. "We are defining what exemplary performance means in that job."

In November 1995, Addicott, who was instrumental in starting the CAT concept at Roberts in 1989, moved her new department to CATs.

"Our department had meetings to define goals, and we got everyone in the department involved," Addicott said. "We needed to increase productivity, turn paperwork around faster, and be nicer to contractors."

Addicott said four problems were identified, and employees signed up for teams to address these issues. The brainstorming sessions were successful.

"The teams came back with ideas and solutions that you wouldn't believe," Addicott remarked. "We would never have known half of the stuff they know if we hadn't asked for their contributions. That's something we never did with the original teams—and we've taken that to the nth degree this time."

The department's efforts have paid off. Employees have increased productivity and seen improvement in customer-satisfaction ratings from contractor scores.

"There must be a business reason for this, and we have seen the payback," Addicott said.

FROM THE CUSTOMERS' PERSPECTIVE

Roberts' customers are just as obsessive about the company's service as Roberts is. Its customers have come to expect certain actions from the organization, which is often why the relationship began in the first place.

Take, for instance, Dennis Salvey, warehouse manager at Pall Manufacturing. A high-volume customer, Salvey's company has used Roberts Express two to three times per week for the past eight years. As a manufacturer of filtration products, Salvey needs the exclusive use of trucks, often immediately.

"Roberts is the best in the business, and they get the job done right," Salvey, said. "I've tried to give the local trucking companies an opportunity for business, but they will be late, or I'll find other freight mixed with mine on the truck. With Roberts, drivers may hit heavy snow or traffic, but they will call to let me know right away. If I'm told at that time, I can let the Planning department know and make adjustments. You don't get that with the competitors."

Late shipments have a tremendous impact on Salvey's company by upsetting the planning schedule. Salvey said goods are produced according to customer requirements, so a late delivery might force Pall Manufacturing to miss a shipment to a customer, which obviously has a sizable effect.

"I didn't pick Roberts Express for the price, but because of the '90 minute call-in service' the company has always adhered to," Salvey said. "And because the drivers are owners/operators, they are a little more careful with the deliveries."

GENERATING SUCCESS FROM NEW TECHNOLOGY

Customer Link has made it possible for Roberts to implement a whole new way of doing business. Rather than sending orders from one department to another, its small, self-directed work teams manage the entire customer service process. The teams share in the responsibility and the glory.

"In a matter of months after installing Customer Link, we were soon showing an 80 percent increase in dispatch productivity—with a goal of 100 percent," Greulich said. "This means there are fewer humans in the seats needed to take more runs."

This customer-focused system also creates a sense of personal involvement. Agents, customers, and drivers—despite the number of miles between them—create a feeling of camaraderie and team effort. Greulich said that connection translates into the kind of service that delights customers.

Customer Link also provides employees and drivers with complete, up-to-the-minute information that allows them to do their jobs better, easier, and faster. In addition to improved productivity, Roberts also has increased loaded miles and other bottom-line measures. From 1982 to 1996, Roberts' staff grew from 17 to 400 to handle a number of annual shipments that has multiplied more than 300 times—from 655 to 220,000.

Roberts Express's proudest honour is the recognition of its Customer Link by the Smithsonian Institution's 1996 Computerworld Smithsonian Awards Program. Customer Link has been deemed "of great historical value" by the Smithsonian and placed in its permanent exhibit "The Information Age: People, Information, and Technology." The Smithsonian looks for organizations that develop innovative uses of information technology that benefit society.

"Everything we do at Roberts is for the customer in some shape or form," Addicott said. "Employees are very involved to make changes for the better. On the whole, it's truly a unique organization. You just have to see it to believe it!"

LESSONS LEARNED

During the years that Roberts Express has been in business, the organization has learned its share of lessons about customer service. While the list is never "finished," there are at least 10 lessons that the company tries to keep in mind—always.

1. We're in the customer-satisfaction business—not the transportation business. Our customers want reassurance and peace of mind as

much as they want a truck or an airplane. Service is what we're really selling.

2. "Service" is a matter of perception, and perceptions can be managed. A company can seem small, no matter how big it is—if it realizes that it is important to customers, and then works hard at it.

3. Customer service is a mission, not a program. That's why we've never had a "quality improvement program" as such at Roberts Express—and never will.

4. The three cardinal rules of customer service: measure, measure, measure. Break any of those rules and your business can be in serious jeopardy.

5. To know where you stand with customers, just ask. Ask as many of them as you can, as often as you can, every way you can.

6. The people closest to the job know it best; when an issue comes up or a change needs to be made, they should be the ones driving the solution—not management.

7. When people are responsible for the whole job, they can see it better—and do it better. In fact, they'll make sure they do it better, because it's their job, their customer.

8. Technology is more than having the latest and greatest. If that new computer system doesn't help you do a better job as far as customers are concerned, it's not worth its gigabytes.

9. It takes people as well as technology to deliver customer service. Even the most advanced phone system falls apart without a friendly voice on the line.

10. Mistakes aren't necessarily bad. You can actually win a customer over by the way you deal with the problem—together.

About the author

VICKI J. POWERS

Vicki J. Powers is a communications specialist and editor at the Houston-based American Productivity & Quality Center. She writes case studies on best-practices organizations for APQC's publications series, *inPRACTICE*.

CHAPTER THIRTY - SIX

Best Practices of a Leader in Banking

BUILDING TOMORROW'S RETAIL BANK TODAY: mbanx, DIVISION OF BANK OF MONTREAL GROUP OF COMPANIES

Jeffrey S. Chisholm, mbanx, Toronto, ON

THE NORTH AMERICAN economy is rapidly converging—coalescing into a single, unified market, driven by a number of important factors, including

- The democratization of information.
- The continuing emergence of a world without boundaries.
- The social and demographic changes influencing our society.
- The accelerating pace of restructuring in the financial services industry.

When my colleagues and I looked at these four trends with what we sincerely hope were clear eyes and good data, we came to a sobering conclusion for a major financial institution. We knew we had to radically change the way we did business, or we could lose our valuable client base to powerful new competitors, such as G.E. Capital and Fidelity Investments, each of which has the marketing expertise and operational scale to dominate segments and move into new products. Fidelity, which is now doing business in Canada, has more assets than the combined assets of the three largest domestic banks in Canada and offers a range of consumer products.

We also knew we had to reinvent our relationship with clients, which meant we had to reinvent our relationship with the employees we count on to create and nurture the client relationship. Both of these critical objectives required us to redesign our business processes and tools.

During the summer months of 1996, Bank of Montreal's management team was reviewing plans for an innovative direct bank pilot project in Calgary that would redefine the relationship with our clients. At the same time, rumours were circulating that Van City was about to take Citizens Bank of Canada national and that the Dutch giant ING Groep NV was going to launch a virtual bank in Canada. Our chairman, Matt Barrett, promptly issued a challenge to turn the pilot into an entirely new national banking enterprise by the fall of 1996. This bold stroke of leadership sent a definitive signal to our clients, employees, shareholders, and competitors that the era of traditional banking in Canada was changing.

Since mbanx jumped onto the Internet in October of 1996, most of the other five large banks have followed. They are doing this through adding on PC banking to their retail offerings. We anticipated this approach and felt we had to distinguish ourselves as an entirely new banking enterprise and not just an "add-on" to traditional banking.

When we were developing the mbanx concept, we asked ourselves how we would compete if we were a monoline competitor (large, single-product provider, for example, of a credit card) coming into this country for the first time. One obvious factor was price, but price was something other financial institutions could probably match.

REINVENTING THE CLIENT RELATIONSHIP

The cornerstone of the relationship with our clients is a unique value proposition. First, mbanx clients have access to a team of specially trained personal portfolio managers 24 hours a day, 7 days a week, 365 days a year to assist them in managing their financial affairs.

Second, our rewards program encourages clients to consolidate their business with us. Our research shows that this would give more than 50 percent of Canadian households with mortgages the ability to have no-fee banking. After crossing a certain dollar threshold, the rewards program would actually put money in their account.

Third, we offer a money-back guarantee. If customers are not satisfied with the service they receive, we refund the monthly fee. Our service-fee guarantee is essentially a monthly referendum on how well we're delivering on our promises. To date, fewer than 1 percent of clients have asked for a refund. In some cases, clients have been surprised to learn that we initiated the refund of their monthly fee because we felt we did not live up to our end of the bargain.

Fourth, I believe the m̲banx culture is critically important to our business. Our employees are free to provide solutions to our clients, as long as their actions are consistent with our five values (described below).

Fifth, m̲banx clients are backed up by the security and convenience of having access privileges at any one of Bank of Montreal's branches in Canada.

We concluded that clients would switch banks if

- Their expectations for instant, accurate information could be met.

- A bank could help them transcend time and space in their financial transactions.

- They could be assured of appropriate security.

So who are the archetypal m̲banx clients? They are time-pressed—so much so that they find it difficult to visit a branch. As a consequence, they already do a heavy percentage of their banking via ABM (automated banking machine) and the telephone. They are financially active, maintaining a range of deposit, loan, and investment connections with the bank. They also travel frequently, and expect and demand seamless service, regardless of whether they are in London, Ontario; the U.S. Midwest; Mexico City; or London, England.

REINVENTING THE EMPLOYEE RELATIONSHIP

It was a challenge to find people with solid traditional banking skills and the entrepreneurial mentality needed to serve our new clients. In order to be first to market, we asked the division heads from our bricks and mortar national branch system to spare 10 or 15 of their best employees for four or five months to fill the portfolio manager positions. As a result, m̲banx hit the ground running when we launched on October 16, 1996. Some of the secondees have since gone back to the branch system and have become "m̲banx ambassadors" to their colleagues across Canada. This has supplemented the extensive internal communication to branch employees about m̲banx and about the new employment opportunities it is creating for bank employees.

We are also undergoing an external recruitment campaign. Our recruiters are looking not only for candidates who have outstanding skills, but also for dynamic client-centric people who want to live and work by our guiding values. While we all hear a lot of talk about values in business these days, I believe that a handful of core values, when deeply believed and broadly adopted, have the power to help create a truly distinctive organization. The five values our employees live by are the following:

1. **Change is good** • Constant innovation • Recognition of creativity • Challenge of old assumptions • Willingness to learn from mistakes • Courage to ask "Why are we doing things this way?"

2. **We believe in better** • Continuous learning • Constant search for ways to improve the quality of clients' financial lives • Providing the resources for employees to grow as they wish • Better compensation for better results

3. **A promise is a promise** • Clarity about our commitments • Clarity about our capabilities • Clarity about the timeliness of our commitments, with clients and with each other

4. **Simple rules that work** • Driving out complexity everywhere in our business, especially in access, communications, and processes

5. **Everyone is important** • For everyone, without exception • Treating all others with the respect we would want for ourselves, all the time

Our new employees undergo an extensive training program. They split their time between the classroom and "the floor" in a "just in time" learning environment. The early floor experience helps plant the seeds of our client service-oriented culture. Professional training staff from Bank of Montreal's Institute for Learning, who are part of the mbanx operating team, have retooled and refined the training process on the basis of feedback from new employees and client-satisfaction measures. As a result, our portfolio managers are better trained, in a shorter period than they were before.

When I think of organizations with employees who are dedicated to providing outstanding client service, Nordstrom, the Seattle-based retailer, comes to mind immediately. We've had a few "Nordstrom moments" of our own at mbanx, which we call the "Wow Factor." For example, when an mbanx client's car broke down recently, he called the mbanx toll-free telephone number because he could not remember the autoclub phone number and didn't carry his card since the membership had lapsed. The mbanx portfolio manager was able to reinstate the client's autoclub membership and arrange for a tow truck to rescue the stranded motorist from the winter elements.

Another portfolio manager recently went the extra mile to help a client get cash for her mother in a remote community not served by Bank of Montreal's retail network. The portfolio manager found out that one of our direct competitors was the only bank with a branch in that village and so walked across the street from our Toronto headquarters to the competitor's branch to make the cash transfer for the client. Employees record these anecdotes about our unrelenting drive to solve client problems on a "Wow Board."

REINVENTING MARKETING/BRANDING STRATEGIES

The extensive mbanx marketing and advertising campaign, which was developed by the bank's public affairs department and Vickers and Benson advertising, began with a "teaser" television commercial showing 300 children in a country scene singing the popular sixties song "The Times They Are A-Changin'." Two weeks later, five new commercials featuring young people were aired, highlighting each one of the five values that our employees have embraced.

mbanx brand recognition was established quickly. Image and awareness have been extremely high. Both aided and unaided awareness of our advertisements among English-speaking Canadians is extremely high. As a result, we are attracting clients from the early adopter segment (people who are comfortable with PC technology and other alternative channels), clients from the existing Bank of Montreal base and, most significantly, clients from other financial institutions.

REINVENTING BUSINESS PROCESS

Strategically, mbanx is not just a logical extension of previous trends in banking, it is an attempt to redefine the banking relationship. ABM technology and telephone banking effectively extended branch hours, but they cannot handle all the complex needs of the modern financial services consumer. mbanx removes all the limitations and constraints associated with time, space, and geography. mbanx, in short, is banking designed to meet the needs of the modern consumer by being totally client-centric, service-driven, and sales-oriented.

The common thread in all claims to virtual banking is technology. Access points such as telebanking, ABMs, or online banking over the Internet are just one component. The real power of technology lies in turning information into knowledge and turning that into insight. We're marrying technology and people to achieve unexpected levels of service quality. We're using tools to replace the drudgery of process with the creativity of people, where our human advantage becomes our competitive advantage. The technology frees resources to deliver the human service people still want.

We're constantly trying to improve and refine business processes. We have reengineered hundreds of business processes to build a more client-focused operating model that fits our values. Recently, we introduced Phone Power's Advanced Performance Management Program, a product that the bank's telebanking group has been using since November 1994. Essentially, this tool examines the productivity and service level of our portfolio managers. It helps turn raw data from automated call distributors and other communications technologies into meaningful information that helps portfolio managers and their coaches identify training gaps. The system is based on three principles:

1. Portfolio managers have the right to know what is expected of them.

2. Portfolio managers have the right to know how the goals will be measured.

3. Portfolio managers have the right to be in a position to improve.

Advances in information technology are helping bankers understand their clients better. While new electronic access channels are driving down the cost structure of banking, new data-mining technologies are sure to revolutionize the business. Data mining allows companies to correlate information from large client databases to gain deep understanding of client behaviour. By understanding patterns of account activity and transaction usage, banks will be able to harness the predictive power of past behaviour to custom-design proactive management strategies.

At mbanx, we are committed to an extensive program of data mining to help our clients. When we know our clients very well, we can figure out how to put things forward that are attractive and profitable to them. Segmentation techniques will be used to group clients with common behaviours. New value propositions can then be tailored specifically to appeal to these clients, thus strengthening their relationship with the bank. Data mining will also fuel our prospecting programs, enabling us to conduct precise client/product propensity profiling.

Ultimately, through the intelligent use of databases and the most advanced database analysis techniques, we want to offer a value-added, customized transaction each and every time. In other words, we intend to truly serve an individual client as a market segment of one. Making a client feel valued as a segment of one is a great untapped discontinuity for the financial services industry, perhaps even most industries. It's a gap that we believe has enormous opportunity, and one that mbanx is trying to fill.

An important part of our process improvement activities is a passion for measurement. We are keenly interested in finding out if we are delivering what our clients want and where we can do better. We rely on client surveys and related techniques to get the information we need. Using internal and external data sources, we are structuring our information systems to electronically deliver timely information on selected performance metrics. Our performance metrics are continually evolving. They include financial and non-financial measures, and cover fundamental categories of performance such as financial results, client perspectives, operating efficiency, innovation capability, employee perspectives, and image effectiveness.

For many years, banking in Canada was a textbook example of a mature industry. Change was incremental at best. Winning market share was expensive and difficult. But today, with the tectonic plates shifting beneath the industry, openings appear and opportunities for growth spring up. mbanx is our response. In the North American context, mbanx is rewriting the rules of the retail banking game. We believe it will be a major driver of growth for the Bank of Montreal Group of Companies.

About the author

JEFFREY CHISHOLM

Jeffrey Chisholm was appointed vice-chairman, Electronic Financial Services, Bank of Montreal, and president of mbanx in 1996. Prior to this appointment, Chisholm served as vice-chairman of Bank of Montreal's Corporate and Institutional Financial Services team, a post in which he was responsible for a $54-billion business.

Born in Erie, Pennsylvania, Chisholm studied business administration at Georgetown University. After earning his bachelor's degree, he joined Chicago-based Harris Trust and Savings Bank. He moved to Toronto in 1984 when Harris was acquired by Bank of Montreal. There he became deputy treasurer. Jeff Chisholm is a director of Grupo Financiero Bancomer SA and Nesbitt Burns Inc.

BOOK REFERENCES
Customer Service

Albrecht K., *At America's Service: How Corporations Can Revolutionize the Way They Treat Their Customers.* Homewood, IL: Dow Jones-Irwin, 1988.

Albrecht K., *Service Within: Solving the Middle Management Leadership Crisis.* Homewood, IL: Business One Irwin, 1990.

Brown, Stan A. *What Customers Value Most: How to Achieve Business Transformation By Focusing On Processes That Touch Your Customers.* Toronto: John Wiley & Sons Canada, Ltd, 1995.

Cartwright, Roger, and George Green. *In Charge of Customer Satisfaction.* Blackwell Publishing, 1997.

Davidow, W.H., and B. Uttal. *Total Customer Service: The Ultimate Weapon.* New York: Harper Perennial, 1990.

Kabodian, Armen J., ed. *The Customer Is Always Right!: Thought Provoking Insights on the Importance of Customer Satisfaction from Today's Business Leaders.* Boston: Harvard Business School Press, 1996.

Leboeuf, Michael. *How to Win Customers and Keep Them for Life.* Berkley Publishing Group, 1989.

Strategy

Brown, Stan A. *Creating the Service Culture: Strategies for Canadian Business.* Toronto: Prentice Hall, 1990.

Broydrick, Stephen C. *The 7 Universal Laws of Customer Value: How to Win Customers & Influence Markets.* Irwin Professional Publishers, 1996.

Burke, Jack. *Creating Customer Connections: How to Make Customer Service a Profit Center for Your Company (Taking Control Series).* Merritt Company, 1996.

Merli, Giorgio. *Breakthrough Management: How to Convert Priority Objectives into Results.* New York: John Wiley & Sons Inc., 1995.

Porter, M.E. *Competitive Advantage: Creating and Sustaining Superior Performance.* New York: The Free Press, 1985.

Wiersema, Fred. *Customer Intimacy: Pick Your Partners, Shape Your Culture, Win Together.* Knowledge Exchange, 1996.

Measurement

Bogan, Christopher, E., and Michael J. English. *Benchmarking for Best Practices: Winning Through Innovative Adaption.* McGraw-Hill, 1994.

Gronoos, C. *Service Management and Marketing: Managing the Moment of Truth in Service Competition.* Lexington, MA: Lexington Books, 1990.

McNair, C.J., et al. *Benchmarking: A Tool For Continuous Improvement (The Coopers & Lybrand Performance Solutions).* Oliver Wight Ltd. Publications, 1994.

Naumann, Earl, and Kathleen Giel. *Customer Satisfaction Measurement and Management: Using the Voice of the Customer.* Nostrand Reinhold, 1995.

Williams, Tom. *Dealing With Customer Complaints.* Ashgate Publishing Company, 1996.

Process Improvement

Brown, Stan A. *Total Quality Service: How Organizations Use It to Create A Competitive Advantage.* Toronto:Prentice-Hall, 1992.

Cooksey C., R. Beans, D. Eshelman. *Process Improvement—A Guide for Teams.* Arlington, VA: Coopers & Lybrand, 1993.

Johansson, Henry J., et al. *Business Process Reengineering: Breakpoint Strategies for Market Dominance.* New York: John Wiley & Sons Inc., 1993.

Technology

Anderson, Kristin. *Great Customer Service on the Telephone (The Worksmart Series).* Amacom Books, 1992.

Bell, Chip R. *Customers As Partners: Building Relationships That Last.* Berrett-Koehler Publishing, 1994.

Bodian, Nat G. *Direct Marketing Rules of Thumb: 1,000 Practical and Profitable Ideas to Help You Improve Response, Save Money, and Increase Efficiency.* McGraw Hill, 1995.

McCafferty, Thomas A. *In-House Telemarketing: The Masterplan for Starting and Managing a Profitable Telemarketing Program.* Probus Publishing Co., 1994.

Shook, Robert L., and E. Yaverbaum, eds. *I'll Get Back to You: 156 Ways to Get People to Return Your Phone Calls.* Boston: Harvard Business School Press, 1996.

Sterne, Jim. *Customer Service on the Internet: Building Relationships, Increasing Loyalty, and Staying Competitive.* New York: John Wiley & Sons, Inc., 1996.

People/Workforce Management

Kanungo, Rabindra N., and Manuel Mendonca. *Compensation–Effective Reward Management (2nd ed.).* Toronto: John Wiley & Sons Canada, Ltd, 1996.

Gillen, Terry. *20 Training Workshops for Customer Care.* Brookfield Publishing Company, 1990.

O'Dell, Susan M., and Joan A. Pajunen. *The Butterfly Customer: Capturing the Loyalty of Today's Elusive Consumer.* Toronto: John Wiley & Sons Canada, Ltd, 1997.

Torrington, Derek, and Jane Weightman. *Effective Management: People and Organization.* Prentice-Hall, 1994.

MAGAZINES

CTI Magazine
A Technology Marketing
Publication
One Technology Plaza
Norwalk, CT 06854 USA
1-800-243-6002
www.ctimag.com

Call Centre Magazine: Technologies & Techniques for Customer Service.
Help Desk. Sales & Support
1265 Industrial Highway
Southampton, PA 18966-9839 USA
(212) 355-2886
www.callcentremagazine.com

Telemarketing Magazine
(See CTI magazine)

Information Week
CPM Media Inc.
National Press Building
529 14th St., N.W., Suite 1170
Washington, DC 20045 USA

Datamation
Cahners Publishing Co.
Division of Reed Elsevier Inc.
275 Washington St.
Newton MA 02158-1630 USA
(617) 558-4281
www.datamation.com

Sales and Marketing Management
Bill Communications Inc.
355 Park Ave, S. 5th Floor
New York, NY 10010-1789 USA
Ph: (212) 592-6200
Fx: (212) 592-6339

The Canadian Business Review
The Conference Board of Canada
255 Smyth Road
Ottawa, ON K1H 8M7
http://www.conferenceboard.ca

*Customer Service Management–
The Journal for Quality and
Service Excellence*
Customer Services Management Ltd.
CSM House, 1 Idle Road
Bradford, BD2 4Q4 UK
(01274) 780780
e-mail: subs@cust-serv.mgmt.com

TeleProfessional Magazine
TelProfessional Inc.
209 West Fifth Street, Suite N
Waterloo, IW 50701-5420 USA
1-800-338-8307

Marketing Magazine
Maclean Hunter Publishing Ltd.
777 Bay St., 5th Floor
Toronto, ON M5W 1A7
www.marketingmag.ca
1-800-668-9215

NEWSLETTERS

Phone-Tap
Canadian Telemarketing Corporation
4 Dearborne Avenue
Toronto, ON M4K 1M7
(416) 466-6943

*Executive Excellence: The Maga-
zine of Leadership Development,
Managerial Effectiveness, and
Organizational Productivity*
Executive Excellence Publishing
1344 East 1120 South
Provo, UT 84606 USA
1-800-304-9782
http://www.eep.com

TeleDIRECTION
Stentor-Teledirection
Main Floor, 410 Laurier Ave. West
Ottawa ON K1P 6H5
(613) 660-3000

*Supervisor's Guide to Quality &
Excellence*
Clement Communications, Incorpo-
rated
Concord Industrial Park,
10 LaCrue Ave.,

Concordville, PA 19331-9987 USA
1-800-459-1680
Internet: editor@clement.com

Customer Service Manager's Letter
Bureau of Business Practice
24 Rope Ferry Road
Waterford, CT 06386 USA
1-800-876-9105
e-mail: bbp/06@q.continuum.net

*Quality Management: Guiding
Product Companies to Quality
Excellence*
Bureau of Business Practice
24 Rope Ferry Road
Waterford, CT 06386 USA
1-800-876-9105
e-mail: bbp/06@q.continuum.net

Executive Report on Customer Satisfaction
The Customer Service Group
215 Park Avenue South, Suite 1301
New York, NY 10003 USA
(212) 228-0246

CSN: Customer Service Newsletter-The Authority on Managing the Customer Service Department
The Customer Service Group
215 Park Avenue South, Suite 1301
New York, NY 10003 USA
(212) 228-0246

Help Desk and Customer Support Practices Report–October 1996
Help Desk Institute
1755 Telstar Drive, Suite 101
Colorado Springs, CO 80920-1017
USA
1-800-248-5667

Strategy
Brunico Communications Inc.
500-366 Adelaide Street West
Toronto, ON M5V 1R9
(416) 408-2300
Internet: hamill@brunico.com

ICSA Journal
International Customer Service
Association
401 North Michigan Ave.
Chicago, IL 60611-4267 USA
1-800-360-ICSA

The Lakewood Report
Lakewood Publications Inc.
50 S. Ninth Street
Minneapolis, MN 55402 USA
Internet: brianmcd1@aol.com

CONTACT
Canadian Professional Sales
Association
145 Wellington Street West
Suite 310
Toronto, ON M5J 1H8
1-800-268-3794
Internet: contact@cpsa.com

Journal of Customer Service in Marketing & Management– Innovations for Service, Quality and Value
William J. Winston, Editor
Haworth Press, Inc.

The Service Report
Anne Petite Associates Ltd.
160 Gildwood Parkway
West Hill, ON M1E 1P4
Ph: (416) 267-2430
Fx: (416) 267-2537

Customer Satisfaction in Practice Benchmarking in Practice
American Productivity & Quality
Center (APQC)
123 North Post Oak Lane, 3rd Fl
Houston, TX 77024-7797 USA
1-800-776-9676 or (713) 681-4020
www.apqc.org

Cowles Report on Database Marketing
Cowles Business Media
11 Riverbend Drive South
Box 4294
Stamford, CT 06907-0949 USA
(203) 358-9900 x351
http://www..simbanet.com

Knowledge/Knowhow
A quarterly publication of Coopers &
Lybrand's Government Consulting
  Practice
1530 Wilson Blvd.
Arlington, VA 22209-2447 USA
(703) 908-1973
http://www.colybrand.com

Customer Focus
A quarterly publication of
The Centre of Excellence in
Customer Satisfaction,
Coopers & Lybrand Canada
145 King St. W.
Toronto, ON M5H 1V8
(416) 869-1130
www.coopers.com

The Outsourcing Monitor
A quarterly publication of the Coopers & Lybrand's Outsourcing Practice
145 King St. W.
Toronto, ON M5H 1V8
(416) 869-1130
www.coopers.com

IDEAS '94
The Centre of Excellence in
Customer Satisfaction,
Coopers & Lybrand Canada
145 King St. W.
Toronto, ON M5H 1V8
(416) 869-1130
www.coopers.com

*IDEAS '95–The Role of
Technology to Enhance Customer
Satisfaction*
The Centre of Excellence in
Customer Satisfaction,
Coopers & Lybrand
145 King St. W.
Toronto, ON M5H 1V8
(416) 869-1130
www.coopers.com

*IDEAS '96–Achieving Break-
through Customer Service—
If It Ain't Broke…Break It*
The Centre of Excellence in
Customer Satisfaction,
Coopers & Lybrand Canada
145 King St. W.
Toronto, ON M5H 1V8
(416) 869-1130
www.coopers.com

First Rate Customer Service
The Economic Press Inc.
Editor: John McDonnell
1-800-526-2554
(201) 227-1224

Direct Marketing News
Lloydmedia Inc.
1200 Markham Road, Suite 301
Scarborough, ON M1H 3C3
(416) 439-4083
e-mail:
75130.2016@compuserve.com
Internet:
http://www.dmlinks.com

QMI Brief
QMI
90 Burnamthorpe Road West
Suite 300
Mississauga, ON L5B 3C3
(905) 272-3920
(No Internet site as yet)

Imprints
The Professional Market Research
Society
(416) 445-9800
e-mail: ocharlebois@bbm.ca

APPENDIX TWO

SUBJECT/CHAPTER INDEX

A Quick-Reference Tool for Making Customer Service a Reality

A customer support strategy based on a single great idea, product or service can easily be duplicated. But a strategy based on a "unique mix" of products and services, enabled by a "unique set" of capabilities cannot be easily copied by competitors. In developing your own customer support strategy, it is highly unlikely that you will focus on one single area or chapter. Rather, you will pull together a unique mix of products and services for your customers. In order to do this, you may draw on several of the ideas and topics discussed in various chapters of this book. The cross-reference that follows will help you find what you are looking for. It identifies broad subject areas as well as the chapters in which they are discussed.

The Keys to Establish Breakthrough Customer Service
A) Consolidation:
- Few Customer Support Centres with few locations, 17, 18
- Single Management Structure, 2, 15,18
- Scaleability—Can expand or contract on demand, 19, 21

B) Integration:
- Ensure a Corporate strategy exists, 1, 2, 3, 4, 12, 18, 32, 35
- Integrate support centre hardware components with related software and databases, 18, 19, 20, 21, 36
- Create a common infrastructure and strategy, 18, 20, 21, 30, 34
- Establish interconnectivity with customers and other departments, 13, 16, 17, 19, 20, 21, 23, 30
- Ensure strong communication links exist across the organization, 2, 5, 16, 29, 32

C) *Workforce Management:*

- Pursue skills-based, cross-functional training, 13, 18, 24, 25, 26, 27
- Base rewards on levels of customer satisfaction, 2, 7, 9, 16, 25, 29, 32, 33
- Establish performance measures/standards, 4, 5, 6, 7, 11, 15, 16, 28, 29, 32, 35
- Measure both efficiency and effectiveness, 2, 4, 6, 7, 15, 28, 29, 32, 33, 35

The Enablers

A) *Process*

- Establishes goals and objectives based on internal and external customer needs, 16, 17
- Create and maintain a visible strategic focus, 1, 3, 5, 16, 31, 36
- Ensure you hear the voice of the customer (internal and external), customer feedback is essential, 2, 5, 7, 9, 10, 11, 16, 17, 35
- Ensure that proper management controls are in place, 15, 28
- Outsource non-core functions; co-source leverageable functions, 14
- Resegment customers on the basis of profitability or customer need, 5, 7, 13, 30, 36
- Process improvement must be systematic and targeted, 2, 7, 12, 26, 31, 32, 35
- Make benchmarking a key learning opportunity, 8, 10, 11, 30
- Provide a full spectrum of distribution channels needed to deliver flexibility and convenience, 18, 36

B) *Technology*

- Use common accessible and integrated databases, 5, 17, 19, 22, 32, 34, 36
- Create a common infrastructure, 5, 18, 19, 20, 21, 32, 34, 36
- Establish on-line links to customers via Internet, 5, 13, 20, 23, 36
- Turn information into knowledge to increase efficiency, create customer profiling and product targeting, and increase profitability, 5, 11, 13, 19, 20, 21, 22, 29, 32, 35, 36

C) *People*

- Change skill sets and increase automation to achieve fewer, but multi-skilled staff and improved efficiencies, 6, 18, 26
- Use cross-functional teams, 6, 24, 25, 26
- Map staff competency against required skills/functions, 4, 5, 24, 25, 29
- Ensure that leaders drive the vision for breakthrough, 2, 4, 16, 27, 29, 33
- Coaching must be an integral part of the process, 2, 4, 24
- Reward appropriate behaviour, celebrate success, 8, 9, 10, 16, 25, 26, 27, 32, 35, 36

INDEX OF CONTRIBUTORS

We would like to thank the following individuals and organizations for their participation in this project. For your benefit we have listed them below.

Bearish, Joan
Chief Administrative Officer
Electronic Commerce
KeyCorp
5000 Tiedeman Road
Brooklyn, OH 44144 USA
Tel: (216) 813-1228
Fax: (216) 813-1514
Reference: Part Four/Chapter 18

Bolton, Hugh
Chairman
Coopers & Lybrand, Canada
145 King Street West
23rd Floor
Toronto, ON
M5H 1V8 Canada
Tel: (416) 941-8212
Fax: (416) 863-0926
E-Mail:
   hugh.bolton@ca.coopers.com
Reference: Part One/Chapter 3

Bound, Bill
Partner
Coopers & Lybrand
1 Embankment Place
London, England
WC2N 6NN
Tel: 171-212-4428
Fax: 171-822-4652
Reference: Part Six/Chapter 30

Brandt, Larry
CCSE Associate Director of
Customer Service
AMP Incorporated
2800 Falling Mill Road M.S.
Box 038-035, P.O. Box 3608
Harrisburg, PA 17105-3608 USA
Tel: (717) 986-7776
Fax: (717) 986-7506
Reference: Part Three/Chapter 16

Brown, Stanley
Partner
Coopers & Lybrand, Canada
145 King Street West, 26th Floor
Toronto, ON
M5H 1V8 Canada
Tel: (416) 941-8459
Fax: (416) 941-8421
E-Mail:
    stan.brown@ca.coopers.com
Reference: Part Three/Chapter 13
    Part Four/Chapter 23

Chisolm, Jeff
Vice Chairman
Electronic Financial Services
Bank of Montreal
55 Bloor Street West, 18th Floor
Toronto, ON
M4W 3N5 Canada
Tel: (416) 927-3326
Fax: (416) 927-6153
Reference: Part Six/Chapter 36

Daly, John
Professor of Communication
University of Texas
2507 McCallum Drive
Austin, TX 78703 USA
Tel: (512) 471-1948
Fax: (512) 471-3504
Reference: Part Five/Chapter 27

Dougherty, Lynn
Senior Editor
Cowles/Simba Report on
    Database Marketing
470 Park Ave. South
New York, NY 10016 USA
Tel: (203) 358-4298
Fax: (203) 358-5825
Reference: Part Six/Chapter 34

Enustun, Turk
Director, Corporate
    Benchmarking
Eastman Kodak Company
243 State Street
Rochester, NY 14650-0244 USA
Tel: (716) 781-5570
Fax: (716) 724-3909
Reference: Part Two/Chapter 10

Fritz, Jerry
Program Director, School of
    Business
University of Wisconsin-Madison
Grainger Hall
975 University Avenue
Madison, WI 53706-1323 USA
Tel: (608) 262-7331
Fax: (608) 262-4617
Reference: Part One/Chapter 4

Finerty, Pat
Manager
Coopers & Lybrand, Canada
145 King Street West, 26th Floor
Toronto, ON
M5H 1V8 Canada
Tel: (416) 869-1130 ext 2619
Fax: (416) 941-8421
E-Mail:
    pat.finerty@ca.coopers.com
Reference: Part Four/Chapter 22

Gallagher, Fred
President
TKM Communications Inc.
60 Columbia Way, Suite 530
Markham, ON
L3R 0C9 Canada
Tel: (905) 470-5225
Fax: (905) 470-7008
Reference: Part Four/Chapter 20

Givens, Karri
Consultant
Coopers & Lybrand, Canada
145 King Street West, 26th Floor
Toronto, ON
M5H 1V8 Canada
Tel: (416) 869-1130 ext 2173
Fax: (416) 941-8421
E-Mail:
 karri.givens@ca.coopers.com
Reference: Part Two/Chapter 10

Green, Jack
Director
Entretel Incorporated
2031 Pen Street
Oakville, ON
L6H 3L2 Canada
Tel: (905) 842-8588
Fax: (905) 842-7954
Reference: Part Five/Chapter 28

Gupta, Suresh
Partner
Coopers & Lybrand
1301 Avenue of the Americas
New York, NY 10019-6013 USA
Tel: (212) 259-2036
Fax: (212) 259-1314
Reference: Part Three/Chapter 15

Hanley, Michael
Partner
Coopers & Lybrand
203 North La Salle St.
Chicago, IL 60601 USA
(312) 701-5811
Reference: Part One/Chapter 1

Kahn, E.J.
Strategic Communications
 Consultant
Coopers & Lybrand
One Post Office Square
Boxton, MA 02109 USA
Tel: (617) 478-5000
Fax: (617) 478-3900
Reference: Part One/Chapter 5

Kendall, Howard
Managing Director
Customer Service Management
 Magazine
CSM House, 1 Idle Road
Bradford, England BD2 4QA UK
Tel: 11-44-168-986-2455
Fax: 11-44-168-986-2999
Reference: Part Two/Chapter 8
 Part Six/Chapter 33

Kressaty, John
Director of Customer Service
North American Consumer
 Products
S.C Johnson Wax
1545 Howe Street
Racine, WI 13403 USA
Tel: (800) 572-0876
Fax: (414) 260-3295
Reference: Part Five/Chapter 24

Kulak, Joe
116 Hoffman Road
Port Murray, NJ 07865, USA
(908) 689-8494
Reference: Part Four/Chapter 19

Lang, Alexandra
Corporate Communications
 Manager
Kaset International
8875 Hidden River Parkway
Tampa, FL 36737 USA
Tel: (800) 735-2788
Fax: (800) 877-1848
Reference: Part Five/Chapter 26

Negrea, Tudor
Partner
Coopers & Lybrand, Canada
145 King Street West, 26th Floor
Toronto, ON
M5H 1V8 Canada
Tel: (416) 941-8476
Fax: (416) 941-8419
E-Mail:
   tudor.negrea@ca.coopers.com
Reference: Part Three/Chapter 14

O'Dell, Susan
President
Service Dimensions
50 Burnhamthorpe Rd. W.
Suite 401
Mississauga, ON
L5B 3C2 Canada
Tel: 604-7324 or (905) 270-3424
Fax: 604-3219 or (905) 563-1974
(long distance)
Reference: Part Five/Chapter 25

Pajunen, Joan A.
Partner
Service Dimensions
50 Burnhamthorpe Rd. W.
Suite 401
Mississauga, ON
L5B 3C2 Canada
Tel: 604-7324 or (905) 270-3424
Fax: 604-3219 or (905) 563-1974
(long distance)
Reference: Part Five/Chapter 27

Parks, Bob
Senior Consultant
Kaset International
8875 Hidden River Parkway
Tampa, FL 36737 USA
Tel: (800) 735-2788
Fax: (800) 877-1848
Reference: Part Five/Chapter 26

Patel, Sandip
Partner
Coopers & Lybrand
One Post Office Square
Boston, MA 02109 USA
Tel: (617) 478-5000
Fax: (617) 478-3900
Reference: Part Three/Chapter 12
   Part Five/Chapter 29

Powers, Vicki
American Productivity and
   Quality Center (APQC)
123 North Post Oak Lane
Suite 300
Houston, TX USA
Tel: (713) 681-4020
Fax: (713) 724-3909
Reference: Part Two/Chapter 11
   Part Six/Chapter 35

Rosen, Joel
Managing Partner
Horwath Management
   Consultants
55 St. Clair Avenue West
Suite 260
Toronto, ON
M4V 2Y7 Canada
Tel: (416) 923-7346
Fax: (416) 923-7606
Reference: Part Two/Chapter 9

Severs, Lorne
Senior Consultant
Coopers & Lybrand, Canada
145 King Street West
26th Floor
Toronto, ON
M5H 1V8 Canada
Tel: (416) 869-1130 ext. 2646
Fax: (416) 941-8421
E-Mail:
   lorne.severs@ca.coopers.com
Reference: Part Three/Chapter 14

Thomson, Jacqui
Market Manager
Symposium Marketing
Nortel Canada
8200 Dixie Road, Suite 100
Brampton, ON
L6T 5P6 Canada
Tel: (905) 863-1449
Fax: (905) 863-8441
Reference: Part Four/Chapter 21

Verma, Sharad
Senior Consultant
Coopers & Lybrand, Canada
145 King Street West
26th Floor
Toronto, Ontario
Tel: (416) 869-1130 ext. 2038
Fax: (416) 941-8421
E-mail:
sharad.verma@ca.coopers.com
Reference: Part Three/Chapter 13

Wilkerson, Dave
Senior Consultant
Coopers & Lybrand
1530 Wilson Blvd.
Arlington, VA 22209, USA
(703) 908-1500
Reference: Part Two/Chapter 7

Yearout, Steve
Partner
Coopers & Lybrand
1530 Wilson, Blvd.
Arlington, VA 22209, USA
(703) 908-1500
Reference: Part One/Chapter 2

ASQC (American Society of
  Quality Control)
See Appendix One
Reference: Part One/Chapter 2

ORDER FORM

To order your free subscription to the Coopers & Lybrand newsletter **"Customer Focus: Delivering Customer Value"** please contact The Centre of Excellence in Customer Satisfaction at (416) 896-1130; fax: (416) 941-8421; e-mail: patricia.everard@ca.coopers.comm, web-site: www.ca.coopers.com

---

Additional Publications Available from Coopers & Lybrand Consulting:

❑ Retail Monitor ❑ Real Estate News

❑ Outsourcing Monitor ❑ Software Industry Views

❑ Pharmaceutical Industry Views

If you would like to receive a complimentary copy of these publications please check the appropriate box and fax this form back to the attention of P. Everard (416) 941-8421.

Name & Title:_____

Company:_____

Address: _____

Telephone: _____ Fax:_____

E-mail: _____